A World Turned Upside Down

A World Turned Upside Down

Social Ecological Approaches
to Children in War Zones

Edited by

Neil Boothby,
Alison Strang,
and Michael Wessells

Kumarian
Press, Inc.

A World Turned Upside Down: Social Ecological Approaches to Children in War Zones

Published in 2006 in the United States of America by Kumarian Press, Inc., 1294 Blue Hills Avenue, Bloomfield, CT 06002 USA

The text of this book is set in 10/12 Janson Text.

Production and design by Joan Weber Laflamme, jml ediset
Proofread by Beth Richards
Indexed by Robert Swanson

Printed in the United States of America by Thomson-Shore. Text printed with vegetable oil-based ink..

∞ The paper used in this publication meets the minimum requirements of the American National Standard for Information Sciences—Permanence of Paper for printed Library Materials, ANSI Z39.48–1984

Library of Congress Cataloging-in-Publication Data

A world turned upside down : social ecological approaches to children in war zones / edited by Neil Boothby, Alison Strang, and Michael Wessells.
   p. cm.
  Includes bibliographical references and index.
  ISBN-13: 978–1–56549–225–7 (pbk. : alk. paper)
  ISBN-10: 1–56549–225–0 (pbk. : alk. paper)
  ISBN-13: 978–1–56549–226–4 (cloth : alk. paper)
  ISBN-10: 1–56549–226–9 (cloth : alk. paper)
  1. Children and war. 2. Child soldiers. 3. Child psychology. 4. Psychic trauma in children. 5. War—Psychological aspects. 6. Emotional problems of children. I. Boothby, Neil. II. Strang, Alison, 1959– III. Wessells, Michael G., 1948–
HQ784.W3.W67 2006
303.6083—dc22

2006020202

15 14 13 12 11 10 09 08 07 06   10 9 8 7 6 5 4 3 2 1   First Printing 2006

CONTENTS

FIGURES AND TABLES

ABBREVIATIONS AND ACRONYMS

CPAN	child protection and action network
CCF	Christian Children's Fund
CDF	Civilian Defense Forces (Sierra Leone)
CRC	Convention on the Rights of the Child
CSC	Coalition to Stop the Use of Child Soldiers
CSVR	Center for the Study of Violence and Reconciliation
DDR	demilitarization, demobilization, and reintegration
FAWE	Forum for African Women Educationalists (Sierra Leone)
HRW	Human Rights Watch
IAGP	Inter-Agency Guiding Principles on Unaccompanied and Separated Children
ICC	International Criminal Court
ICRC	International Committee of the Red Cross
IDP	internally displaced person
IGO	intergovernmental organization
IRC	International Rescue Committee
LRA	Lord's Resistance Army (Northern Uganda)
NGO	nongovernmental organization
NPA	National Plan of Action for Palestinian Children
OCHA	Office for the Coordination of Humanitarian Affairs (UN)

PRCS   Palestinian Red Crescent Society

PTSD   post traumatic stress disorder

PWG   Psychosocial Working Group

RSC   Refugee Studies Centre

RUF   Revolutionary United Front (Sierra Leone)

SCF   Save the Children

STDs   sexually transmitted diseases

UN   United Nations

UNHCR   United Nations High Commissioner for Refugees

UNICEF   United Nation's Children's Fund

WCLAC   Women's Center for Legal Aid and Counseling
              (Palestine)

INTRODUCTION

Over the past fifty years we have witnessed more wars than any of us care to count, over 150 since World War II; at least twenty-four continue to rage as we write. While journalists and political observers have followed the "big" war in Iraq with impressive care, it is the small, hidden wars—nearly all fought in poor countries—in which human suffering is often most staggering. Until recently, the rivalry of the United States and the Soviet Union loomed in the background of almost all insurgencies and counter-insurgencies. But now it is the Third World's enormous underclass that has been presented with a bitter choice: the M-16 or the AK-47, and the politics of the supplier of one or the other.

Despite the end of the fifty-year Cold War, and talk of a New World Order, violence and displacement continue to be realities in the lives of poor people around the globe. Today's estimates say there are more than seventeen million refugees living outside their own countries and another twenty-five million internally displaced people. At least half of these forced migrants who are fleeing wars and ethnic conflict are children—most of whom have been exposed directly or indirectly to violence. One study of refugee children who had sought asylum in Europe, for example, found that 60 percent of them had been exposed to violence (Montgomery and Foldspang 2005). Children displaced *within* war-affected countries may be exposed to violence and additional tragedies in even greater numbers and for longer periods of time. In Rwanda a 1996 survey found that 96 percent of children interviewed had witnessed violence; 80 percent had lost a family member; and 70 percent had seen someone killed or injured (Machel 2001). No longer are wars fought on battlefields by opposing armies. Today the village is the battleground of change, and children caught in the cross fire are now the main victims of war.

More children than ever before are carrying guns in today's wars. A recent initiative by human rights advocates identified thirty-six countries where children comprise significant percentages of national

1

standing armies, guerrilla groups, or both (Human Rights Watch 2005). But the child soldier is only the most visible manifestation of a much broader concern. Children today also are caught in the ideological struggles that accompany political and ethnic strife. Different sides teach their own solutions to the ills of a given nation, trying to capture the loyalty and imagination of one generation of girls and boys so that a particular vision of "progress," "justice," or "nationhood" will be imbued into succeeding generations. Guerrilla organizers use highly impoverished circumstances to politicize villages and recruit boys and girls to their cause. At the same time, governments often force children from these very same rural zones into national armies. Youth wings of liberation movements and political parties are increasingly being militarized and used to terrorize civilians in a number of nations. The inability to ensure children's neutrality and safety from political strife is a principal cause of refugee flight.

We, the authors and editors of this book, come to these matters not as journalists or human rights advocates, but as psychologists who have spent over two decades working with children in war zones in Asia, Africa, Latin America, and Europe. Over the years we have seen child survivors of political and ethnic conflicts wobble into camps for refugees and displaced persons physically exhausted and thoroughly subdued, speechless, and, it seemed, emotionless—unable or unwilling to cry, to smile, to shout, to laugh, or to show any feelings other than a kind of stoic weariness. Given time and stability we also have seen how remarkably sturdy, self-reliant, and hopeful many of these same children eventually become. In the end we have been struck more by their purposeful striving toward psychological health than we have by the occasional collapse of their minds.

During our work in different regions of the world we also have seen one or another group of war-affected children declared by the media to be "traumatized," "emotionally stunted," a "lost generation," "beyond the pale," or worse, "future barbarians." As so-called experts on the spot, we often have been asked to comment on these pronouncements and, more often than not, have responded that we do not yet know how these children will turn out as adults; for better or worse that will depend more on the opportunities provided or denied to them now than on any one of the events of their recent pasts. But what do we mean by "depends"? Does it mean that exposure to violence does not leave a deep emotional scar? Or that the moral reasoning of young boys and girls who as child soldiers killed other human beings is not perniciously altered? Or that loss of family and home does not permanently affect one's psychological outlook? What about the literature indicating war victims can suffer a lifetime of traumatic symptoms or that abused children grow up to become abusers?

We do not mean to say that girls and boys are not hurt by exposure to violent acts, or that the pain of losing a mother or father to war ever disappears, or that children eventually forget war-related events altogether. But there are factors other than the events and circumstances children encounter in war that help to shape their immediate responses as well as their subsequent growth and development. Consider, for example, this snapshot of two Afghani infant girls one of us spent time with while working in Kabul before the American invasion of Afghanistan. Both survived Taliban-instigated bombardments of their neighborhood. Initially, the thundering explosions startled the sleeping babies, who began crying. One was picked up by her mother, held closely in her arms, comforted with words and songs, and eventually fell back to sleep. The other baby girl was left alone. No one comforted her; she cried and cried until, exhausted, she fell back asleep on her own. She remained agitated and continued to cry for several days, and her mother found it difficult to get her to eat, sleep, or maintain regular routines.

The same war event resulted in very different short-term reactions. One infant's mother was able to intervene and soothe her daughter, thereby mediating significantly the frightening effects of the rockets' explosions, eventually demoting them to the category of "routine." But the second baby girl's family was not available and, precisely because no one came to her aid, she became increasingly terrified. This real-life example begs the question: Is it the event per se that determines a child's response to war-related events? Or is it more a matter of what human support is available before, during, and after the event?

Consider the longer-term outcome of a boy named Israel, a former child soldier in Mozambique. Israel was twelve years old when he was abducted by Renamo (see Chapter 7), taken to a guerrilla base camp, and systematically dehumanized and trained to kill. He spent the next one and a half years raiding rural villages, until he was captured by government forces and placed in a rehabilitation center in Maputo, the nation's capital. Today, Israel, now thirty-two years old, is married and a father of two. His wife says he is a good husband and provider. His children are healthy and attend school, something Israel was denied. He serves as head of his community's equivalent of a PTA (Parent Teachers Association) and is referred to as a good neighbor by his fellow villagers because "he always offers help to those in need." Why is this former child soldier not a violent, abusive, or irresponsible adult? In other words, what went right when so much of his child-hood went wrong?

Just as the presence of an attentive mother insulated an infant from the frightening effects of an aerial bombardment, there were impor-tant people in Israel's life who helped him both to endure and to recover from these awful events. Before the abduction Israel had a strongly religious mother who maintained a loving but disciplined routine of daily caregiving. During his time with Renamo, Israel did what he was told; to do otherwise would have led to his immediate death. But he also secretly prayed nightly to his God to forgive him for the sins he was forced to commit during the day. After leaving the guerrilla group and participating in the rehabilitation program in Maputo (where he was perceived to be a positive peer leader), Israel was reunited with his older sister and her family (his mother had died), who were also supportive. So, too, were neighbors, traditional heal-ers, and other members of the community network. As one village elder points out, psychological recovery and healing are collective acts:

> "[Israel] was torn from us by a great evil. When he returned several years later, we knew he was different and that the war had changed him. But he was our son, and we welcomed him back with open arms. When he had problems, we were patient. When he did well, we congratulated him. When he needed chickens and cloth for his cleansing ceremony, we gave them to him. When he found a wife, we helped him build his house. Today, he is just like everyone else. Now he helps others as much as we helped him. That's how it works here."

At a conceptual level, then, we are pointing out that the nature of war-related experience differs enormously from child to child. Some will endure episodic shelling of their villages but be spared exposure to violence; others will become separated from their families during flight and arrive in refugee camps alone. Some will witness the killing of family members; others will be tortured, sexually abused, or forced into fighting units. An understanding of how children are affected by war must begin by clarifying the important distinctions among type, degree, and duration of traumatic events.

Social ecologies

Children's development is shaped by the material, social, and cultural contexts of their lives. Uri Bronfenbrenner (1979; 1986) has contributed significantly to our understanding of how long-term relationships (what he calls proximal interactions) are critical in shaping children's immediate responses to adversity as well as longer-term outcomes. Indeed, in our own work with war-affected children we have found "systems"—such as the family, school, and peer group, in which children are involved in continuous, face-to-face interactions with familiar people—to be key determinants of war-affected children's developmental outcomes. What emerges through the social ecology lens is a dynamic picture of how children develop amid changing social, political, economic, and cultural worlds that offer a mixture of protection and risks to children's rights and well-being.

In some of today's war zones, systems that are normally sources of support and protection, such as the family, become sources of risk and developmental damage. Religious leaders and institutions may also enable psychological well-being and recovery or, conversely, politicize children's pain to the point that they are willing to strap dynamite around their waists and sacrifice their own lives to kill members of the "other" side. Carving out an economic niche for a family, which is difficult enough in peaceful settings, becomes even more challenging in conflict zones; exploitative child-labor practices and child prostitution may increase significantly in poverty-riddled refugee and displaced persons encampments.

Although the emphasis is on external influences and socialization processes, the social ecology perspective also portrays children as actors rather than as passive victims. Children in war zones make choices about how they live, negotiate their roles within groups, and actively engage and cope with the stresses and risk they face. Indeed, the relation between war-related events and subsequent child outcomes may also be mediated by powerful developmental processes. The domains of subjective experience, cognitive appraisal, feelings of empowerment and competence, different coping and attributional styles, and complexities of identity, meaning, and purpose contribute enormously to how children are affected by armed conflict.

The ecological framework has important implications for strengthening the psychosocial supports of children in war zones. In contrast to individualized approaches, an ecological conceptualization suggests that the impacts of war are socially mediated. In this view psychosocial assistance to war-affected children occurs not through the provision of therapy by outsiders but through holistic support from insiders. For separated children, family reunification is in itself a key psychosocial support. One of the main themes of this book is that in war zones, psychosocial assistance is often best provided through family and community-based supports that are guided by a holistic, socially situated understanding of children's well-being. Indeed, in many ways this book is premised on the belief that well-conceived psychosocial programs can shift the balance from destructive to health-promoting forces by activating social support and taking advantage of children's innate resilience.

PWG conceptual framework

This book is more than just a product of its authors. It is rooted in the work of a group of colleagues who have come together regularly over the past few years to share our experiences and our thinking. This group—the Psychosocial Working Group (PWG)—brings together an international consortium of academic institutions and humanitarian agencies, and it involves experts from across the psychosocial field who are committed to supporting best practice in psychosocial interventions.[1] It was first initiated with the support of the Andrew Mellon Foundation in 2000 in response to a widening recognition of the effects of conflict on people's mental health and social well-being. The approaches to addressing these acute and chronic needs were many and diverse, embracing solutions from medication to ritual cleansing ceremonies, and from war crimes tribunals to sewing circles. Yet so many important questions went unanswered. Which of these approaches is most effective and in what situations? How can we tell? Do we do any harm, and what are we trying to achieve anyway? What is psychosocial well-being?

The PWG undertook the task of developing a conceptual framework to encompass the breadth of understandings of psychosocial needs and responses to those needs. It provided the hub for a consultation process not aspiring to comprehensiveness but to diversity, embracing the very different perspectives in the field and people's different roles, from field worker to policy maker. Our lively discussions soon engaged not only with the practical and theoretical challenges of working in this field, but also the ethical dilemmas faced again and again by those attempting work with cultural sensitivity and yet encountering clashes of culture. How can a humanitarian worker combine the aim to empower local people and support deployment of culturally appropriate resources in a situation where cultural practices lead directly to serious human rights abuses? It was clear that any analysis of psychosocial interventions must address these moral and political realities. With the invaluable support of a great many wise and experienced colleagues, drawing on the previous social ecological framework presented in the work of Bronfenbrenner (1979; 1986) and others, a model has gradually evolved that is elaborated on in the PWG Conceptual Framework (PWG 2003). This framework has been used to map the contribution of psychosocial interventions, identify gaps in our knowledge, and define a research agenda (PWG 2002). It is this understanding of psychosocial well-being and psychosocial interventions that provides the rationale for the contributions to this volume.

The PWG model is based on several fundamental principles, which are discussed below.

Attention to context

The effect of conflict on a person's psychosocial well-being is best understood in relation to his or her context. In the context of war it is primarily the circumstances that are the source of the problem—not the individual's inability to cope. Behaviors that could be classified as trauma symptoms should rather be seen as normal responses to abnormal circumstances. (This surely must be true by definition where 95 percent of the population is classified as demonstrating post traumatic stress disorder, thus creating a "norm" for this situation [de Jong 2000].) This view is coherent with the elaboration of the ecological perspective by Miller and Rasco, who suggest that "many types of mental problems, including most of the displacement related distress experienced by refugees, are best understood as reflecting problems in the relationship between the demands of settings in which people live and the coping or adaptive resources at their disposal" (Miller and Rasco 2004).

It follows that any analysis of psychosocial well-being that will lead to fruitful insights must help us to understand the context. Furthermore, any attempt to address the problem should address the context. There is a danger that by focusing on the individual as the locus of change we actually do even further damage. A therapeutic approach can pathologize normal behavior; it may suggest to the individuals concerned that their own responses are to blame for their suffering, carrying stigma and reinforcing a sense of failure, loss, and dependence.

Attention to meaning

What affects the way we cope with circumstances? Is it purely the severity of the experiences themselves? The case for psychosocial intervention is often made by reporting the number and nature of the traumatic events to which a child has been exposed. Indeed, quite a number of assessment tools also rely on such lists. However, our experiences and those of our colleagues suggest that this does not really reflect the severity of the impact. Take Israel, the young Mozambican introduced earlier. We saw that the impact of his experiences was mitigated by the acceptance and support of family and friends, along with the self-acceptance attained through his personal religious faith. Both aspects enabled him to retain a sense of personal identity and integrity that protected him from the potential destruction of both his psychological and social worlds.

It was not just the nature of the events to which Israel was exposed and the experiences he had (of witnessing and taking part in killings) that determined his long-term well-being, but the meaning that he and those around him attached to those events. Experiences are mediated through social context, religion, and ideology. For these reasons the PWG takes an ecological approach, addressing the needs of people affected by conflict within the wider context of their community.

Active engagement

As people, children, and communities we engage with the challenges we face. Even the apparent withdrawal into passivity can be seen as an attempt to make life more bearable. Our responses may be more or less helpful, but it is a mistake to ignore the fact that the primary actors are those who have been directly affected.

A resource-based model

The PWG framework is fundamentally a model of resource—in contrast to a deficit model, which looks at loss or dysfunction. It supports the resources available to a community in addressing the challenges that it faces. While there are myriad ways to look at a community and recognize the resources that are available to it—economic, environmental, geographic, historical, to name but a few—we have identified three core resource domains most pertinent to defining psychosocial well-being. The framework understands psychosocial well-being in terms of the domains of human capacity, social ecology, and culture and values.

Human capacity

Conflict and displacement frequently lead to a loss of human capacity within the community. This domain is taken to constitute such resources as the physical and mental health of community members and the skills and knowledge of people (which can be referred to as the *human capital* of the community). Events can clearly reduce such human capacity by many means. Physical disability, loss of skilled labor, and social withdrawal and depression all serve to degrade human capacity, as do less tangible effects, such as a reduced sense of control over events and circumstances.

Social ecology

The circumstances of war and seeking refuge also lead to a disruption of the social ecology of a community, involving social relations within families, peer groups, and religious and cultural institutions; links with civic and political authorities; and so on (which can be referred to as the *social capital* of the community). Targeted disruption of such structures and networks is often the central focus of contemporary political and military conflict (Summerfield 1999).

Culture and values

Events may also disrupt the culture and values of a community, challenging human rights, cultural values, mores, and so forth (which can be referred to as the *cultural capital* of the community). Conflict can threaten cultural traditions of meaning that unite and give identity to a community (Wessells 1999). Conflict can also serve to reinforce hardened images of other political or ethnic groups, encouraging escalation of violence and hatred (Kostorova-Unkovska and Pankovska 1992).

FIG. INTRO–1. FACTORS INFLUENCING PSYCHOSOCIAL WELL-BEING

While psychosocial well-being is appropriately defined with respect to the three core domains of human capacity, social ecology, and culture and values, the loss of physical, economic, and environmental resources also has a major impact on well-being in many refugee settings. Availability and depletion of such resources thus define the broader context within which individuals, families, and communities protect their well-being.

Resilience

This model provides a useful framework for considering processes of coping, resilience, and recovery in war-affected communities (Strang and Ager 2003; Ager, Strang, and Abebe 2005). Hobfoll (1998) argues that investment and exchange of resources characterize the coping response of a community, that is, the active engagement of the community in addressing the consequences of conflict through the use of remaining, available resources to replace resources that have been lost. Skills are utilized to provide protection. Cultural values are used as a basis to reestablish social connections. Social networks are exploited to develop livelihoods.

So, to what extent does this model move us toward answering the questions we have posed? We have argued that psychosocial well-being can be seen as the ability to deploy resources effectively to cope with the challenges that a community faces. We have suggested that the resource domains of human capacity, social ecology, and culture and values together make up the core of psychosocial well-being. It follows that the focus of psychosocial intervention should be to support a community as it deploys these resources. Often, psychosocial intervention is prompted by a perception that a community's resources alone are insufficient to cope with the disruption and challenges it faces. The PWG framework suggests that psychosocial well-being can be effectively supported through interventions that enhance resources within all three domains and facilitate their interaction.

Fundamentally, the model recognizes the centrality of those who have themselves been affected by conflict in coping with its impacts. The need is not for restoration but for transformation to address the challenges of the future. Often, it is the inequities of what went before that provided the seeds of the conflict (Adjukovic 2001). Those of us seeking ways to help would best see ourselves as facilitators, offering our own resources and perspectives but ultimately empowering people to choose their own way forward.

This formulation elaborates the complexity of the relationship between those who are directly affected by conflict (the affected community) and those who seek to help (the external community).[2] It is clear that the external humanitarian community brings its own resources of human capacity, social ecology, and culture and values to a situation. Effective humanitarian interventions must acknowledge the differences in style, perspectives, and values of the various participants and implement programs through a process of negotiation. Yet so often these differences remain unacknowledged, programs are imported wholesale, and communities are left feeling abused by the humanitarian "invaders."

We hope our readers will find this book helpful. Previous literature on war-affected children (e.g., Apfel and Simon 1996; Cairns 1996; Leavitt and Fox 1993; Straker 1992) has focused mainly on how to provide psychosocial support. In addition, these works reflect the research emphasis of the late 1980s and early 1990s on trauma and mental illness. The work of the PWG acknowledges that these dimensions are important but also emphasizes that the impacts of war on displaced children cannot be conceptualized adequately within a trauma or mental-illness framework. For separated children, for example, trauma may be less the issue than the current lack of protection and problems meeting basic needs, such as food and shelter. Similarly, displaced children often report that their greatest stress is being teased at school due to their poverty, poor dress, or different language. Child soldiers often report that their biggest obstacle to reentering civil society lies not in healing from traumatic experiences but in earning a living and reconciling with their communities. These and related issues indicate the need for more holistic, socially contextualized approaches to understanding and assisting war-affected children—the benchmark of the social ecological portion of the PWG framework, which is the focus of this book.

Book overview

The following chapters analyze key components of the social worlds of children in violent settings, and our authors address them with detailed examples and the stamp of firsthand experience. We adopt the somewhat arbitrary age limit of eighteen to define the upper limit of childhood, which includes adolescence. Each author more or less follows this Convention on the Rights of the Child (CRC) age-determined definition of childhood, even though we acknowledge that the boundaries of childhood are often determined differently, based on historical, social, cultural, and political contexts.

In Chapter 1 Kathleen Kostelny provides a culturally grounded framework for understanding the lives and development of children in war zones. She opens with an analysis of the culture bias that permeates the study of war-affected children and invites critical reflection on how Western theories can be misapplied. To reduce these problems, she argues that culture must be at the center of one's analysis and programmatic actions.

The importance of the family to child well-being is enshrined in the CRC, as well as in most of the other significant international norms and standards. But does the protective role of the family really hold up in situations of armed conflict? In Chapter 2, Alastair Ager examines the value of the family as an explanatory concept regarding the social ecologies of children and war. He delves into the varied meanings of family and the different forms the structure can take, asking finally if there is any consistent understanding of what family is and is not? He then considers the contention that families, in addition to supporting well-being, can provide a context for abuse and neglect. Evidence for the sexual exploitation and malign socialization of children is also reviewed. The chapter concludes with an analysis of the appropriateness of the family as a locus for humanitarian intervention. The key functions for families in such contexts are identified. While families provide a potentially significant resource for children's well-being in the context of emergencies, such functions are seen as being potentially fulfilled by other social structures (for example, sibling and peer support) that may be more accessible in such settings. The conclusion also addresses the limitations of a purely functional framework of family.

Amy Hepburn, in Chapter 3, addresses the tragic problem of child-family separation as a persistent and predictable aspect of war and mass population movements, discussing the kinds of separation that occur, their causes, and the response of international and voluntary agencies. She provides an overview of the problem of separated children in emergencies, reviewing several historical case studies and describing some of the efforts agency personnel have taken and the problems they have encountered. She then deals with the psychological vantage point, looking in particular at the effects of loss and separation, other trauma, and care and placement concerns. In the final section she identifies effective interventions used to address and prevent family separation in conflict with an emphasis on tracing and reunification activities, as well as interim and durable solutions for care.

In Chapter 4 Susan McKay explores the issue of gender in the context of armed conflict and child soldiering and examines the specific, gender-mediated effects on girls who become members of fighting forces. She begins by discussing varying cultural perceptions of girlhood and how conflict often blurs the demarcation between childhood and adulthood for girls. She then provides an overview of what little is known about girls' roles and experiences as child soldiers and the physical, psychosocial, and economic impacts upon their lives when they return to civilian life. McKay points out the ways in which current humanitarian efforts fall short in assisting girl soldiers with reintegration into communities and calls for gender justice to help restore hope and dignity in former girl soldiers.

In Chapter 5 Cairo Arafat and Thahabieh Musleh embark on research to learn how children in the West Bank and Gaza are dealing with the conflict that permeates their lives. Their findings reveal that the majority of children do not feel safe; nor do they believe their parents can protect them. Almost half of the children had personally experienced or witnessed violence. But the study also found that most Palestinian children continue to exhibit positive signs of resiliency and remain largely optimistic about their personal futures. Schools are playing a pivotal role in the daily lives of children and remain "institutions of hope" for most of them. The chapter concludes with a discussion on how schools could evolve into "multi-functional centers" where girls and boys could study, play, and socialize throughout the day.

Chapter 6 explores the contributions youth make to conflict reproduction and peace building through their peer group interactions. Looking at narrative data collected in Northern Ireland since the Belfast/Good Friday Peace Accord, Siobhán McEvoy-Levy examines how youth are creating political meaning. The stories the young people construct, the frames and metaphors they use to describe their experiences of violence and attitudes to peace, and the dynamics of the focus groups themselves capture a process of collective meaning-making and illustrate how conflicts are reproduced. These narratives also create new knowledge about young people's needs and perceptions, and more generally, they critique and prescribe for peace. The chapter argues that active participation of youth in such activities can not only produce useful, nuanced, and new knowledge about conflict, but might also constitute an empowering practice—an experience of inclusion—that will be significant in breaking cycles of violence.

In Chapter 7 Neil Boothby's research on the adult outcomes of Mozambican child soldiers offers rare insights into how a group of boy soldiers have fared over time. It takes place in rural, southern Mozambique, where formal health and social welfare systems are either dysfunctional or nonexistent. In this "where there is no doctor" scenario, extended families, neighbors, community leaders, self-help safety nets, and traditional healers have stepped to the fore and enabled most of these former child soldiers to return to their communities and live meaningful and productive lives. Boothby discusses how a social ecological perspective can inform efforts to promote the reintegration of former child soldiers back into civilian life and identifies specific interventions that appear to have helped support positive adult life outcomes.

Michael Wessells continues the focus on child soldiers in Chapter 8, but from the perspective of livelihoods. The first part of the chapter examines lack of livelihoods as a prominent feature of the social ecology that enables child recruitment into armed groups. It then explores the pivotal role of livelihoods in the reintegration of former child soldiers. Using program case studies from Sierra Leone, Wessells provides concrete examples of how livelihoods supports enable reintegration, while also addressing wider cultural and social ecologies that shape the process of reintegration. The chapter concludes with reflection on the connections between livelihoods programs and the wider tasks of economic and political reconstruction that are necessary for building peace and social justice.

In Chapter 9 Michael Wessells and Alison Strang discuss the role of religion and political ideology as a resource for individuals and communities who have been affected by war. It focuses on young people's engagement with religious activities and examines individual factors in relation to religious commitment. It also examines the negative influences of extreme ideology and organizations in situations of conflict, and how organized violence challenges the moral development of older children and adolescents. Case studies show how older children from different war zones either have utilized religion to constructive ends (for example, come to terms with the existential meaning of a lost loved one) or, conversely, have been drawn toward extreme ideologies and groups to seek restitution and revenge.

The concluding chapter, written by Carl Triplehorn and Catherine Chen, identifies key lessons learned during organized efforts to protect children growing up amid conflict. It addresses both on-the-ground programs and practices that have made a positive difference in the lives of war-affected children, as well as international advocacy efforts to place the protection of children in armed conflict more squarely on the United Nations' Security Council peace-and-security agenda. The authors examine significant shortcomings in the international community's response to children in armed conflict and describe what is required to move child care and protection interventions to a more central focus on the international community's humanitarian response agenda.

Acknowledgments

We would like to thank the individuals and institutions that make up the PWG for their inspiration and assistance in moving this volume forward. We admire what you do in the world to help children through some of the ugliest moments in history—and have learned a great deal from you all through our PWG work together. We also want to thank Sara Saad El-Dein, Trina Vithayathil, and Bree Akesson, our most able research assistants, based within the Mailman School of Public Health's Program on Forced Migration and Health at Columbia University. And we are truly grateful to Carolyn Makison and the Andrew J. Mellon Foundation, whose vision and generosity have contributed significantly to a global effort to professionalize the field of humanitarian practice, including in the area of psychosocial response. While the final destination has not been reached, the journey has indeed begun!

Finally, we have been asked over the years how we reconcile the fact that we have been blessed with healthy sons and daughters who have grown up in the midst of relative peace and security while so many girls and boys we have come to know have not. We have never known how to respond to this question (other than with reflection or prayer), and we won't attempt an answer here. Suffice it to say that the discrepancy between our professional lives and private lives has heightened our own awareness of how children enter the world full of potential, and how fate and circumstance, in turn, can nurture, stunt, or crush this potential. We dedicate this book, then, to our children (Peter, Thomas, Nathaniel, Gordon, Elspeth, Rachel, and Aaron) and their generation, in hopes that the world they inherit as men and women will be a bit better off than the world they found as children.

Notes

[1] The membership of the Psychosocial Working Group comprises five academic partners (Institute for International Health and Development, Queen Margaret University College, Edinburgh; Joseph Mailman School of Public Health, Columbia University; Program in Refugee Trauma, Harvard University; Solomon Asch Centre for the Study of Ethnopolitical Conflict, University of Pennsylvania; Refugee Studies Centre, University of Oxford) and five humanitarian agencies (Christian Children's Fund; International Rescue Committee; Médecins sans Frontières–Holland; Mercy Corps; and Save the Children–US).

[2] The polarization between affected and external communities is a simplification to add clarity to the model. It is acknowledged that there is a continuum of degree to which communities are affected by any conflict situation.

References

Adjukovic, D. 2001. Welcome address, ISHHR annual conference, Cavtat, Croatia. June.

Ager, A., A. Strang, and B. Abebe. 2005. Conceptualising community development in war-affected populations: Illustrations from Tigray. *Community Development Journal* 40 (2): 158–68.

Apfel, R. J., and B. Simon, eds. 1996. *Minefields in their hearts: The mental health of children in war and communal violence.* New Haven, CT: Yale Univ. Press.

Bronfenbrenner, U. 1979. *The ecology of human development: Experiments by nature and design.* Cambridge, MA: Harvard Univ. Press.

———. 1986. Ecology of the family as a context for human development: Research perspectives. *Developmental Psychology* 22: 732–42.

Cairns, E. 1996. *Children and political violence.* Cambridge: Blackwell.

De Jong, K., M. Mulhearn, N. Ford, S. van der Kam, and R. Kleber. 2000. The trauma of war in Sierra Leone. *The Lancet* 355 (June 10), 2067–68.

Hobfoll, S. 1998. *Stress, culture, and community: The psychology and philosophy of stress*. New York: Plenum.

Human Rights Watch. 2005. Stop the Use of Child Soldiers->Facts. Available on the humanrightswatch.org website.

Kostorova-Unkovska, L., and V. Pankovska. 1992. *Children hurt by war.* Skopje, Macedonia: General Children's Consulate of the Republic of Macedonia.

Leavitt, L. A., and N. A. Fox. 1993. *The psychological effects of war and violence on children*. Hillsdale, NJ: Erlbaum.

Machel, G. 2001. *The impact of war on children*. Vancouver, British Colombia: UBC Press.

Miller, K., and L. Rasco, eds. 2004. *The mental health of refugees: Ecological approaches to refugee mental health*. Upper Saddle River, NJ: Erlbaum.

Montgomery, E., and A. Foldspang. 2005. Seeking asylum in Denmark: Refugee children's mental health and exposure to violence. *The European Journal of Public Health* 15 (3): 233–37.

PWG (Psychosocial Working Group). 2002. *The Psychosocial Working Group Research Agenda*. May. Available online.

———. 2003. Psychosocial intervention in complex emergencies: A conceptual framework. Available online.

Straker, G. with F. Moosa, R. Becker, and M. Nkwale. 1992. *Faces in the revolution: The psychological effect of violence on township youth in South Africa*. Athens, OH: Ohio Univ. Press.

Strang, A., and A. Ager. 2003. Psychosocial interventions: Some key issues facing practitioners. *Intervention* 1 (3): 2–12.

Summerfield, D. 1999. Sociocultural dimensions of conflict and displacement. In *Refugees: Perspectives on the experience of forced migration*, ed. A. Ager, 111–35. London: Continuum.

Wessells, M. G. 1999. Culture, power and community: Intercultural approaches to psychosocial assistance and healing. In *Honoring differences: Cultural issues in the treatment of trauma and loss*, ed. K. Nader, N. Dubrow, and B. Stamm, 276–82. New York: Taylor and Francis.

1

A CULTURE-BASED, INTEGRATIVE APPROACH

Helping war-affected children

Kathleen Kostelny

Introduction

Analyses of war-affected children have been dominated by theories from Western psychology, and much of the humanitarian work on behalf of these children reflects a Western perspective. Although Western psychology has yielded an impressive body of science and practice, it embodies the Enlightenment values of individualism. In conceptualizing how children have been affected by armed conflict, this lens leads people to focus on individual impact, when effects on children are mediated by their social ecologies, such as families, peers, and communities. Even our understanding of the child and these ecologies is culturally constructed. One cannot assume the universality of Western constructs of children, families, and communities.

For this reason it is vital to reflect deeply on issues of culture—to probe indigenous understandings of childhood, well-being, and healing practices—and to explore the power relations that lead to the imposition of Western approaches to mental health and intervention. Lack of awareness of these issues leads to violations of the "do no harm" imperative that should guide all humanitarian assistance to war-affected children.

This chapter provides a culturally grounded, ecological framework with which to view child development in war zones. Divided into three sections, the chapter first provides a critical analysis of the cultural bias inherent in many analyses of war-affected children. It examines issues of power asymmetry between the "helpers" and the "helped," how Western interventions can be misapplied in war zones, and the importance of placing culture at the center of understanding and working with children. Second, it presents an ecological systems framework that demonstrates the importance of social ecologies such as family, peer groups, civic groups, and community institutions. The framework incorporates a transactions perspective that paints a picture of children's dynamic, changing social ecologies and illuminates the risks and protective factors within them. The chapter concludes with a discussion of the ways an ecological approach can reduce risks and strengthen psychosocial supports for children, families, and communities through holistic, community-based interventions.

Cultural bias and its implications

What is childhood in a war zone? How do children and their caretakers make sense of their experiences? What indigenous practices exist for healing the wounds of war? The overwhelming majority of the child-development literature, psychological research, and interventions regarding war-affected children have a Western perspective that emanates mainly from North America and Europe. It cannot be assumed that such a perspective applies in other regions of the world, however. Since Westernized approaches address neither the indigenous understandings of childhood nor the experiences of children throughout most of the non-industrialized world—particularly children affected by war—a broader approach is called for (Boyden 1990).

While childhood is defined by the Convention on the Rights of the Child (CRC) as the period from birth through eighteen years of age, many non-Western cultures view the period quite differently. In many countries throughout sub-Saharan Africa, after a young person has completed traditional initiation rites (around the time of puberty), he or she is no longer considered a child and begins assuming adult responsibilities. Moreover, views of childhood, youth, and adulthood also depend on specific roles that one has assumed in one's culture. For example, in East Timor unmarried males are considered youths through their thirties, while married sixteen-year-old girls are viewed as adults. In addition to having different conceptualizations of when a child becomes an adult, many developing societies diverge from industrialized societies in their views of children's roles, responsibilities, and expected behaviors. In these societies young boys are expected to contribute to the household resources by tending animals, farming, or working outside the home, and young girls are expected to spend much of their day doing domestic chores such as cleaning, cooking, and caring for younger children.

Additionally, a key difference between Western and indigenous views of childhood is the focus on the individual versus the collective. While Western ideas of childhood view the child as an autonomous entity or as developing into one, in other countries (including most war zones) children's identities are defined mainly in terms of their social relations and social roles; people have collective identities that honor the good of the group over any individual good (Triandis 2001).

Western definitions of child development address the physical, cognitive, social, and emotional competencies necessary to engage fully in family and society (Aber et al. 1997), but cultural competencies, including the spiritual, are also crucial aspects of development (Garbarino et al. 1991; Wessells and Monteiro 2004). To engage fully in family and society, children need to be anchored in the knowledge and life skills of their community and culture (Garbarino and Kostelny 1996b).

Power asymmetry

In humanitarian work outsiders are typically called in at the beginning of emergencies to assess the situation and analyze how children have been affected. They bring with them the label of expert and the enormous prestige associated with their degrees. Local people, often desperate to get any help they can and feeling inferior, eagerly accept the diagnoses offered by the outsiders. These analyses frequently guide the interventions, which ultimately reflect Western assumptions and approaches. When working in war zones, one must be conscious of the power asymmetry that frequently exists between the persons providing psychosocial intervention and the persons receiving them. Historically, developing nations have been exploited and colonized by countries in the Western hemisphere. Imposing Western interventions is an act of "psychological imperialism" that marginalizes local belief systems and undermines cultural ways of dealing with psychosocial stresses (Anderson 1996; Dawes 1997; Wessells 1999; Wessells and Kostelny 1996).

This power asymmetry is evident when local people defer to the "wisdom" of Western experts while silencing their own knowledge and methods of healing. Frequently they are embarrassed about their "primitive" beliefs and practices. It is not uncommon for local people who have been educated in Westernized universities to shed their indigenous knowledge and traditions for "scientifically based" practices. Sharing knowledge, power, and decision making with local communities is crucial in correcting such power asymmetry.

Limits of Western approaches

In contrast to the traditional focus of psychology on individuals, families, and small groups, armed conflict and poverty are macro-level problems that require a focus on whole communities, ethnic groups, and nations, taking into account the larger social, economic, and political context (Martin-Baro 1994; Reichenberg and Friedman 1996; Wessells and Dawes 2006). For example, in East Timor, where the political conflict destroyed social trust between neighbors and communities, it was not productive to focus on individuals without taking into account the larger situation. Following the 1999 referendum young East Timorese men who were employed in the Indonesian army fought against their neighbors and destroyed important community structures, including homes, churches, and schools. The resulting divided communities and communal wounds required communal interventions that focused on rebuilding a positive community and reestablishing traditions and norms (Kostelny and Wessells 2004).

Concepts of mental health and mental illness also vary across cultures. Western psychology has focused on mental illness and concepts of trauma and post traumatic stress disorder (PTSD). Although the PTSD concept has been validated and has value in some contexts, a focus on trauma can marginalize other effects of war such as mistrust, hopelessness, social exclusion, and the current stresses of daily life. The diagnosis of PTSD, a product of Western psychiatry and psychology, does not usually fit well into local concepts of mental health and well-being (Honwana 1997, 1998, 1999; Marsella et al. 1996; Nader, Dubrow, and Stamm 1999). For example, research in Angola found that symptoms of PTSD were not correlated with dysfunctionality (Eyber and Ager 2004), in contrast with the United States, where dysfunction is one of the criteria used to define PTSD. In many non-Western cultures the somatic symptoms typically associated with PTSD, such as sleep disturbances, intrusive thoughts, and hyper-vigilance, are seen not as the result of experiencing a single traumatic event in the past but as part of current personal, social, and spiritual stresses and problems.

For example, in Mozambique a young girl cannot sleep at night because she hears the voice of her dead father, asking why she did not perform a burial ritual for him. Seen from a Western trauma model, this girl is experiencing the intrusive thoughts and sleep disturbances reflective of PTSD and stemming from her father being killed. Seen from Mozambique cosmology, her father's spirit is unable to transition to the next world without the burial ritual and will cause problems for her and the entire community. Within this culture the problem is seen as spiritual discord that is highly communal.

Focusing on specific life-threatening events and the resulting trauma ignores the chronic, macro stressors that are part of the fabric of life in most war zones—such as poverty (Dawes and Donald 1994; Straker 1987). Moreover, such terminology "medicalizes" and "pathologizes" individuals, and even whole populations, when it is the political and social systems that are dysfunctional (Punamaki 1989; Wessells 1999). Imposing Western concepts and interventions may be not only inappropriate but also unethical because it can cause harm to individuals, families, and whole communities.

The Western focus on trauma and mental-illness approaches issues from their negative aspects, when it may be more appropriate and effective to focus on positive aspects of functioning and well-being. A well-being model takes into account physical health as well as the social, spiritual, economic, and political (Ahearn 2000). Furthermore, a well-being model emphasizes people's capacity for coping and self-reliance rather than stigmatizing them and creating dependency by viewing them as victims. In Afghanistan, for example, even though many people had suffered decades of war, were politically and socially repressed under the Taliban, had experienced drought and food insecurity, and had been forced to flee their homes and communities, most appeared to be functioning well as defined by local social and cultural norms (Wessells and Kostelny 2002). Moreover, traumatic events are mediated by belief systems and cosmology, contributing to conceptions of functionality and well-being (Wessells

1999, Honwana 1997). In this example, Afghans reported that their Islamic faith along with family and community support had been key factors in helping them cope.

Culture

All children are part of a culture that shapes their development, provides meaning, transmits beliefs and values, and structures roles and responsibilities (Vygotsky 1986). Culture is not monolithic but dynamic and constantly changing, and among cultures there are differences of gender, class, and a host of other social factors. When trying to understand the situation and development of war-affected children, culture must be central to all analyses and interventions. However, while making culture central, it is important not to romanticize it and unconditionally accept all cultural practices. Harmful cultural practices exist—such as female genital mutilation and child sacrifice—and one must be vigilant in ensuring that children's rights and protection are not violated.

Understandings of child development, mental illness, mental health, and healing practices vary widely among cultures (Adler and Mukherji 1995; Gielen, Fish, and Draguns 2004). Moreover, how children interpret their experiences is culturally scripted, based on the beliefs, values, and practices within their society. In many war zones spiritual dimensions are essential in interpreting experiences and providing meaning. For example, girls in Sierra Leone who were abducted and repeatedly raped by multiple members of the Revolutionary United Front (RUF) during the armed conflict were regarded by themselves and their community as "contaminated," "unmarriageable," "unsuited for business," and having "unstable minds." These effects were seen as results of "violation of the bush" (Kostelny 2004). In African cosmology the bush is sacred, and its violation by sexual activity not only affects the girls but also brings misfortune in the form of crop failures and other community calamities. In contrast, a girl who is raped outside of the bush or a girl who is abducted but not raped may have a different interpretation of events and not be as stigmatized by her community.

Healing practices also vary by culture and are grounded in local beliefs. Indigenous healing practices in war zones often contain spiritual dimensions, which may include rituals, prayer, meditation, and reading sacred texts. Practices typically used in Western mental-health settings—such as emotional expression through talking—may be inappropriate, or even harmful, in a different cultural context. In many countries it is not emotional expression or talking through past traumatic events but culturally prescribed rituals that are required for healing and social reintegration. In many African countries children who have been soldiers must undergo rituals conducted by a traditional healer to restore spiritual harmony. In Angola a former boy soldier must participate in a ritual in which he is cleansed with flour, and a chicken must be sacrificed and its blood put on the door frame of a hut symbolic of his past. Also, the boy must put the clothes he wore as a soldier in this hut and then, as the hut and clothes are burned, he is told not to look back and not to talk about his experiences. For this society, talking about the past, a common Western practice, is to invite bad spirits into the community, causing calamities for all members (Honwana 1999). While some Western interventions may be of value, they must be carefully tailored to fit the context and integrated with local methods.

Ecological framework

The central tenet of ecological approaches is that children develop in a social milieu in which family, peers, teachers, and the wider community are part of the fabric of their day-to-day lives (Bronfenbrenner 1986). Economic, cultural, and political forces from the macro environment shape children's development as well. During armed conflict children's psychosocial well-being depends on a number of factors: the type and frequency of current stressors, their developmental level, their inner resources and coping strategies, the availability of support from the family and community, past experiences of risks and supports, and the meaning given to their experiences (Cairns 1996; Garbarino and Kostelny 1996b; Wessells 1998). When trying to understand the lives of children growing up in war zones and the impact of the above factors on their psychosocial well-being, it is helpful to incorporate a framework drawing upon both ecological and transactional models. Such a framework offers a dynamic picture of how risk factors and protective factors in the child's physical, social, and cultural environments contribute to, or impair, psychosocial well-being at different stages of the life cycle (Sameroff 1991; Sameroff and Fiese 2000).

Moreover, children are active participants in their social milieu, with the capacity for change (Garbarino et al. 1992). Children make choices about how they live, negotiate their roles within groups, and actively engage and cope with the stresses and risks they face. Children shape ongoing interactions in their family and community as they bring their capacities and past experiences to new interactions and situations. For example, in Afghanistan, after the fall of the Taliban, when girls were allowed to go to school again, some teachers insisted that girls have school uniforms and denied access to girls who did not have them. Although the girls' families were poor and could not afford uniforms, some girls persisted in walking great distances to school every day and "reasoned" with the teachers until the teachers let them in class (Wessells and Kostelny 2005).

Risk and protection

War zones expose children to a mixture of discrete risks, such as attack and displacement, and chronic risks, such as poverty and lack of access to health care. These risks can have adverse emotional, social, spiritual, and physical effects on children. Because of the urgency of meeting basic needs in emergency situations, attention is usually focused on ameliorating the impact of physical risks—such as illness, lack of shelter, or danger of attack. However, most physical risks also have impacts at the social, emotional, and spiritual level. A child in Afghanistan who is injured by a landmine has a physical injury but also may suffer the emotional impact of a lost limb and social stigmatization from peers. A child in Kosovo who has to flee home and country and become a refugee, not only loses a home—a physical place of refuge and source of emotional well-being—but also loses his or her social identity, social status, and culture.

Because war zones present multiple risks to children, their situation cannot be understood in terms of single events such as displacement from home, stepping on a landmine, or the death of a parent. In this respect a risk-accumulation model provides useful insights into the plight of children in conflict and post-conflict situations (Garbarino and Kostelny 1996a). This model asserts that as risks accumulate, the likelihood of damage to children increases exponentially. For example, the accumulation of three or more risks can produce ten times as much damage as a single risk factor (Rutter 1985).

These multiple, ongoing risks can occur at the family, community, and societal levels. At the family level children may suffer the loss of a parent or destruction of their home. Frequently children also do not have access to emotionally available adults, as parents and other community caretakers are frequently overwhelmed with basic survival, seeking shelter, food, and water. Moreover, among mothers in war zones, high levels of depression have been reported, and this has repercussions for children, including insecure attachment relationships with their caregivers (Garbarino and Kostelny 1996b).

At the community level children may be forced to flee their village, have their school destroyed, or be made to participate in activities that rupture their social bond with their community. In a number of countries, including Sierra Leone, Liberia, and Uganda, children were captured and then forced to attack their neighbors, causing social mistrust and disruption and effectively ensuring that the children would not be able to return to their communities (Wessells, forthcoming).

At the societal or macro level policies may be instituted that close schools or deny education and rights, as was the situation for girls under the Taliban in Afghanistan. Even after the fall of the Taliban, cultural norms in rural areas dictate that boys and girls have separate schools. Thus, where there is only one school in a village, and cultural norms do not allow young girls to walk unaccompanied, girls are still denied access to education (Wessells and Kostelny 2002).

Risks and supports operate in a dynamic fashion. While the accumulation of risk factors can negatively affect well-being, a child's resilience and coping capacities, as well as protective factors—including social supports within the environment—can increase a child's chances for positive outcomes (Garbarino, Kostelny, and Barry 1998). Resilience—the ability to adapt and function effectively in the face of adversity—does not imply that children are unaffected by their experiences, but rather that they have coped effectively with their experiences and are functioning in ways that are appropriate for their situation and culture. Protective factors for children include nurturing relationships with caretakers, supportive relationships with peers, meaningful interactions with adults, cognitive and emotional stimulation, and the opportunity to take part in cultural beliefs and practices.

Individual factors that promote resilience in children include a high level of cognitive functioning and temperaments that can adapt to changes in environment—such as displacement from home and school closures (Garbarino et al. 1992). Children learn coping skills and strategies that enable them to adapt and to manage adversity. For example, children who have experienced stressful events may seek out friends or supportive adults for advice and comfort, or participate in healing rituals and ceremonies. In Tamil Nadu, children who had lost friends in the December 2004 tsunami sought the help of adults in their community to conduct a tree-planting ritual that honored their friends and restored spiritual harmony (Kostelny and Wessells 2005).

At the family and community levels one of the most important protective factors for children is a relationship with at least one emotionally available adult (Werner and Smith 1992). When parents are not available, another family member or a member of the community—such as teacher, spiritual leader, or neighbor—can fill this role. Furthermore, the more people invested in the child, the greater the likelihood of positive outcomes. Informal networks of women, groups of youth, and religious figures are usually sources of social and emotional support for children. Community institutions, such as schools and places of worship, provide opportunities for social support as well as grounding in one's culture.

At the macro level, cultural traditions during difficult and stressful events provide emotional, social, and spiritual support that restore the rhythms of life, impart meaning, and lessen symptoms such as anxiety and fearfulness. Many individuals turn to spiritual leaders and healers during stressful times. In East Timor, a predominantly Catholic society, local people reported that their faith had been a crucial factor in helping them sustain horrific attacks and the destruction of their homes and communities by the Indonesian paramilitaries. Additionally, local staff who were able to partake in a religious service after their churches had been destroyed reported a restored sense of solidarity, lessened anxiety, hope that things were returning to normal, and restored spiritual harmony (Kostelny and Wessells 2002).

In conflict zones, then, children's well-being and level of resilience depend on the balance of risks and protective factors in their lives. While nearly all children in war zones are affected by stressful and traumatic events, certain groups, because of greater risks and fewer supports, are more vulnerable than others. Such vulnerability often results from the weakening or absence of family, community, and other social support systems. These vulnerable groups include displaced children, orphans, separated children, working children, sexually exploited children, and disabled children. Such vulnerable groups could benefit from additional psychosocial support.

Psychosocial interventions

An ecological framework is also useful in understanding how psychosocial supports for children in war zones can be strengthened through humanitarian assistance. Psychosocial support is often best provided through holistic, culturally grounded, family-based and community-based methods. To construct culturally relevant approaches, it is essential to use and to learn from local approaches, placing culture at the center of psychosocial work.

Local communities can often contribute a rich array of cultural resources to psychosocial assistance provided by international organizations. These resources include traditions, human resources, community processes, and tools (Nader, Dubrow, and Stamm 1999; Wessells 1999). Traditions provide support, ensure continuity, and bestow meaning during difficult events. Human resources—groups of women, elders, parent groups, teachers, religious leaders, traditional healers, as well as other leaders and persons of influence in the community—offer wisdom and expertise and can become active agents of community-based projects. Community processes include talking with key people, working within local power structures, and listening to different groups, increasing the likelihood that there will be community buy-in of the intervention. Tools include specific practices for healing, such as rituals, ceremonies, and singing and dancing.

Since these resources reflect values, beliefs, and cultural traditions, they give voice to and honor local people and thus are more sustainable than "off the shelf" or "copy and paste" methods imported from the West. It is local communities, using their cultural resources and supports, that are central to psychosocial well-being (Wessells and Monteiro 2004). Even though these resources may be disrupted during and after war, the role of outsiders should be to help restore traditions by assisting in community empowerment and building local capacity through facilitation, training, and technical assistance (Wessells 1999). In addition to drawing on cultural resources, interventions need to be holistic and engage community-based strategies that ensure empowerment and broad local participation. The engagement of local people, who themselves guide processes of collective planning and action, is at the heart of the community mobilization process that supports children's well-being (Boothby 1996).

Holistic approaches also link emotional and social support with meeting basic needs of food, shelter, and physical reconstruction. In difficult circumstances physical reconstruction and development are also psychosocial, offering tangible manifestation of improvement and building hope for the future (Boothby 1996). Additionally, holistic approaches also address the needs of the entire community and can include providing vocational training, teaching life skills, offering literacy classes, and providing links with jobs.

A good example of a large-scale, psychosocial intervention in a post-conflict setting that addressed risks through an ecological approach is the program that was implemented in Afghanistan by three NGOs—ChildFund Afghanistan (the Afghan arm of Christian Children's Fund), International Rescue Committee, and Save the Children–US—as part of the NGO Consortium on the Care and Protection of Children. Decades of war and extreme poverty, combined with frequent natural disasters such as drought, earthquakes, and floods, had by the late 1990s made Afghanistan's the world's largest refugee crisis. Most of the six million Afghan refugees in neighboring countries lived in abject poverty and overcrowded camps, fueling their desire to return home. Also, there were nearly two million internally displaced people who lacked the refugee protections extended under international law.

The opportunity for return and resettlement came following the overthrow of the Taliban in October 2001. However, most villages had been destroyed or plundered, and government services and capacities could not address the enormous needs throughout the country. Amid the displacement and chaos of war, most community-planning mechanisms had fallen dormant. Returning to their villages, most adults struggled to obtain food and to meet basic needs, leaving little time for attending to children. Child protection was a significant issue because many children were at risk, not only because of their war experiences, but also because of their current life situations, which included exposure to landmines and unexploded ordnance, early marriage of young girls, child soldiering, disability, dangerous labor, and trafficking (Wessells and Kostelny 2002).

To address these problems on a national scale and to avoid duplication of efforts, in 2002 the Consortium created a national child-protection program to improve the protection, well-being, and development of Afghan children through the reduction of risks, increased access to services such as education, and strengthened mechanisms and capacities for child protection at family, community, and societal levels. The program, using a geographic spread strategy—with the three agencies focusing in different locales—emphasized holistic, community-based psychosocial assistance and child protection. By mobilizing communities on a large scale, it hoped to strengthen civic society and weaken the grip of local warlords and commanders, who controlled access to basic goods and services and who continued to militarize the country.

In the first three years of the program, over twenty-five thousand children participated in formal and nonformal education programs. From a psychosocial standpoint, education is essential because it normalizes life, enables social integration, offers adult guidance, provides the basic life skills and competencies that support resilience, and increases life options, thus creating hope in difficult circumstances. In post-conflict situations education is itself a significant source of child protection (Nicolai and Tripplehorn 2003). Much of the education occurred nonformally in child-centered spaces, which were set up in tents or structures such as mosques and organized by community volunteers selected by local villages for their commitment to and skill in working with children. In Afghanistan nonformal education was essential because many villages did not have a school and girls were prohibited from walking unaccompanied outside their village.

In addition to teaching basic literacy skills, educating about health and hygiene, and spreading messages about landmines, the child-centered spaces also engaged children in expressive, culturally grounded activities such as singing, dancing, and storytelling. Additionally, a key part of the education work was training teachers to recognize and support war-affected children, referring the most severely affected for more specialized support. To build government capacities for education, consortium partners worked closely with Ministry of Education officials to limit the use of harsh, corporal punishment in schools, to integrate participatory teaching methods into teacher training, and, where possible, to transition away from temporary child-centered spaces toward the construction and use of new schools.

To build local capacities for child protection and mobilize communities around supporting children, the consortium partners worked in more than 150 villages through local volunteer groups. First, local program staff led groups of approximately ten children

seven to thirteen years of age in drawing maps that included all the
dwellings and geographic landmarks in their village and then indicating any places that were dangerous, where accidents happen, or where
children were afraid to go. Consistent with Afghan norms, separate
groups were held for girls and boys, which was also useful in highlighting gender differences in risks to children. This child-participa-
tion process aimed at building children's leadership and helping
children become agents of their own protection.

Next, the children prioritized the risks and presented them to the
community through a method of their choosing, such as drama, song,
art, or discussion. The presentation typically evoked considerable
excitement and interest, creating a venue for discussion of how to
organize and address the risks that children had presented. The local
staff then facilitated a dialogue about establishing a local committee
of people who would serve as catalysts and mobilizers to help the
village address the risks. The dialogue featured issues of inclusive-
ness, the value of children's participation, and the importance of including people or subgroups who live in the social margins of the
village, usually due to ethnicity, class, or disability status.

It was these discussions that led to the formation of the volunteer
groups, called child well-being committees, which consisted typically
of ten people, half of whom were under eighteen years of age. Staff
provided initial training on child protection and then made regular
follow-up visits for purposes of ongoing support and capacity building. Over time, the committees acquired skills in monitoring protection risks, reaching out to marginalized and vulnerable children, and
reporting abuses. Working with village groups, they conducted dialogues and activities to raise village awareness of children's situations
and means of supporting them. The committees also mobilized youth
to participate in community-selected civic-works projects such as school
construction, bridge repair, and installation of wells. Reports thus far
indicate that youths' participation in these projects, designed in part to
give them a positive role, boosts their sense of civic responsibility, promotes hope for the future, and elevates their status in the community.

Since child protection requires the formation of wide networks
for monitoring, reporting, and action, this program also built national capacities for child protection through the construction of local and regional child protection and action networks (CPANs). The
CPANs consisted of representatives of NGOs, youth associations,

government ministries, intergovernmental agencies such as UNICEF and UNHCR, and other groups that work in diverse areas, have contact with children, and were willing to incorporate a protection component into their work. For example, groups that focused on building shelters addressed child protection by having the community select the poorest, most vulnerable families as the first recipients for shelter assistance. Similarly, youth associations incorporated into their work messages that raised awareness about issues of trafficking, which were increasing in Afghanistan. The regional CPANs were connected with the national CPAN, which worked closely with the Afghan government on issues of child protection. Because they formed a national network, the CPANs offered a powerful venue for strengthening child protection on a national scale.

Although it is too early to discern its impact clearly, the program has brought about a significant increase in education participation, in part through the reduction of risks such as the use of harsh, corporal punishment in the schools. It has also raised awareness of protection risks, created processes for reducing risks, and created activities that have engaged young people in community service and the development of life skills that build a sense of hope. Also, the program has reduced some of the physical and psychological risks to children. While programs that work on this scale do encounter challenges in logistics, program consistency, and backup support —and these problems were amplified in Afghanistan due to the increasingly dangerous and fluid security situation—this program nevertheless illustrates how those interested in psychosocial assistance can contribute to national reconstruction efforts by working in a collaborative manner and in partnership with local people.

Conclusion

An important step in improving psychosocial assistance for war-affected children is the development of ecologically oriented, culturally grounded approaches. At present, there is strong rhetoric about the importance of developing ecological approaches and taking culture seriously. Too often, however, this rhetoric does not match reality, and many programs in the field continue to have excessively individual approaches that feature mostly Western methodology.

At the same time, it would be inappropriate to dismiss the value of Western approaches. The question is one of balance. In order to develop the field of psychosocial assistance in war settings, it will be valuable to think of blending and even integrating Western and local approaches in ways that fit local concepts and practices related to children's social ecologies.

References

Aber, L., M. Gephart, J. Brooks-Gunn, and J. Connell. 1997. Development in context: Implications for studying neighborhood effects. In *Neighborhood policy*, Vol. 1, *Context and consequences for children*, ed. J. Brooks-Gunn, G. Duncan, and L. Aber. New York: Russell Sage Foundation.

Adler, L. L., and B. R. Mukherji, eds. 1995. *Spirit versus scalpel: Traditional healing and modern psychotherapy*. Westport, CT: Bergin and Garvey.

Ahearn, F. 2000. Psychosocial wellness: Methodological approaches to the study of refugees. In *Psychosocial wellness of refugees*, ed. F. Ahearn, 3–23. New York: Berghahn.

Anderson, M. B. 1996. Humanitarian NGOs in conflict intervention. In *Managing global chaos: Sources of and responses to international conflict*, ed. C. A. Crocker, F. Hampson, and P. Aall, 343–54. Washington, DC: U.S. Institute of Peace Press.

Boothby, N. 1996. Mobilizing communities to meet the psychosocial needs of children in war and refugee crises. In *Minefields in their hearts: The mental health of children in war and communal violence*, ed. R. J. Apfel and B. Simon, 149–64. New Haven, CT: Yale Univ. Press.

Boyden, Jo. 1990. Childhood and the policy makers: A comparative perspective on the globalization of childhood. In *Constructing and reconstructing childhood: Contemporary issues in the sociological study of childhood*, ed. Allison James and Alan Prout. Philadelphia: Palmer Press.

Bronfenbrenner, U. 1986. Ecology of the family as a context for human development research perspectives. *Developmental Psychology* 22: 723–42.

Cairns, E. 1996. *Children and political violence*. Cambridge: Blackwell.

Dawes, A. 1997. *Understanding conflict and promoting peace: Contributions from South Africa*. A special issue of peace and conflict. Mahwah, NJ: Lawrence Erlbaum Associates.

Dawes, A., and D. Donald. 1994. *Childhood and adversity: Psychological perspectives from South African research*. Cape Town: David Philip.

Eyber, C., and A. Ager. 2004. Researching young people's experiences of war: Participatory methods and the trauma discourse in Angola. In *Children and youth on the front line: Ethnography, armed conflict and displacement*, ed. J. Boyden and J. de Berry, 189–208. New York: Berghahn.

Garbarino, J., et al. 1992. *Children and families in the social environment*. New York: Aldine de Gruyter.

Garbarino, J., and K. Kostelny. 1996a. The effects of political violence on Palestinian children's behavioral problems: A risk accumulation model. *Child Development* 67: 33–45.

———. 1996b. What do we need to know to understand children in war and community violence? In *Minefields in their hearts: The mental health of children in war and communal violence*, ed. R. J. Apfel, and B. Simon. New Haven, CT: Yale Univ. Press.

Garbarino, J., K. Kostelny, and F. Barry. 1998. Neighborhood-based programs. In *Violence against children in the family and the community*, ed. P. Trickett, and C. Schellenbach, 287–314. Washington, DC: American Psychological Association.

Garbarino, J., K. Kostelny, and N. Dubrow. 1991. *No place to be a child: Growing up in a war zone*. Lexington, MA: Lexington Books.

Garbarino, J., N. Dubrow, K. Kostelny, and C. Pardo. 1992. *Children in danger: Coping with the consequences of community violence*. San Francisco: Jossey-Bass.

Gielen, U., J. Fish, and J. Graguns. 2004. *Handbook of culture, therapy, and healing*. Mahwah, NJ: Lawrence Erlbaum.

Honwana, A. 1997. Healing for peace: Traditional healers and post-war reconstruction in Southern Mozambique. *Peace and Conflict: Journal of Peace Psychology* 3: 293–306.

———. 1998. *"Okusiakala Ondalo Yokalye": Let us light a new fire*. Luanda: Christian Children's Fund/Angola.

———. 1999. Non-western concepts of mental health. In *The refugee experience*, Vol. 1, ed. M. Loughry and A. Ager, 103–19. Oxford Univ. Refugee Studies Programme.

Kostelny, K. 2004. What about the girls? *Cornell International Law Journal* 37 (3).

Kostelny, K., and M. G. Wessells. 2002. *Mapping local cultural resources for psychosocial support in East Timor: A pilot study*. Richmond, VA: CCF International.

———. 2004. Internally displaced East Timorese: Challenges and lessons of large-scale emergency assistance. In *The mental health of refugees: Ecological approaches to healing and adaptation*, ed. K. Miller and L. Rasco, 128–225. Hillsdale, NJ: Erlbaum.

———. 2005. Psychosocial aid to children after the Dec 26 tsunami. *The Lancet* 366 (9503).

Marsella, A., M. Friedman, E. Gerrity, and R. Scurfield, eds. 1996. *Ethnocultural aspects of posttraumatic stress disorder*. Washington, DC: American Psychological Association.

Martin-Baro, I. 1994. *Writings for a liberation psychology*. Cambridge: Harvard Univ. Press.

Nader, K., N. Dubrow, and B. Stamm, eds. 1999. *Honoring differences: Cultural issues in the treatment of trauma and loss*. New York: Taylor and Francis.

Nicolai, S., and C. Triplehorn. 2003. The role of education in protecting children in conflict. London: Humanitarian Practice Network.

Punamaki, R. 1989. Political violence and mental health. *International Journal of Mental Health* 17: 3–15.

Reichenberg, D., and S. Friedman. 1996. Traumatized children. Healing the invisible wounds of war: A rights approach. In *International responses to traumatic stress*, ed. Y. Daniele, N. S. Rodley, and L. Weisaeth. Amityville, NY: Baywood.

Sameroff, A. 1991. The social context of development. In *Becoming a person*, ed. M. Woodhead, P. Light, and R. Carr, 167–89. London: Routledge/ The Open University.

Sameroff, A., and B. Fiese. 2000. Transactional regulation: The developmental ecology of early intervention, in *Handbook of early childhood intervention*, 2nd ed., ed. J. Shonkoff and S. Meisels. New York: Cambridge Univ. Press.

Straker, G. 1987. The continuous traumatic stress syndrome: The single therapeutic interview. *Psychology and Sociology* 8 (1): 48–79.

Triandis, H. 2001. Individualism and collectivism: Past, present, and future. In *The handbook of culture and psychology*, ed. D. Matsumoto. New York: Oxford Univ. Press.

Vygotsky, L. 1986. *Thought and language*. Cambridge, MA: MIT Press.

Werner, E., and R. Smith. 1992. *Overcoming the odds: High risk children from birth to adulthood*. Ithaca, NY: Cornell Univ. Press.

Wessells, M. G. 1998. Humanitarian intervention, psychosocial assistance, and peacekeeping, in *The psychology of peacekeeping*, ed. H. Langholtz. Westport, CT: Praeger.

———. 1999. Culture, power, and community: Intercultural approaches to psychosocial assistance and healing. In *Honoring differences: Cultural issues in the treatment of trauma and loss*, ed. K. Nader, N. Dubrow, and B. Stamm, 276–82. New York: Taylor and Francis.

———. Forthcoming. *Stolen childhoods*. Cambridge, MA: Harvard Univ. Press.

Wessells, M. G., and A. Dawes. 2006. Macro-level interventions: Psychology, social policy, and societal influence processes. In *Handbook of international psychology*, ed. M. Stevens and U. Gielen. Westport, CT: Praeger.

Wessells, M. G., and C. Monteiro. 2004. Psychosocial assistance to internally displaced people in Angola: A child focused, community-based approach. In *From clinic to community: Ecological approaches to refugee mental health*, ed. K. Miller and L. Rasco. Upper Saddle River, NJ: Erlbaum.

Wessells, M. G., and K. Kostelny. 1996. *The Graça Machel/U.N. study on the impact of armed conflict on children: Implications for early child development.* New York: UNICEF.

———. 2002. *After the Taliban: Assessing the needs of children in northern Afghanistan.* Richmond: Christian Children's Fund.

———. 2005. Assessing Afghan children's psychosocial well-being: A multimodal study of intervention outcomes. Edinburgh: Christian Children's Fund, Oxford Univ., and Queen Margaret's Univ. College.

2

WHAT IS FAMILY?

The nature and functions of families in times of conflict

Alastair Ager

The family in policy and practice

The family is central to current understandings of the welfare of children; however, this emphasis can preclude other social ecological structures in children's lives that are equally or sometimes more important. The initial sections of this chapter explore the reasons for and against viewing the family as the cornerstone of war-affected children's well-being.

This centrality of family is reflected in a wide range of international conventions and policy statements. The United Nations Convention on the Rights of the Child (CRC), for instance, sees the family as key in ensuring the well-being of children: "The child, for the full and harmonious development of his or her personality, should grow up in a family environment" (CRC 1989, preamble).

Indeed, a conviction regarding the role of the family is at the heart of its rationale: "The family, as the fundamental group of society and the natural environment for the growth and well-being of all its members and particularly children, should be afforded the necessary protection and assistance so that it can fully assume its responsibilities within the community" (CRC 1989, preamble).

Protection of and assistance to the family is seen as a key strategy in protecting children. It is the family's job to provide adequate care, and families need to be equipped for this task. The role envisioned

39

for the state is an enabling rather than directing one: "States Parties shall respect the responsibilities, rights and duties of parents or, where applicable, the members of the extended family . . . to provide, in a manner consistent with the evolving capacities of the child, appropriate direction and guidance" (CRC 1989, Art. 5).

Such emphasis on the role of families in protecting and nurturing children is found in many other policy documents relevant to the experience of children affected by war. For example, the UNHCR Policy on Refugee Children again emphasizes the accountability of parents for their children and the strategy of the state supporting children by supporting their parents:

> A principle of international law fundamental to this policy is the primary responsibility of parents or legal guardians to care for children. Moreover, States are responsible for protecting the human rights of all persons within their territory, including refugee children, and for providing *adults accountable for these children with the support necessary to fulfill their own responsibilities.* (UNHCR 1993, para 18, emphasis added)

Within these guidelines the responsibilities of parents are justified explicitly by emphasizing the dependence of children—physical, economic, and psychological—on their families:

> Three interrelated factors contribute to the special needs of refugee children: their dependence, their vulnerability and their developmental needs. . . . Children . . . are dependent upon their parents or other adults to provide the basic necessities for their survival. Moreover, they are . . . legally dependent on their parents or guardians for appropriate guidance and direction. (UNHCR 1993, para 10)

The stories in the following paragraphs, however, illustrate the potential fragility and complexity of this physical, economic, and psychological dependency.

In Sierra Leone a young mother who had been abducted, raped, and impregnated by members of an armed group cares for her one-year-old girl. Although both mother and child are HIV-positive and the mother lacks steady income, the mother is the child's only source of food, protection, and health care. Enrolled in an NGO program on income generation, she learns new skills marketable in the local area and says, "I love my baby and will take care of all her needs."

A ten-year-old Afghan boy, Mohammed, attends school in the morning, tends his family's animals in the afternoon, and occasionally sells small items in the streets to help support his family. Mohammed defines his identity in terms of his family, introducing himself to others as the son of his father and other ancestors. His developing identity relates closely to his role as a worker in the family. As in many developing countries, Afghan children are integral parts of a family labor system in which all family members contribute to family income. For Mohammed, who finds meaning in his work, being a good son means supporting his family and taking care of elders and infirm family members.

Seeing children as vulnerable and dependent upon their families (though perhaps significantly contributing to the income of the family) has clear implications for humanitarian practice. Children are reached—and conceptualized—through the social context of their family. It is this social unit that supports the well-being and development of the child, so it is this social unit that is the focus of support and intervention:

[These are the] central principles which will guide . . . UNHCR staff. . . .
(b) preserving and restoring family unity are of fundamental concern;
(c) actions to benefit refugee children should be directed primarily to enable primary care-givers to fulfill their principal responsibility to meet their children's needs;
(d) . . . child-focused activities . . . should be carried out with the full participation of their families. (UNHCR 1993, para 26)

Such statements place the family as central to our understanding and promotion of the well-being of children. But is such a preeminent position for the family justified? Are there other social ecological structures in these children's lives that are of equivalent or perhaps even greater importance?

Deemphasizing the role of the family

In recent years a number of analyses have argued that the preeminent place given to the family in such statements may indeed be unjustified (e.g., Nordstrom 1997; Boyden and Mann 2000). This is not to say that the family cannot play a key role in the protection and support of children, but does it deserve to be a cornerstone of our approach to analysis and intervention?

In reviewing processes of socialization of children, Dawes and Donald (1994) suggest that there is often an uncritical acceptance of the role and power of parents in shaping the experience of children. They note how approaches that emphasize the role of parents often convey, as Robert D. Hess stated, a "concept of adult life as a relatively monolithic structure of norms and sanctions with immense power to impress its expectations on the developing child" (Richter 1994, 35).

This is not to say that there are not settings in which parents have significant influence and power. Rather, it is to acknowledge that this may not always be the case, at least when there are many competing sources of power and influence. Thus Dawes and Donald suggest that such expectation of parenting "is a difficult concept to apply in a . . . complex, differentiated and pluralistic society . . . [where] there are several intersecting socializing units, including the family, school and neighborhood [that] . . . diffuse the impact of any single socializing unit" (Dawes and Donald 1994).

A view of the family, and especially parents (or guardians), as the key focus for understanding children's well-being is challenged here by greater awareness of the *plurality* of socializing forces in the lives of children. Another consideration challenging analysis and intervention unduly focused on the family is that of the *autonomy* of children.

While the CRC places significant emphasis on the responsibilities of families, as described earlier, this convention has also fostered greater awareness of the autonomy of children. In fact, the convention asserts that children's participation is a key principle and that children's views should be not only heard but given "due weight" (CRC 1989, Art. 12). Working within the framework of the convention inevitably leads to discussions of the power of children to shape their lives and the manner in which, as children's autonomy grows, the influence of family is diminished. The developmental transition involved in this process is reflected in the following UNICEF policy guidance:

> It is in fact essential that children be provided with the necessary options that exist and the consequences of such options such that they can make informed and free decisions. Providing information enables children to gain skills, confidence and maturity in expressing views and influencing decisions. (UNICEF 2000)

The increasing establishment of autonomy is not only conceived as a developmental goal as suggested here, however. It can be promoted both as a human right and, indeed, as a pragmatic assessment of the importance of children's own resources. Particularly in unstable environments, but potentially in many other circumstances also, there are calls for interventions to be based on a "view of children as agents of their own survival and development . . . [and] even of self-sufficiency in children" (Boyden and Mann 2000). A number of agencies now place child agency—and its promotion and protection—at the core of their humanitarian and developmental agendas (e.g., CCF 2004).

The plurality of socialization influences on the lives of children and a growing appreciation of the potential value of children's autonomy both call into question the central role of the family in our understanding of how to promote the psychosocial well-being of children affected by armed conflict. The following sections thus consider the evidence for retaining the family as the central construct in our analysis and intervention.

The family as an explanatory concept

Variation in the meaning of family

Is it meaningful to talk of *family* at all? The term is widely used to denote a grouping of adults and dependent children. However, with such diversity within and across societies, is there anything consistent about our understanding of the term? The paragraphs below describe "families" that were displaced because of the conflict in sub-Saharan Africa.

The Jeketes live in a refugee settlement on the edge of a village. Mrs. Jekete lost her husband, daughter and eldest son in the civil war. She shares her weekly food ration with her sole surviving son—and only living close relative—thirteen-year-old Paulo. Paulo is not in school and tries to get work to buy food and basic commodities for himself and his mother. He sleeps in a friend's house, under a plastic sheet that serves as a blanket.

Gabrielle Namalomba, fifteen, lives with her mother, aunt, and two brothers in a house provided by her uncle when his family fled to a neighboring country. She enjoys school and hopes to get a job in an office with the company that employed her grandfather.

Julius Sitola, fourteen, lives on the street with his brother, Thomas, who is sixteen. They lost contact with their parents during an invasion of their district by rebel forces and assume that they were killed. They make a living on the streets through some trading and petty crime, and are beginning to befriend a number of other street children.

Joseph, a thirteen-year-old Ugandan boy, became head of his household after his parents died of AIDS. He oversees the well-being of his six younger brothers and sisters. An excellent student, Joseph still dreams of attending university, though for now his primary goal is to care for his siblings.

In terms of the social ecology of the children living in these families, despite significant commonalities in experience and circumstances, the relationships and resources available are enormously diverse. Does it make sense to talk of family as if it were a definable structure in the lives of children when such diversity exists?

Data not only testify to the variation in the structures of families, but also in the expectations of their roles across cultures. Consider, for example, experience of this African woman bringing up children as a refugee in Scotland:

"Back home I wouldn't be alone to deal with this. . . . In Africa, I would say, the child is brought up by the whole family, even the whole village. If a neighbor sees a child doing something wrong, he will punish him for me and I won't say, 'no, you've done wrong,' so the child is well protected. If I talk to him or her and he seems not to listen, his aunt will talk to him,

and so on. But then that's different from here." (Ager 2002, parent 1,
transcript 1)

Here, both the boundaries of what constitutes the family and the
roles and responsibilities of its members are seen to depend on the
setting. "Back home" one set of expectations applies; "here" another
set applies.

Consistencies in the meaning of family

Although such evidence challenges simplistic generalizations about
families, legal and economic definitions establish some commonality.
As the policy statements referenced earlier demonstrate, dependency
is commonly fundamental to defining the legal relationship of adults
to children. Similarly, in the economic sphere, the household is widely
used as a framework to define familial relationships and commitments.
Principles such as sharing a common meal or sleeping under the same
roof are generally taken to have sufficient local meaning and external
validity to be used as a common measure of household membership
and obligation across cultures.

However, from a psychosocial perspective, parental behavior and
mutual expectations of parent and child vary widely across cultures,
making generalizations about parenting hazardous. Nonetheless,
Hundeide has proposed the commonality of "a contract between parent and child . . . negotiated within cultural norms and practices"
(Hundeide 1991); that is, while there is wide variation in specific behaviors and roles, there is—at a certain level of abstraction—a common task that is addressed at the familial level by parents and other
caregivers.

Figure 2–1 is a schematic representation of the process of child
socialization that locates this task between direct personal experience
and learning mediated by wider societal structures and institutions,
such as school, religion, and government. Children's understanding
of the world develops as a result of action within it. Children learn
directly from such interaction, but much of their learning is mediated, or interpreted and shaped, by others. The family is the locus for
a key part of this process of mediation, passing on knowledge regarding social mores, expectations, and effective behavior. Within this
schema such family-mediated experience is valuable to the extent that

FIG. 2–1. CHILD SOCIALIZATION

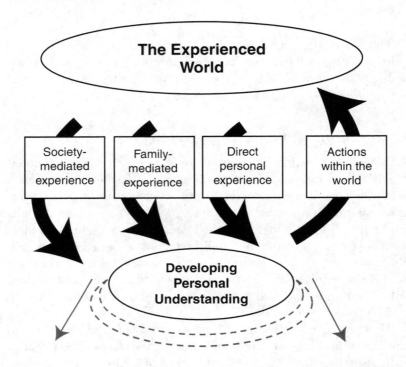

it is both more efficient and secure than relying on direct experience and also more intense and focused than societal mediation.

This idea that there are—at a sufficiently high degree of abstraction—common socialization processes at work across widely varying settings is also at the heart of the conceptualization offered by Steven E. Hobfoll. Hobfoll talks of "individuals-nested-in-families-nested-in-social organization" to describe the social ecological context shaping the experience of individuals. He sees that actions and values can be construed as "nested" within other structures, with the family serving as a key layer of "nesting" between the individual and wider social institutions (Hobfoll 1998).

Despite wide variation in the behaviors and values expected of families in differing settings, there seem to be broad economic, social, and psychological justifications for considering the family as an appropriate unit of analysis. However, the theoretical conceptualization that has had greatest influence in our own more recent work (e.g., Ager,

Strang, and Abebe 2005)—and which has clear synergies with the ecological focus of this book—is drawn from analysis of the notion of social capital.

Social capital is a concept that reflects the resources available to individuals as a result of their connection to others. It can be used to understand a wide range of social processes affecting the well-being of communities (Ager, Strang, and Abebe 2005). There are a number of different formulations of social capital, but Michael Woolcock's is perhaps the most helpful: "Woolcock's (1998) model of social capital facilitates analysis across various levels by presenting a comprehensive framework that incorporates four dimensions of social capital: strong ties between family members and neighbors; weak ties with the outside community and between communities; formal institutions (including laws and norms); and state-community interactions" (Colletta and Cullen 2000, 6).

It is the first two of these dimensions that are of greatest relevance for our current analysis, with the first most clearly equating to family structures: "Strong ties (integration) form the primary building blocks of society, uniting nuclear and extended family members and neighbors. These relations, predominantly based on kinship, ethnicity and religion are largely protectionist, defense mechanisms that form a safety net for basic survival" (Colletta and Cullen 2000, 6; see also Granovetter 1973; Gittell and Vidal 1998).

In many analyses, including our own (Ager and Strang 2004; Ager, Strang, and Abebe 2005), such ties are specified as social bonds, given their fundamental role in providing individuals a firm social foundation for action. Such bonds are contrasted with social links: "Weak ties (linkages) are more networked and associational and connect people to the outside community. . . . These cross-cutting relations are often affiliated with offensive measures, such as civic engagement and economic enterprise, that give people the strategic advantage they need to move ahead" (Colletta and Cullen 2000, 6).

The development of social bonds is generally seen as important in providing capacity to develop and exploit social links (Ager, Strang, and Abebe 2005). The family provides a protective network of social relations, a defensive foundation upon which active, wider engagement can be built.

Although we need to provide for wide variation in its incarnation across cultures, a key "place" for the family in these various understandings is connecting individual children's capacities and needs with the wider social institutions that they need to access. Whether it is through Hobfoll's vision of individuals nested in families nested in social organization (1998), through the role of social bonds, or through some other conceptualization, we can see families playing a key mediation role, supporting the development of competencies and understandings in children so that they may move confidently and effectively into the wider social world. But what evidence is there of the effectiveness of such processes in the context of conflict and displacement? Does the social ecology of the family provide a key protective structure for war-affected children?

The family as a resource for war-affected children's psychosocial well-being

A historic and influential claim regarding the protective influence of family on war-affected children is based upon Freud and Burlingham's 1943 work with evacuated and non-evacuated children during the Second World War. Their findings supported the resilience of children in the face of exposure to bombing raids when the family was able to play a mediating and protective role. Conversely, there was greater vulnerability in children separated from families (and potentially less exposed to the war) through evacuation. This led them to conclude:

> War acquires comparatively little significance for children so long as it only threatens their lives, disturbs their material comfort, or cuts their food rations. It becomes enormously significant the moment it breaks up family life and uproots the first emotional attachments of the child within the family group. (in Ressler, Boothby, and Steinbock 1988, 149)

Ressler, Boothby, and Steinbock's report on field experience with war-affected children broadly supports this conclusion, though controlled studies as rigorous as Freud and Burlingham's 1943 work have been rare. A number of correlational studies have established that family intactness is positively associated with measures of psychological well-being (Rumbaut 1991; Ager, Ager, and Long 1995). Also, it has consistently been found that parental coping predicts children's resilience (McCallin 1996; Laor et al. 1997). Ivanka Zivic has concluded

that "the best predictor of positive outcomes for the child who sur-
vives intensive stress is the ability of important adults around him or
her, primarily parents, to cope" (Zivic 1993, 711).

Raija-Lena Punamaki has conducted perhaps the most thorough
program of research in this area in recent years, focusing on the experience of children and their parents in the Palestinian Occupied
Territories (Punamaki 1990; 2000a). Her work has shown the close
potential relationship between family functioning and the social and
emotional well-being of children, clarifying how parenting style, for
instance, can mediate negative psychological impacts of exposure to
conflict (Punamaki 2000b). However, Punamaki expresses concern
that such findings be interpreted with an appropriate understanding
of the broader impact of war on family functioning:

> It has been claimed that a young child does not suffer emotion-
> ally from war experiences at all if the parents, and especially the
> mother, is able to maintain a stable relationship and if the se-
> cure structure of family life is not shaken. This statement is ut-
> terly unrealistic because war, by its very nature, disturbs and
> breaks up family life. It is often precisely the demands which
> war makes on families that produce disturbing effects on a child's
> psyche. (Punamaki 1987, 27)

While data have established that families can serve as a buffer for
children in the context of war, Punamaki's observations clarify that
such protection is not guaranteed. War—directed as it often is at
"unpicking" the fabric of people's social and cultural lives (Summerfield
1999)—creates a clear threat to families' ability to provide the mediation role outlined in the previous section. Such a perspective may be
helpful in interpreting data that are at odds with the findings reported
earlier regarding the protective influence of family. Loughry and
Nghia, for instance, found that "while the unaccompanied returnee
children have lived for an average of two years in harsh confined conditions, without their parents, and at a vulnerable age, this study has
found no significant difference between the returnee children and
their local counterparts who never left Vietnam" (Loughry and Nghia
2000, 171).

Although this finding may be seen to point to the resilience of unaccompanied children (an issue explored in more detail later), it can also
be taken to indicate the lack of protection provided by Vietnamese

families in a context of conflict. While families can serve a protective function, there are contexts in which such function is compromised. Indeed, it needs to be acknowledged that there are circumstances in which the family not only fails to protect but serves as a locus of harm.

When families do more harm

Kostarova-Unkovska and Pankovska, for example, document the key role played by families in socializing children into the stereotypes and prejudice that enabled and fueled inter-ethnic conflicts in the Balkans (Kostarova-Unkovska and Pankovska 1992). In her study of family functioning in the Palestinian Occupied Territories, Khamis found that 16 percent of Palestinian households showed rates of maltreatment (emotional abuse, emotional neglect and "corrupting") indicative of psychological abuse (Khamis 2000). While child characteristics, parental demographics, and economic hardship were each predictive of higher rates of abuse, the most significant predictor of abuse was the methods of socialization (including discipline) chosen by parents. This work confirmed the findings of earlier studies (e.g., Garbarino and Kostelny 1996), which reported significant risk to Palestinian children living in abusive families.

In war zones families may pose some of the greatest risks to children. In Northern Afghanistan, following the Taliban's defeat, significant numbers of poor families arranged marriages for daughters as young as eleven years of age, often to men in their fifties (Wessells and Kostelny 2004). Although such forced early marriages bring economic benefits to the family, they carry high risks of maternal mortality, post-birth complications, and subsequent family violence. In many war zones it is not uncommon for families to marginalize particular children, such as disabled children, who are stigmatized by the community and unable to earn an income, or to exploit children by sending them to the streets to sell rather than sending them to school.

Although evidence supports the potential of the family as a resource protecting the psychosocial well-being of war-affected children, it is clear that such protection is not a given. The context of war and conflict can not only erode the effectiveness of protection but also can distort the powerful socializing influence of the family toward abusive and malign effects.

The family as a locus for humanitarian intervention

This section considers the implications of the preceding analysis for seeing the family as a key locus for humanitarian intervention to aid children affected by armed conflict. It draws on the model elaborated on in this book's introduction and developed by the Psychosocial Working Group (PWG 2003). The PWG model presents a framework for analyzing needs and resources in conflict settings, and identifying appropriate response strategies. The psychosocial well-being of a community is understood with respect to three core domains: human capacity, social ecology, and culture and values (see Figure Intro–1). Reflecting Hobfoll's analysis, war-affected communities are considered actively to deploy resources from each of these domains in addressing their needs. Communities recognize that responding to the threats and losses associated with conflict means making use of all the skills, capacities, linkages, culture, and values available to them (Hobfoll 1998).

The work of the PWG argues for humanitarian responses that build upon such mechanisms of engagement, bolstering the process of recovery through investment in the resources of human, social, and cultural capital (PWG 2003; Ager, Strang, and Abebe 2005). In terms of this analysis, then, the place that the family has in humanitarian response depends upon its role in the process of community engagement and recovery.

Key functional tasks of the family

The roles and responsibilities of families will—as noted earlier—vary across settings, but the above analysis helps us define the key tasks that families will usually be required to carry out. These tasks are best understood with respect to the mediation role elaborated on earlier, whereby families enable individuals to connect to the resources of the wider community in which they are nested (Hobfoll 1998). Without mediation, children cannot (easily) access the knowledge, skills, relationships, and values that may be present in their environment. The function of a family is to help children develop into individuals able to access the wider resources of the community.

Combining the analysis of resources offered by the PWG framework with the concept of mediation, these key tasks of the family involve providing children access to the four core domains of resources illustrated in Figure 2–2. These core domains are provision of an economic foundation for meeting physical needs, promoting care, and providing protection; fostering basic skills and competencies; fostering social access; and transmission of cultural knowledge and values.

First, the family is paramount in providing care and protection for children. A primary aspect of this is providing an economic environment in which basic physical needs are met. Young children do not have the ability to access such resources themselves. By adulthood, individuals are generally expected to have acquired the capacity to access such resources (maybe in cooperation with others). The family is tasked with enabling this transition from resource dependence

FIG. 2–2. KEY TASKS OF THE FAMILY

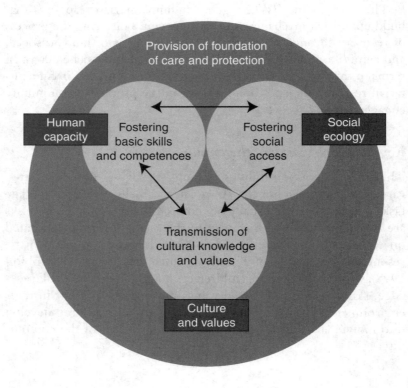

to resource provision. It is important to emphasize this notion of transition, and the influence of context on its nature and pace. The economic dynamics of households vary widely, and assuming that children are economic "dependents" on parents and other elders, while common in the West, is globally uncommon. Children typically play a significant economic role within households in the developing world, sometimes through external earnings, but usually by fulfilling domestic (for example, water collection and sibling care) or other tasks (for example, supervision of animals), which frees adult time for other activities. In terms of the framework described here, the key task of the family is to create a sufficiently sound economic foundation to meet physical needs of family members. This may appropriately utilize the capacities of children but will be harmful for children if their labor disrupts opportunities for gaining other resources, such as appropriate social development, education, and skills.

Providing a foundation of care and protection is, of course, not limited to such economic considerations. It also includes protecting children from disease and outside threats such as crime, sexual assault, and forced recruitment. Of no small importance are psychosocial dimensions, such as providing a safe context in which children form attachments to their parents or caretakers, thereby fulfilling a key developmental task that provides a foundation for healthy, subsequent relationships (Bowlby 1969; Grossman, Grossman, and Waters 2005). What all these elements share is that they provide a foundation upon which other resources can be built.

The three other key tasks for the family relate to developing resources in the domains of human capacity, social ecology, and culture and values. In terms of human capacity, community institutions such as school clearly play a great part in developing skills and knowledge. The task of the family is to enable children to develop basic skills and competencies that allow them to access such institutions—for them to behave knowledgeably and competently within their community—so that they may be able to learn from its rich resources. Within the family children learn positive values, trust, and skills of empathy and cooperation that subsequently shape their engagement with their communities and societies.

In my work with parents of intellectually impaired children in Malawi during the 1980s, I was initially struck by how different the goals of these parents seemed to be compared to those of parents in the UK. Whereas UK parents would typically want their disabled children to dress and feed themselves, their Malawian counterparts prioritized such things as respectfully greeting visitors to the village. However, on reflection, these behaviors served a similar function in the two very different cultures. These tasks were examples of the most basic skills and competencies that would allow their children to engage effectively within their community.

A child needs skills and competences—a degree of human capital—to begin to engage with the wider resources of the community. But social connections are also required. The family frequently provides the initial basis of such connections through the relationships, status, and identity of relatives and the social group to which the family belongs. These are the "strong ties" (Colletta and Cullen 2000) or "social bonds" (Ager, Strang, and Abebe 2005) that underpin the longer-term development of "social bridges" (into other communities) or "social links" (into institutions of the state). To the extent that conflict disrupts the capacity of families to address these crucial tasks, this model thus provides a framework for considering priority interventions to protect children in times of war.

The fourth key task for the family in this model is the transmission of basic cultural knowledge and values. Children will directly experience local culture and values through their interactions with the world and, over time, come under the influence of a range of educational, religious, and civic institutions that shape such understandings. The family, however, commonly functions as a mediator of cultural understanding: modeling, explaining, and codifying cultural expectations and values. The family is again functioning to equip a child for effective engagement with wider community and societal institutions, this time through acquisition of core cultural knowledge and values. Typically, values about the family itself will be a key part of the cultural message that is transmitted. The role of the family in modeling appropriate attachment, care, and respect is valued as a central tenet by many cultures.

The following story illustrates how conflict can interfere at multiple levels with these key tasks of family:

Hind, fourteen, lives with her parents and two younger brothers in the town of Qalqilya, in the north part of the Occupied Palestinian Territories. A barrier assembled by the Israelis encircles her home, and her parents are now unable to visit relatives in nearby towns. The "wall" has significantly disrupted social connections with friends and family that are important to Hind's social development. The classes that she attended in cultural dance—which her parents had valued for educating Hind in traditional songs and dances—have also been disrupted, eroding her access to "cultural capital."

Although this formulation is driven by the PWG framework for understanding psychosocial well-being and intervention, it reflects a number of issues addressed earlier in the chapter. It reflects Woolcock's idea of the social bonds of the family providing a secure foundation for the more "offensive" functions required for socioeconomic activity (for example, farming, trading, formal employment). It also clearly reflects Hobfoll's understanding of families providing a mediation role by being "nested" within the wider community (and having individuals "nested" within them) (Hobfoll 1998). This identification of tasks also fits in well with the CRC notion of children's participation in decision making in a manner reflecting the "evolving capacities of the child" (CRC 1989, Art. 5). The key tasks of the family are about equipping children to access broader resources (for themselves and their household). The "evolving capacities of the child" are not incidental to the tasks of the family but a significant product of them.

Implications for intervention

What implications does this functional framework have for planning, implementing, or evaluating interventions?

Multiple potential points of intervention

One of the key strengths of the PWG framework is that it clarifies how—through the processes of community engagement by investment of resources—interventions targeted in one domain can have impacts on others. A psychosocial intervention establishing vocational skills in demobilized combatants will affect more than just human capacity. Such skills can bring not only material benefits but broaden social linkage and reinforce cultural values of self-worth and household provision. The framework thus suggests multiple points of potential intervention, all sharing the overall goal of strengthening psychosocial well-being. In principle, it suggests a taxonomy of interventions: those seeking to promote well-being by primarily targeting the strengthening of material conditions, or human, social, or cultural capital.

The importance of a family's economic foundation

The framework demonstrates clearly how the economic resources of a family underpin its capability to develop the human, social, and cultural capital of children. Interventions targeting the economic conditions of war-affected families can therefore be expected to have wider impacts. There is considerable evidence that in resource-poor environments children are recruited to assume roles within families that may serve short-term labor needs but disrupt longer-term developmental outcomes. The increase in household labor imposed by water and fuel-wood shortages in Malawian refugee camps contributed significantly to the trend of girls quitting school (Ager, Ager, and Long 1995). Pressure to ensure adequate supervision of domestic animals has been cited by children in Afghanistan as a major factor interfering with engagement in both school and play (SCF 2001).

Framework for appraisal of resource loss and availability

Intervention planning is frequently shaped by discussions of the relevant balance between needs and strengths. By focusing on functional resources and their development, the framework provides a single structure for identifying areas where conflict has led to the depletion of resources and areas where significant resources are intact. The logic of the framework is that capacities are supported so that communities invest what they have to recover what they have lost.

Where family structures and functioning are relatively unimpaired, the family can be a key resource across all domains. In other situations the impact of conflict will have impaired family functioning in one domain (for example, forced displacement disrupting social connections and leaving family members isolated). In such circumstances it generally makes sense for interventions to support families in recovering capacity in this area (in the example above, by supporting the development of community links in displaced persons' camps). In other circumstances family structures and functioning may be so disrupted (for example, with large numbers of unaccompanied minors) that intervention needs to focus on addressing the key functional tasks by other means. For example, some child-headed households may be effective in supporting the human, social, and cultural development of children (Putter 2004) but require targeted intervention in the form of economic support.

Emphasis on development of agency and engagement

The focus of the framework is on equipping individuals for effective action within communities—whether through families or otherwise. The emphasis is on the development of agency and the support and resources required for such development. Resources are not simply acquired; they are invested to develop other resources. In this way all interventions need to be framed in terms of how they will support active processes of engagement within communities, with an emphasis on how they build upon existing resources and strategies (Ager, Strang, and Abebe 2005).

This emphasis on the development of agency from the foundations of family has an important consequence: it clarifies that promoting child agency is in no way incompatible with promoting the role of the family. Effective families promote the capabilities of children, and confident, capable children can more effectively engage with their families, as illustrated below:

Nedim, eight, enrolled in a program for children displaced from his hometown in Bosnia-Herzegovina, across the border from Macedonia. He was very quiet and withdrawn in the early weeks of the program. The program involved lots of structured activities but increasingly involved children in taking responsibility for planning sessions and deciding on their focus. After several months Nedim had acquired a range of skills that helped him deal with conflicts and disagreements, and he generally felt more confident in dealing with difficult situations. The development of such human capacity helped him to build wider social connections with other children. He also became more confident at home, and began to reestablish a previously strong relationship with his grandfather. Nedim loved to hear his grandfather's stories of life back in Bosnia-Herzegovina when he was a boy of Nedim's age.

Acknowledgment of the diverse means of providing family support

The presented model, rather than defining the family as a structure, defines it functionally: the family is whatever provides an economic foundation for meeting physical needs, fosters basic skills and competencies, fosters social access, and transmits core cultural knowledge and values. For the majority of children these functions will be fulfilled by relatives in structures approximating established models of family. For many, however, and particularly in the context of the familial disruption associated with civil conflict, "family" will be provided by a wide range of social relationships. The extent to which arrangements are effective is largely an empirical question, and the model provides the four criteria by which such effectiveness can be evaluated.

Concluding considerations

To conclude, I want to consider two issues arising from the preceding analysis that were raised at the time of its initial presentation at a PWG meeting and have been raised by readers of subsequent drafts: Where is love? and What is good?

Where is love?

The family is not only central to our understanding of policy and practice for children affected by armed conflict, but it is also at the core of our understanding of nurture and care. For many, the purpose of the family is to show love, and, through the development of appropriate attachment, create in children a sense of security and acceptance. The functionalist approach of the preceding analysis appears to offer little room for such understanding.

There are essentially two responses to this concern. First, it can be argued that the functions of the family identified in the analysis do indeed reflect key elements of love. Families can be seen to express their love for children through care and protection. Also, some of the basic skills and competencies acquired through family support are emotional security, identity, and self-worth. We can see the trusting and confident social relationships established within the family as a template for establishing wider social networks. We can see an awareness of and concern for the needs of others as a fundamental value established through family socialization. In other words, love is here, it is just being expressed in a functionalist vocabulary.

This is all true, to some extent, but there is another, complementary response. The analysis presented is a model for understanding key functions of the family and how we can best support children affected by armed conflict. It is not a comprehensive account of family.

In particular, it is explicitly a functional analysis, looking at the *tasks* of families, not at the *experience* of them. A model that sought to identify the dimensions of experience within the family would necessarily take a very different form. Love is not considered in the presented analysis, not because it is irrelevant to families, but because we are concerned here more with tasks than experience.

What is good?

A perhaps more telling concern is that the analysis offers no insight into the appropriateness of family processes or child outcomes—or what is "good." As a functional analysis of tasks, it draws attention to available resources and their utilization rather than the ends to which such resources are put. Such functional analysis has the advantage of being sufficiently free from context and assumption that it is applicable across a wide range of settings. But there is danger in offering an analysis so neutral that it does not engage in discussions of appropriateness in settings where war exposes key issues of morality, justice, and rights.

It was noted earlier that families can serve as institutions of malign socialization, but the presented model and analysis of the mediating role of families provide little in the way of a moral compass to judge the appropriateness of parenting and children's behavior. The concept of psychosocial well-being—defined here in terms of availability of human, social, and cultural capital—provides a technical standard. However, a child soldier may, for instance, have acquired significant skills and knowledge, social connection, and a clear ideology to sustain him or her as a combatant. Technically, such socialization may be effective and congruent with the demands of a conflict-impacted area. But is it a "good" outcome for the child?

Many would assert that it clearly is not. However, any challenge to the appropriateness of this socialization—to the view that this represents a "good" outcome—has to come from outside a functionalist paradigm. Within such a paradigm, if it "works," it is deemed effective, and therefore appropriate. Any challenge to this logic has to be made from a position where actions and choices are evaluated on a broader horizon than their being adaptive to the demands of the current situation.

While humanitarian agencies often work with functionalist paradigms (Adelman 1999), agencies and workers alike generally seek a basis for evaluating against wider moral, ethical, and humanitarian values. Such values may be derived from a range of sources, from government-ratified conventions to religious or political commitments. The framework presented here is neutral on these issues. However, readers will necessarily bring their own moral agendas to bear in its application to the experience of civil conflict and war.

References

Adelman, H. 1999. Modernity, globalization, refugees, and displacement. In *Refugees: Perspectives on the Experience of Forced Migration*, ed. A. Ager, 83–110. London: Continuum.

Ager, A., and A. Strang. 2004. Indicators of integration: Final report. Home Office Development and Practice Report 28.

Ager, A., A. Strang, and B. Abebe. 2005. Conceptualising community development in war-affected populations: Illustrations from Tigray. *Community Development Journal* 40 (2): 158–68.

Ager, W. 2002. Refugee families in Scotland: A case study. Master's diss., Univ. of Edinburgh.

Ager, A., W. Ager, and L. Long. 1995. The differential experience of refugee women and men. *Journal of Refugee Studies* 8 (3): 263–87.

Bowlby, J. 1969. *Attachment and loss*, vol. 1, *Attachment*. New York: Basic Books.

Boyden, J., and J. Mann. 2000. Resilience, vulnerability, and coping in children affected by extreme adversity. Background paper for Refugee Studies Centre consultation on children in adversity. Oxford: RSC.

Brehm, S., and A. M. Kassin. 1996. *Social psychology*. 3rd ed. Boston: Houghton Mifflin.

CCF (Christian Children's Fund). 2004. Child poverty: A conceptual framework. Report for CCF by Jo Boyden. Richmond, VA: CCF.

Colletta, N., and N. Cullen. 2000. *Violent conflict and the transformation of social capital*. New York: World Bank.

Convention on the rights of the child. 1989. New York: United Nations.

Dawes, A., and D. Donald. 1994. *Childhood and adversity: Psychological perspectives from South African research*. Cape Town: David Roberts.

Garbarino, J., and K. Kostelny. 1996. The effects of political violence on Palestinian children's behavioral problems. *Child Development* 67: 33–45.

Gittell, R., and A. Vidal. 1998. *Community organizing: Building social capital as a development strategy*. Thousand Oaks, CA: Sage.

Granovetter, M. 1973. The strength of weak ties. *American Journal of Sociology* 78: 1360–80.

Grossman, K., K. Grossman, and E. Waters. 2005. *Attachment from infancy to adulthood*. New York: Guilford.

Hobfoll, S. 1998. *Stress, culture, and community: The psychology and philosophy of stress*. New York: Plenum.

Hundeide, K. 1991. *Helping disadvantaged children: Psycho-social intervention and aid to disadvantaged children in third world countries*. London: Jessica Kingsley.

McCallin, M. 1996. *The psychosocial well-being of refugee children: Research, practice, and policy issues*. 2nd ed. Geneva: International Catholic Child Bureau.

Khamis, V. 2000. Child psychological maltreatment in Palestinian families. *Child Abuse and Neglect* 24: 1047–59.

Kostorova-Unkovska, L., and V. Pankovska. 1992. *Children hurt by war*. Skopje, Macedonia: General Children's Consulate of the Republic of Macedonia.

Laor, N., L. Wolmer, L. Mayes, A. Gershon, R. Weizman, and D. Cohen. 1997. Israeli preschool children under Scuds: A 30-month follow-up. *American Academy of Child and Adolescent Psychiatry* 36 (3): 349–55.

Loughry, M., and N. X. Nghia. 2000. Returnees to Vietnam: The well-being of former unaccompanied minors. In *Psychosocial wellness of refugees*, ed. F. L. Ahearn, 153–78. Oxford: Berghahn.

Nordstrom, C. 1997. *A different kind of war story*. Philadelphia: Univ. of Pennsylvania Press.

Punamaki, R-L. 1987. Psychological stress of Palestinian mothers and their children in conditions of political violence. *The Quarterly Newsletter of the Laboratory of Comparative Human Cognition* 9: 116–19.

———. 1990. Relationships between political violence and psychological responses among Palestinian women. *Journal of Peace Research* 27: 75–85.

———. 2000a. Measuring suffering: Conflicts and solutions in refugee studies. In *Psychosocial wellness of refugees*, ed, F. L. Ahearn, 105–30. Oxford: Berghahn.

———. 2000b. Personal and family resources promoting resiliency among children suffering from military violence. In *Health hazards of organized violence in children (II): Coping and protective factors*, ed. L. van Willigen, 29–42. Utrecht: Pharos.

Putter, C. 2004. Unfolding tragedies: The impact of mother's death on her kin and community: An ethnography from Southern Malawi. Doctoral diss., Queen Margaret Univ. College, Edinburgh.

PWG (Psychosocial Working Group). 2003. Psychosocial intervention in complex emergencies: A conceptual framework. Available online.

Ressler, E. M., N. Boothby, and D. J. Steinbock. 1988. *Unaccompanied children*. New York: Oxford Univ. Press.

Richter, L. 1994. Economic stress and its influence on the family and care-taking patterns. In *Childhood and adversity: Psychological perspectives from South African research*, ed. A. Dawes and D. Donald, 28–50. Cape Town: David Roberts.

Rumbaut, R. G. 1991. The agony of exile: A study of the migration and adaptation of Indochinese refugee adults and children. In *Refugee children: Theory, research, and services*, ed. F. L. Ahearn and J. L. Athey, 53–91. Baltimore: Johns Hopkins Univ. Press.

SCF (Save the Children). 2001. Afghanistan's children speak to the UN special session, 19–21 September 2001. Peshawar: SCF.

Summerfield, D. 1999. Sociocultural dimensions of conflict and displacement. In *Refugees: Perspectives on the experience of forced migration*, ed. A. Ager, 111–35. London: Continuum.

UNHCR (United Nations High Commissioner for Refugees). 1993. UNHCR policy on refugee children. Executive Committee of the High Commissioner's Programme, 44th Session, EC/SCP/82. Geneva: UNHCR.

UNICEF (United Nations International Children's Emergency Fund). 2000. Fact sheet: The right to participation. Available on the unicef.org website.

Wessells, M. G., and K. Kostelny. 2004. A preliminary study of qualitative measures of Afghan children's coping strategies. Richmond: CCF International.

Zivic, I. 1993. Emotional reactions of children to war stress in Croatia. *Journal of the American Academy of Child and Adolescent Psychiatry* 32: 709–13.

3

RUNNING SCARED

When children become separated in emergencies

Amy Hepburn

Introduction

In nearly every war and large-scale humanitarian emergency through-out history, children have been separated from their families. The tragedy of separation knows no boundaries of culture, religion, or ethnicity. Whether the crisis is a natural disaster, such as the 2004 Asian tsunami, or an armed conflict, such as the 1994 Rwandan genocide, mass population displacements put children at considerable risk for physical hardship and emotional distress. This distress is exacerbated by the dislocation of a child from his or her family or community.

In any given emergency the number of children separated from their families has ranged from a few hundred to several hundred thou-sand. At the end of World War II, approximately 50,000 children were believed homeless in most European countries (Ressler, Boothby, and Steinbock 1988). In 1994, over 100,000 children living in Rwanda and other neighboring countries were separated from their families—the largest population of separated children from any single conflict in Africa (Brown 1995).

While the number of separated children in emergencies is histori-cally underestimated, it is widely accepted that children have higher mortality rates than adults, and unaccompanied children, in particu-lar, have the highest mortality rates overall. Such children are also the most vulnerable to recruitment into armed forces, trafficking into forced labor or prostitution, and other egregious forms of physical, psychological, and sexual abuse. As a result, a comprehensive understanding of the developmental, psychological, and protection needs of children in such situations is essential to informing effective policy and programming responses.

The following discussion offers a synthesis of research, literature, and select case and field experiences to increase awareness of the developmental and psychological vulnerabilities of separated children and to better inform programs and policies for assistance. The belief that family, as a social ecology, should provide a vital and holistic environment for the healthy emotional and physical development of children is the foundation for this discussion.

This chapter is divided into three sections. The first section provides an overview of the definitions, nature, and scope of the problem of separated children in emergencies. The second section explores the psychosocial effects of separation in emergencies and examines specific trauma, care, and placement concerns. The third section identifies interventions used to address and prevent family separation in conflict, with an emphasis on tracing and reunification activities as well as interim and durable solutions for care.

The nature and scope of separation in emergencies

Defining the separation of children in emergencies

Given the many circumstances in which children become separated from their families in emergencies, the international community, including local and international nongovernmental and governmental organizations, has sought consensus on the definitions that guide its policies and programs. To address this, the Inter-agency Working Group on Unaccompanied and Separated Children was created in 1995 by the International Committee of the Red Cross (ICRC), the United Nations High Commissioner for Refugees (UNHCR), the United Nations Children's Fund (UNICEF), and a select number of international NGOs. This working group subsequently issued the Inter-Agency Guiding Principles on Unaccompanied and Separated Children (IAGP), which has become a significant collaborative document in guiding current and future policy and field operations. The

IAGP offers the following agreement on definitions based on international human rights, humanitarian, and refugee law:

- A *child* means any person under the age of 18, unless under the (national) law applicable to the child, majority is attained earlier (Convention on the Rights of the Child, or CRC, Article 1).
- *Separated children* are those separated from both parents, or from their previous legal or customary primary care-giver, but not necessarily from other relatives. These may, therefore, include children accompanied by other adult family members.
- *Unaccompanied children* (also called unaccompanied minors) are children who have been separated from both parents and other relatives and are not being cared for by an adult who, by law or custom, is responsible for doing so.
- *Orphans* are children, both of whose parents are known to be dead. In some countries, however, a child who has lost one parent is called an orphan. (IAGP 2003, 13)

In practice, the terms *separated* and *unaccompanied* are often used interchangeably. According to the Statement of Good Practice for Separated Children in Europe issued in October 2000, the term *separated* is preferred because it better defines the situation of children who are "without the care of their parents or legal guardians, and as a consequence suffer socially and psychologically from this *separation*" (Hannan 2003, 8). For the purpose of this chapter, the term *separated* will be used to encompass both those children that are separated from families or primary caregivers and those who are unaccompanied, unless the context of the discussion indicates otherwise.

Types of separation

While the circumstances of each family separation are unique and vary from crisis to crisis, comparative research suggests that similarities can be drawn in the ways in which children and parents separate and the causes of these separations. In general, the separation of children from their families can be grouped into two primary categories: involuntary and voluntary. The distinction between these two groups is useful in that it provides important insight into the intent of the parent/child separation, the possibility of preventing such separation in the future, and whether reunion is desirable or even possible. With more complete information, it may be possible—even in emergencies—to prevent further family separations or rapidly reunify families that have been dislocated only briefly (Hepburn, Williamson, and Wolfram 2004).

Involuntary and voluntary separations can be grouped into nine categories, based on intent and circumstances: (1) abducted, (2) lost, (3) orphaned, (4) runaway, (5) removed, (6) abandoned, (7) entrusted, (8) surrendered, and (9) independent (Ressler, Boothby, and Steinbock 1988).

Involuntary separations

Involuntary separations indicate that the separation has taken place against the will of the parents. These separations include those situations in which children are *abducted* or physically taken from the parents against their will; *lost* or separated accidentally from their parents; *orphaned* or living in a new care situation due to both parents being deceased; *runaways*, where children intentionally leave parents without their consent; or *removed* from their parents as a result of the loss or suspension of parental rights.

Voluntary separations

In contrast, voluntary separations occur with the parents' consent. These separations include those situations in which children are *abandoned* or deserted by parents with no intention of reunion; *entrusted* or voluntarily placed in the care of another adult or in an institution by parents who intend to reclaim them; *surrendered* by parents who have permanently given up parental rights; or *independent* and living apart from their parents with their consent.

Few of these categories are mutually exclusive, as the circumstances under which the separation takes place may change over time. Given the variable nature of separations, it is critical to assess individually each child's separation experience as accurately as possible to determine both the intent of the parent and the child at the time of separation and to evaluate the possibility of a future reunion, taking into account the wishes and best interests of the child. An important caveat to this assessment is that parents (if alive) and children must be found in order to conduct the most thorough review; to this end, effective tracing mechanisms are needed, which will be discussed in more detail in the final section of this chapter.

Causes of separations

While the circumstances that cause separation in emergencies are varied, both field experience and research suggest that the vast majority of separations occur for the following seven reasons: (1) social, psychological, and cultural factors; (2) parents' inability to provide care; (3) emergency-related circumstances; (4) perceived opportunities; (5) military and government policies; (6) relief interventions; and (7) child initiatives (Ressler, Boothby, and Steinbock 1988).

Social, psychological, and cultural factors refers to the causes of separations that occur both in non-emergency and emergency settings. Examples of these separations include the abandonment of children born out of wedlock or unwanted due to their gender, and the neglect of children born with disabilities. *Parents' inability to provide care* and *emergency-related circumstances* refer to the many facets in which a parent provides for a child and how that provisory role is often compromised in emergencies. Imprisonment, conscription into armed forces, famine, disease, and work opportunities that require parents to travel far from home are examples of circumstances that affect parents' ability to provide adequate supervision and care for their children. Single-parent status and abject poverty are highly correlated to this cause of separation. *Perceived opportunities* refers to the assumption of many parents during emergencies that their children will have more opportunities for educational and economic gain if they do not remain within the family structure or local community.

Military and government policies refers to policies adopted by national and local governments or militias with the specific intention of separating children from their families, such as the abduction or drafting of children into armed forces. *Intervention* refers to the unintended consequences of humanitarian assistance, including distribution systems in emergencies, which may cause family separations. For example, in the aftermath of a natural disaster or the chaos of a mass evacuation, relief agencies may move children to safe zones or hospitals without consulting family members. Once separated, few children, especially those that are very young, have the proper documentation for immediate reunification. Furthermore, the structure of aid disbursement, including access to educational and health services, may also encourage separations if they only provide opportunities for separated children and are not open to the participation of all children in the community. *Child initiatives* refers to the deliberate separation of children from their parents, family, and community. This most often occurs with older adolescents who wish to escape conscription into a conflict, seek economic or educational opportunity elsewhere, or extract themselves from a difficult or hazardous family environment.

Rwandan example

On April 6, 1994, a plane carrying the presidents of Rwanda and Burundi was shot down, commencing one hundred days of brutal killing, torture, and rape that would result in the genocide of approximately 800,000 men, women, and children. The reasons behind this conflict were complex and dated back to policies created during the colonial rule of the Belgian regime from 1914 to 1962, which fostered distrust and inequality between the country's two primary ethnic groups, the Hutu and the Tutsi.

Following this genocide approximately 100,000 children were separated from their families and sought refuge in camps and orphanages in Rwanda and neighboring countries (Brown 1995). Given the scale and nature of the crisis in Rwanda, over the last decade many lessons were learned regarding the types and causes of family separations in emergencies—many of which were seemingly preventable. The causes of separation varied greatly from village to village and child to child. However, some common methods and causes of involuntary and voluntary separations emerged.

Regarding involuntary separations, as would be expected, many children were orphaned when their parents were killed in the attacks. For example, of 8,628 children living in centers for unaccompanied children in 1994, 41 percent (3,552) believed both parents to be dead, 35 percent (3,043) did not know the status of their parents, and the remaining 23 percent believed at least one parent to be alive or were unwilling or unable to express any opinion (Brown 1995). In addition to those orphaned, many children became separated from families in the process of fleeing violence; others were coerced to join the conflict as combatants. A 1994 large-scale cholera outbreak in Rwandan refugee camps in Goma, Zaire, was also responsible for the separation of large numbers of children, as more than 12,000 were placed in children's centers and an estimated 4,000 to 6,000 more were placed with local Zairean families (Brown 1995).

Unintentional separations were also documented as a result of uncoordinated humanitarian assistance; for example, it was reported in at least one Rwandan city that families were not given prior notice of when trucks would arrive to take them to refugee camps from the town. When the trucks arrived, they departed immediately, leaving behind children who had been sent by parents to secure firewood or water. During this period there were also reports that some well-intentioned international NGOs medically evacuated children out of camp settings for treatment without being accompanied by family members. Furthermore, in the process of relocating one Rwandan refugee camp in April 1995, several young children were unable to keep pace with their parents along the road or became lost at resting stations. Approximately 1,600 children became separated from their parents during this time, about one-third of whom were under five years old (Brown 1995).

In addition, children were surrendered voluntarily by their families during this period for a host of psychological and physical reasons. For example, some mothers who had babies born of rape were unwilling or unable to care for their children and abandoned them in maternity hospitals. Other mothers handed off young children to international organizations or NGOs for safekeeping when it appeared that their own physical safety was at risk. The proliferation of children's centers and care institutions prompted many impoverished families to drop off children they felt could be better cared for in group settings.

Protection and the physical and emotional needs of children separated in emergencies

Once children become separated from their families, a variety of risk factors begins to accumulate that threatens their physical, emotional, and psychological well-being. Access to quality educational and health services may be inhibited by their age and unaccompanied status, putting them at further risk for exploitation by adults. If children are unable to access food and medical services in a timely manner, they are at a high risk of malnutrition, making them more susceptible to disease and injuries, especially in crowded environments. Children under five years of age are particularly vulnerable to the negative effects of poor nutrition and inadequate developmental care (Hepburn, Williamson, and Wolfram 2004).

During emergencies all children require assistance to secure their physical and emotional well-being, but separated children in particular endure a significant amount of psychological stress due to fear, loss of identity or feeling of belonging, and a heightened sense of physical and emotional disorientation. While discussed in more detail in the following section, such emotional stressors have a profound effect on the physical and emotional well-being of children, who may become overwhelmed with the immediate responsibility for their own survival. In such situations concentrated efforts to promote normal recovery from traumatic events are essential, and more specialized psychological assistance may be necessary for a small percentage of children.

Particularly vulnerable children

In the case of separated children, three groups—children with disabilities or chronic illness, such as HIV/AIDS; girl children; and those living in child-headed households—are particularly vulnerable to abuse and exploitation and require targeted assistance, protection, and oversight in emergency settings.

Children with disabilities or chronic illness are at a high risk of abandonment or physical and emotional abuse as parents or caregivers feel overwhelmed by their responsibility to provide care in the given circumstances. In most conflict or post-conflict camp settings, specialized health and social services are not readily available to children with special needs, and foster families may be reluctant to assume the responsibility for their care.

In addition to the psychological stress of this method of rejection, children living with disability or illness are vulnerable to being placed in institutions for long periods of time where overburdened caregivers are unable to provide the necessary attention to ensure that their basic physical and emotional needs are met.

Girls are more likely to be abused, raped, or recruited as domestic laborers or sexual slaves. They are at a high risk for contracting HIV/AIDS and other sexually transmitted diseases. As noted in a 1996 Human Rights Watch Report on sexual violence during the Rwandan genocide:

Testimonies from survivors confirm that rape was extremely widespread and that thousands of women and girls were individually raped, gang-raped, raped with objects such as sharpened sticks or gun barrels, held in sexual slavery (either collectively or through forced "marriage") or sexually mutilated . . . including mutilation of the vagina and pelvic area with machetes, knives, sticks, boiling water, and in one case, acid. (Human Rights Watch 1996)

In addition to the exploitation and abuse noted above, it is also common in emergencies for older children, both female and male, to assume the primary responsibility of care for younger siblings or friends. These child-headed households often subsist in abject poverty with little physical, material, or psychosocial support. Children, who just days before were dependent on parental support and care, are suddenly required to assume a provider role with little or no preparation. Such a transition is overwhelming for children who are struggling to meet their own immediate needs as well as those for whom they are caring. As one Congolese boy who was caring for his twelve-year-old sister and four-year-old niece described it: "What choice do I have? I am fifteen years old. I do not know how to raise these girls. I do not know how to look after them. I can take care of myself but I cannot take care of them. Sometimes, I do not know what to do. Without me, they would have no food to eat, no place to sleep. But what can I do?" (Mann 2003, 29).

To better protect these exceptionally vulnerable children, specific attention should be given to developing a comprehensive protection framework; while the theory and legal foundation for such a framework is discussed in more detail below, it should also include practical elements such as flexible educational opportunities, vocational training, income-generating activities, and the creation of community-awareness programs designed to educate community members on the specific hardships these children may face and how they can be best supported.

Protection framework

As noted previously, the protection, survival, and well-being of all children in emergencies is of paramount importance. However, separated children in particular require special protection consideration under international law due to their unaccompanied status.

The protection of separated children is addressed in a comprehensive international legal framework including a number of legal conventions and their respective protocols. These conventions include the Fourth Geneva Convention—particularly Article 47, which establishes family reunification as a priority in times of armed conflict; the 1959 Declaration of the Rights of the Child; the United Nations Convention on the Rights of the Child (CRC); and the Convention relating to the Status of Refugees. According to international law all children are entitled to (1) the right to a name, legal identity, and birth registration; (2) the right to physical and legal protection; (3) the right not to be separated from their parents; (4) the right to provisions for their basic subsistence; (5) the right to care and assistance appropriate to their age and developmental needs; and (6) the right to participate in decisions about their future (IAGP 2003).

Central to the understanding of children's rights and protection within an international context is the "best interest principle," as articulated in the CRC: "In all actions concerning children, whether undertaken by public or private social welfare institutions, courts of law, administrative authorities or legislative bodies, the best interests of the child shall be a primary consideration" (CRC 1989, Art. 3). The best-interest principle should constitute the basis for decision-making for all separated children in emergencies. Honoring this commitment requires that a child's best interests, wishes, and opinions be both sought and considered at every stage of assistance. Research and practice suggest that determining the best interests of a particular child requires a highly individualized assessment, and as a result, every effort should be made from the onset of an emergency to "prevent further developmental harm . . . by protecting whatever psychological, social and cultural ties the child may still possess" (Ressler, Boothby, and Steinbock 1988, 248).

Using the best-interest principle and international law as foundational building blocks, the IAGP outlines a protection framework that describes three complementary types of protection activities to assist separated children in emergencies. The activities are grouped into three categories: responsive action, remedial action, and environment building (IAGP 2003). These categories are not mutually exclusive but rather inclusive of the compendium of activities necessary to address and protect children fully in the most adverse circumstances. *Responsive action* refers to activities that attempt to prevent or alleviate the immediate effects of a specific pattern of abuse. *Remedial action* refers to efforts aimed at restoring a child's sense of dignity through rehabilitation, restitution, and reparation. And, *environment building* references activities intended to create a political, social, and legal environment conducive to the protection of separated children over the long term (IAGP 2003). This framework provides a useful rubric for integrating and balancing the immediacy of children's short-term survival needs with long-term protection goals in an emergency context.

The emotional and social impacts of separation in emergencies

All children in emergencies face a unique set of pressures that may compromise their psychosocial well-being. However, children separated from the comfort, safety, and support of their families and communities during conflict are at increased risk of acute psychosocial stress. The manifestations and projected recovery from this stress depend largely on the temperament, nature, and previous family background of the child; the age of the child at the time of separation; the adversities the child experienced after the initial separation; and the presence or absence of relief assistance for the child and its efficacy (Ressler, Boothby, and Steinbock 1988). The rapid reunification of children to a stable family and community environment with adequately trained adult caregivers fosters appropriate attachment behavior, which increases resiliency and decreases psychological vulnerabilities.

Importance of family and community during conflict

Both family and community play essential roles in helping children through the trauma of conflict. Family and stable environments provide the security and stability children crave throughout their childhood and particularly during times of insecurity and conflict. The attachments in family relationships and the familiarity of language and cultural and religious traditions in a community allow children to explore and develop holistically. It is therefore common, even in stable periods, for temporary separation from their families or communities to provoke great anxiety in children at any age.

Children in conflict situations are particularly attuned to their need for emotional and physical security, intense physical contact, and reassurance from parents. Without the security of these familiar attachments, children struggle emotionally to compensate for their loss, manifesting a variety of physical and psychological effects. Many assume that children's exposure to violence, deprivation, or physical harm during conflict is the most damaging experience to their psychosocial health. But, in fact, research suggests that it is the actual separation or anticipation of separation from their families that most threatens children's psychological health. Anna Freud and Dorothy Burlingham summarize: "War acquires comparatively little significance for children so long as it only threatens their lives, disturbs their material comfort, or cuts their food rations. It becomes enormously significant the moment it breaks up family life and uproots the first emotional attachments of the child within the family group" (Freud and Burlingham 1943, 149).

Specific effects of separation and loss

A child's experience of separation and loss in conflict is compounded by multiple environmental, developmental, and situational factors. Two of the most significant external factors influencing the psychosocial recovery of separated children in conflict are the age of the child at the time of separation and the presence or absence of adequate adult caretakers. Our understanding of the significance of adult care in the development of a child's sense of security, trust, and resilience is rooted in the seminal work of John Bowlby on the psychological concept of attachment (Bowlby 1973). Attachment is understood in both practice and literature as the psychological bond between a child and his or her parent or primary caregiver; the concept of attachment behavior is described as the development of this bond over time (Mann 2001). While the presence of appropriate adult care is particularly important for young children (under five years old), who require a significant amount of one-on-one attention to meet their basic developmental need for attachment, it remains a highly correlated factor for psychosocial well-being for children of all ages.

The developmental importance of establishing significant attachments in the first twenty-four months of life is well documented (Grossman, Grossman, and Waters 2005). However, the bonding that occurs during this period tends to be more biologically predisposed than attachments that are formed later in development. As children develop emotionally and cognitively, their ability to form attachments is influenced by a more sophisticated analysis of biological and external factors, such as the continuity and quality of their care. For example, one study noted that children less than one year old tended to demonstrate stable attachment behaviors very quickly, usually within the first two weeks of life, while children older than one year of age took significantly longer (Dozier, Manni, and Lindhiem 2005).

The weakening of attachment behavior is one of the greatest psychological risks of family separation for children less than five years old. As one researcher noted, "The security of the early attachment bond predicts a child's ability to adapt to future developmental tasks (such as forming relationships with peers and non-parent adults) and psychosocial stressors (for example, separation from a parent)" (Macksoud, Aber, and Cohn 1990, 220). Children less than five years old are at the greatest risk of weakening their attachment behavior if not placed in the care of at least one adult relatively soon after the initial separation. Such young children who experience repeated disruptions in care tend to find it difficult to develop appropriate socialization skills; they feel powerless, fearful, and overwhelmed by their sense of dislocation. Children in these situations may regress developmentally and verbally, as demonstrated by periods of intense crying, excessive thumb-sucking, or bedwetting, among other issues. Older children in this group may also have repeated nightmares or terrors, and fear of actual or imaginary objects (Ressler, Boothby, and Steinbock 1988).

Research suggests that older schoolage children and adolescents tend to be better able to handle the psychological stress of separation due to a number of factors, including a growing sense of independence and more advanced cognitive and emotional development. Furthermore, children who have demonstrated the ability to form positive peer relationships have been shown to be particularly resilient and less likely to manifest their psychosocial distress in the form of depression, aggression, or moodiness (Mann 2001).

All children require targeted, age-appropriate assistance and attention to avoid long-term psychological disturbances. In particular, children whose separation is complicated by extreme deprivation, emotional stress, preexisting conditions such as mental retardation and depression, or exposure to violence and abuse—such as witnessing the murder of a parent or family member—are at far greater risk for long-term psychological and adjustment disorders and may require more specialized or clinical support.

Encouraging resiliency in children

While the effects of separation and loss for children in conflict are profound, the resiliency of children in crisis should not be understated. Research suggests that most children recover from their distress symptoms if they originated from stable family environments, were afforded the opportunity to form new adult attachments relatively quickly following their separation, and continue developmentally appropriate activities. For particularly young children and infants the presence of consistent maternal affection during infancy has been noted to affect greatly the resiliency of the child later in life (Ainsworth 1973).

Noting these protective factors, every effort should be made to prevent voluntary separations (as discussed in more detail in the following section) and maintain familial relationships within communities by providing material assistance, food, and other essentials in conflict settings. Religion, cultural traditions, language, and school settings all provide supportive coping strategies by virtue of being familiar. As noted previously, when the initial loss or separation is compounded by extreme adversity, the risk of long-term psychosocial disturbance goes up dramatically. While some of these difficulties are inevitable in wartime environments, others are preventable, such as the absence of physical protection in camp settings and repeated disruptions in care.

While lengthy stays in refugee camps or institutional settings may be temporarily unavoidable in certain conflict settings, it is important to recognize that such settings rarely encourage resiliency and recovery, particularly when the adult-to-child ratio is low. Furthermore, the research literature suggests that children living in institutional care are often isolated, stigmatized by their "orphan" status, and may lack the opportunity to develop the social skills necessary for their successful reintegration into the broader community (Tolfree 2003).

For example, research on Salvadoran children living in institutional care throughout the civil war revealed that while the material care in most facilities was acceptable, particularly with regard to hygiene, the emotional aspects of care were severely lacking:

> The children who grew up in orphanages often felt unloved, unwanted and lonely. Physical and emotional abuses were all too common, especially in some of the institutions. Additionally, children were branded as orphans and subject to strong social discrimination. . . . The young people claimed the treatment depended too much on individuals rather on institutional responsibility. Caretakers were not screened or trained adequately to deal with children. Much less were they equipped to handle cases of children who have suffered trauma. (Sprenkels 2002, 100–101)

Given the inherent limitations of institutional care in conflict settings, both foster and peer-group care may offer more viable interim and durable care solutions, as discussed in more detail in the next section.

Interventions

Effective programming for separated children in emergencies includes activities designed to prevent separation, and, when those are unsuccessful, assisting children in the reunification process through appropriate assessment, care, and protection. As noted earlier, children should be reunited with families as soon as possible following separation unless it is not believed to be in their best interest. In determining a child's best interest, agencies should take into account the amount of time a child has spent in his or her current situation with individualized adult care, the amount of time the child was with his or her family prior to separation, the length of separation, the overall quality of care the child is receiving from the current caregiver, and the child's own wishes (if age appropriate) (Ressler, Boothby, and Steinbock 1988).

Once reunification is determined to be in the child's best interest, components of successful reunification programs generally include situational assessments, identification, documentation and registration, tracing, verification and monitoring, and evaluation. Utilizing all of these components ensures that the reunification process is both thorough and sensitive to children's developmental and protection needs and best interests. Maintaining the confidentiality and privacy of the family during the process is essential, particularly in areas of active conflict and ethnic cleansing such as Rwanda, where publicizing children's identity could have cost them their life.

Prevention of separation

In times of conflict every effort should be made to prevent both voluntary and involuntary separations. Voluntary abandonment can be lessened by ensuring that distribution systems are equitable and that food, water, medical, educational, and social services are available for all families. In addition, specific efforts should be made to support children in their own communities and identify particularly vulnerable families, such as single-parent or child-headed households and households caring for children with disabilities or affected by illness such as HIV/AIDS.

While the CRC requires all children to be registered at birth, approximately one-third of all births worldwide are not (IAGP 2003). Therefore, a large number of separated children are undocumented and at risk of losing their identity, becoming stateless, and sacrificing the guaranteed protection by any state to ensure their basic legal rights and security. Thus, a concerted effort should be made to register each child upon birth according to international, local, or customary law. To assist in this process, UNHCR field offices have the right to facilitate birth registration by written attestation for the facts of birth. Red Cross and Red Crescent societies also assist local personnel in issuing certificates of birth for refugee children (Hepburn, Williamson, and Wolfram 2004).

If movement is organized by a third party or agency and taking place in motorized vehicles, field staff should make every effort to register all passengers and note their familial associations and to provide drivers with these rosters to assist with camp registration. Planned medical evacuations should always take place with parental consent, and children should travel with a family member whenever possible. When it is not possible, children should have their name and family information written in a file (so long as it will not place them at further risk). Children should also be evacuated to the facility closest to their community, and the maintenance of familial communication should be a high priority (Hepburn, Williamson, and Wolfram 2004).

Interim and durable care options

Once separation occurs and immediate reunification options are exhausted, a situational assessment is necessary to account for and document the number of separated children in a given setting; their protection and care needs; the involuntary or voluntary nature of their separation; and the procedures for acting in their best interests through the establishment of an effective tracing program and interim (short-term) and durable (long-term) care options.

Interim and durable care options in conflict situations should be culturally appropriate, encourage age-appropriate development, and allow siblings to stay together. Such options usually include (1) foster care, (2) peer groupings or group-home care, (3) institutional care, and (4) adoption. Given the unpredictable nature of life and family structures in conflict, all of these care settings may be planned with agency or government support or spontaneously created. For example, following a mass movement and a subsequent separation, a neighbor family or family from outside the immediate displaced community may take a child into its care without the involvement of a third party. Although such situations are made without prior arrangement, they still require monitoring and oversight to ensure the well-being of the child in the new setting.

Foster care

Anecdotal and qualitative evidence suggests that fostering provides children essential attachment opportunities; even severely distressed children, schoolage and younger, adapt well psychologically and physically to foster settings when the family setting is developmentally appropriate, respects the child's right to education and play, and integrates the child into the familial environment without discrimination (Dona 2001; Ressler et al. 1988; Sprenkels 2002).

Such positive fostering experiences have been well documented in a number of emergency settings, including El Salvador, where researchers noted that children in some cases demonstrated a strong reluctance to reunify with their biological families after establishing lasting attachments with their foster families (Sprenkels 2002). In contrast, some families may view their responsibility to care for foster children as a temporary obligation, as was noted in Rwanda where some families were reported to have returned their foster children to institutions upon their repatriation (Dona 2001).

While research suggests that fostering within the family context has the potential to address adequately children's developmental, social, and emotional needs, separated children in this environment still face a heightened risk of discrimination, abuse, exploitation, and loss of educational opportunities. As a result, extensive family assessments, sensitization trainings, and preparation prior to placement are necessary, and the close supervision of foster children by field staff is critical (Tolfree 2003).

Peer-group care

Peer-group care is often advocated to address the special needs of adolescents in times of family separation and armed conflict. Adolescence is a particularly trying time for most young adults, and their growing pains are only exacerbated by conflict and separation. As a result, many adolescents have trouble adjusting to the new familial and parental structures of fostering situations and appear more suited to peer-group care.

In many cases peer-group care consists of a small number of teenagers or adolescents living together under the supervision of one adult who acts as a parental figure (Hepburn, Williamson, and Wolfram 2004). In such settings the adolescents' basic needs are provided for, yet they are encouraged to become independent young adults. Peer-group settings are often viewed as both practical and viable care alternatives for adolescents at a unique and vulnerable crossroads in their lives. A large peer-group care arrangement for separated Sudanese children in an Ethiopian refugee camp, Pignudo, was described in the following way:

> At the start of the Pignudo refugee camp, about 14,818 separated children lived in 12 different groups. The number of children staying in each group ranged between 1,000 and 1,350, the groups being divided into *tukuls*, or huts, each accommodating 3 to 5 children . . . Each group had an average of 12 adult caretakers, one being a head caretaker. . . . The caretakers were

expected to be adult role models to be emulated by the children in order for them to grow into responsible adults. . . . The children were also encouraged to elect their own leaders who, together with caretakers, managed the groups. (Derib 1998, 6)

While peer-group care, as in the above example, has the flexibility to adjust to the changing needs of adolescents during an important developmental period in their lives, it is not without its challenges. As with any care arrangement, it is heavily dependent on the presence of good adult role models. In the absence of these role models, adolescents have limited positive behavior to emulate; this can lead to disciplinary problems, poor coping strategies, and limited academic performance. Furthermore, without appropriate adult supervision adolescents are vulnerable to a host of protection concerns, such as recruitment into armed militias and sexual exploitation (Derib 1998).

Institutional care

Institutional care, as discussed in the previous section, is often viewed as a final yet necessary resort in many conflict settings. While institutional care is rarely, if ever, an optimal long-term solution for care, in particularly turbulent times the stability of a temporary stay in an institutional care facility may be the only option immediately available to satisfy a child's basic needs for food, water, rest, and general safety.

Considering the serious developmental concerns associated with institutional care noted previously, all institutional centers caring for children should be carefully monitored and evaluated on a regular basis to ensure that the children are being cared for and enjoying the same opportunities and rights as other children in the community. Furthermore, institutional facilities created during emergencies, particularly periods of armed conflict, should be considered temporary, have trained staff, and maintain a high adult-to-child ratio to ensure appropriate oversight and care of the children (Hepburn, Williamson, and Wolfram 2004).

Adoption

Adoption, both intra-country and intercountry, is the most permanent and therefore the most personally and politically delicate of all durable care solutions. Adoption is defined as the permanent and legal or customary transfer of parental rights and responsibilities to the adopter (Hepburn, Williamson, and Wolfram 2004). Traditionally, intra-country adoptions take place after foster-family placements have been deemed successful and all parties seek to make the situation legally permanent. In contrast, intercountry adoptions usually take place between families and children who have had little or no contact prior to placement and limited opportunity to ensure compatibility (Ressler, Boothby, and Steinbock 1988). Considering this, intercountry adoption is viewed as a last resort by the international community, to be used only when interim and long-term placements within the affected community are exhausted or unsatisfactory.

According to the IAGP, adoption should only be considered and pursued when (1) there is no reasonable hope of successful tracing and family reunification; (2) a reasonable period (usually at least two years) has passed during which all feasible measures have been taken to trace parents or other relatives; (3) the parent or guardian provides free and informed consent; and (4) the child gives free and informed consent, if age appropriate (IAGP 2003, 55).

Tracing and family reunification efforts

Following the completion of a situational assessment, tracing and family reunification should be initiated within a short time period. Tracing and reunification efforts can assume many forms, including informal tracing by family and community members, which usually takes place without agency assistance; formal, large-scale tracing, which relies on the collaboration of multiple international organizations, local agencies, and NGOs; and cross-border tracing, involving extensive cooperation from the ICRC, which maintains a mandate to trace across international borders.

The ICRC and the UNHCR are considered the lead international agencies with a responsibility to assist with the tracing and reunification of children separated in emergencies. The ICRC is charged with the specific mandate of implementing Article 74, "Reunion of Dispersed Families," of the Geneva Convention. As part of this mandate it houses and coordinates the Central Tracing Agency, which "directs and coordinates all activities related to restoring family links, reuniting families and searching for missing persons" (Hepburn, Williamson, and Wolfram 2004).

The UNHCR is mandated by the United Nations to respond to forced migration emergencies and to assist all persons fleeing persecution across international borders. The UNHCR has affirmed its core obligation to protect refugee children within the context of the CRC and identifies the reunification of families in conflict as a key protection concern. While the UNHCR and the ICRC are often well situated to initiate tracing and reunification efforts in emergencies, the most effective and efficient programs are collaborative and rely on extensive assistance from both international and local NGOs (Hepburn, Williamson, and Wolfram 2004; Brown 1995).

While approaches to tracing differ according to the emergency, the majority of comprehensive tracing efforts contain the following elements: identification, registration and documentation, tracing, verification, family reunification, and follow up. According to the IAGP:

- Identification is the process of establishing which children have been separated from their families or other care-givers, and where they may be found.
- Registration is the compilation of key personal data: full name, date and place of birth, father's and mother's name, former address and present location. This information is collected for the purpose of establishing the identity of the child, for protection and to facilitate tracing.
- Documentation is the process of recording further information in order to meet the specific needs of the child, including tracing, and to make plans for his or her future. This is a continuation of the registration process and not a separate undertaking.
- Tracing, in the case of children, is the process of searching for family members or primary legal or customary care-givers. The term also refers to the search for children whose parents are looking for them. The objective of tracing is reunification with parents or other close relatives.
- Verification is the process of establishing the validity of relationships and confirming the willingness of the child and the family member to be reunited.
- Reunification is the process of bringing together the child and family or previous care-provider for the purpose of establishing or re-establishing long-term care.

- Follow-up is the term used to refer to a range of activities for children and their families to facilitate their reintegration. These activities may include social and economic support. (IAGP 2003, 31–39)

Tracing and reunification efforts in emergencies have had varying degrees of success depending on a host of organizational and cultural factors, including the sustainability of scarce donor resources. Case examples of formal mass tracing efforts include those in Albania, in which the names and descriptions of children were broadcast over the radio, printed in the newspapers, and shown on television. Radios were distributed to displaced populations, and special frequencies were designated for the broadcast of tracing information. In Rwanda the radio was used to communicate new methods for tracing and reunification and to inform parents and families where to find and share information on missing children (Hepburn, Williamson, and Wolfram 2004).

In Goma, Zaire, photo-tracing efforts were successful in reuniting several refugee Rwandan children with their families. Photographs were reproduced through color photocopying and arranged several to a page by commune or origin where possible. The compilation of photos was then sent to New York, reproduced, and distributed widely among camps and villages. UNICEF established a database and supported office staff to handle all claims and to coordinate the program. While several initial positive identifications turned out to be in error, the photo-tracing efforts expedited the reunification of a number of families, particularly those with children under two years old (Brown 1995).

In August 2004 the ICRC launched a program in Liberia entitled "Help Us Come Home," which included posters and small booklets containing pictures of 343 Liberian children registered by the ICRC in Cote d'Ivoire, Ghana, Guinea, Liberia, Nigeria, and Sierra Leone. The goal was to reunite them with their families. These books were distributed at markets, school, hospitals, and refugee camps in Liberia and surrounding countries. Local ICRC delegates also performed a play to help communicate the purpose of the project to the larger community and to convey the importance of supporting such tracing efforts. Programs such as these have been instrumental in reuniting more than six hundred children with their families (ICRC 2004).

Programming challenges in conflict

While many tracing programs experience some degree of success, in the reunification process as noted above, the necessarily cooperative and culturally sensitive nature of the process presents significant challenges. The most commonly cited institutional challenges plaguing many such programs include inefficiency, interagency discord, poor collaboration, and lack of sustained donor support. In emergencies, and particularly in conflict situations, it is difficult to coordinate and come to a mutual understanding of the different roles and responsibilities that each agency must assume to establish a rapid-response tracing and reunification program. Basic programmatic decisions, critical to the long-term sustainability and success of the program, include which forms and criteria to use in the registration process; how to coordinate and monitor donor support; which local, regional, and international actors to include in the tracing process; and whether to use one or more central databases.

Furthermore, agencies must struggle to keep their autonomy, complement other agencies' efforts and honor their own mandates, while collaboratively acting in the best interests of the children. For example, the ICRC is obligated to maintain its neutrality in all of its operations; as a result, it may be reluctant to share information with certain agencies, particularly government ministries, that may be well positioned to assist in certain cases. Sustaining tracing and reunification efforts with financial and human capital beyond an initial emergency phase is another concern as donor pressure increases and new emergencies arise.

Finally, while many commonalities exist between tracing and reunification programs, agencies are required to orient each program to address the nuances of the specific emergency and to be culturally sensitive and practical in their design and implementation. As noted in an ICRC report of tracing and reunification activities for children separated during the Rwandan genocide, the collection of appropriate registration information was fraught with difficulties as

- a family name common to family members is extremely rare;
- most people at best know their year of birth; only 2.5% were able to state their exact date of birth, i.e., including month and day;

- a Rwandan's identity (name) is usually made up of one or two first names of either Christian or Islamic origin, followed by a Kinyarwanda term or name; the fact of having the same name or names as someone else does not imply kinship. (Merkelbach 2000)

Conclusion

Children separated from their families during conflict are among the most vulnerable in the world. Without the protection of their parents or primary caregivers, they are at risk of the worst forms of exploitation and abuse. Furthermore, the effects of separation on children's psychosocial development are exacerbated when children are unable to form necessary attachments with adult caregivers.

The international community, including international, national, and local actors, is charged by international law to protect and care for separated children in a comprehensive manner. All assistance should be integrated into a framework that balances the needs of separated children with all children affected by conflict so as to avoid unnecessary jealousy, stigmatization, or incentives for additional family separations.

In the absence of family care, the timely establishment of appropriate community-based interim and durable care solutions for separated children cannot be overstated; however, it is critical to acknowledge that many family separations during conflict are preventable, and family unity should be maintained whenever possible. When family separations do occur, the rapid establishment of tracing and reunification programs is essential, and the reintegration of children into stable and caring family and community environments should be a top priority in any conflict setting.

All children deserve the opportunity to grow and develop in an environment that encourages their strengths and fosters their resiliency during difficult periods. From birth, their lives are entrusted to their families and communities for safekeeping with the promise of a better future. When the social safety net of these protective factors is torn by instability and conflict, all members of the international community become their guardians. Every effort should be made to honor this obligation.

References

Ainsworth, M. 1973. The development of infant-mother attachment. In *Review of child development research*, vol. 3, *Child development and social policy*, ed. B. M. Caldwell and H. N. Ricciuti, 1–94. Chicago: Univ. of Chicago Press.

Bowlby, J. 1973. *Attachment and loss*, vol. 2, *Separation*. New York: Basic Books.

Brown, M. 1995. Family tracing and reunification case study: Rwanda. In *Children separated by war: Family tracing and reunification*, ed. M. Brown, H. Charnley, and C. Petty. Save the Children Conference Report. London: Save the Children UK.

CRC. 1989. *Convention on the rights of the child*. New York: UN General Assembly.

Derib, A. 1998. *Group care and fostering of Sudanese children in Pignudo and Kakuma refugee camps: The experience of Save the Children Sweden from 1990 to 1997*. Stockholm: Save the Children Sweden.

Dona, G. 2001. *The Rwandan experience of fostering separated children*. Stockholm: Save the Children Sweden.

Dozier, M., M. Manni, and O. Lindhiem. 2005. Lessons from the longitudinal studies of attachment. In Grossman, Grossman, and Waters, *Attachment from infancy to adulthood: The major longitudinal studies*,.

Freud, A., and D. Burlingham. 1943. *War and children*. New York: Medical War Books.

Grossman, K., K. Grossman and E. Waters, eds. 2005. *Attachment from infancy to adulthood: The major longitudinal studies*. New York: Guilford.

Hannan, L. 2003. *A gap in their hearts: The experience of separated Somali children*. Nairobi: UN Office for the Coordination of Humanitarian Affairs, Integrated Regional Information Networks.

Hepburn, A., J. Williamson, and T. Wolfram. 2004. *Separated children: Care and protection of children in emergencies—A field guide*. Save the Children US Children in Crisis Field Guide Series. New York: Save the Children Federation.

Human Rights Watch. 1996. "Shattered lives: Sexual violence during the Rwandan genocide and its aftermath." Available on the hrw.org website.

IAGP (Inter-Agency Guiding Principles on Unaccompanied and Separated Children). 2003. Geneva: ICRC, UNHCR, UNICEF, International Rescue Committee, Save the Children UK, and World Vision International.

ICRC (International Committee of the Red Cross). 2004. "Liberia: New ICRC tracing campaign," *ICRC News*, no. 04/144 (August 12). Available on the icrc.org website.

Macksoud M., L. Aber, and I. Cohn. 1990. Assessing the impact of war on children. In *Minefields in their hearts: The mental health of children in war and communal violence*, ed. R. Apfel and B. Simon, 219–30. New Haven, CT: Yale Univ. Press.

Mann, G. 2001. *Networks of support: A literature review of care issues for separated children*. Stockholm: Save the Children Sweden.

———. 2003. *Not seen or heard: The lives of separated refugee children in Dar es Salaam*. Stolkholm: Save the Children Sweden.

Merkelbach, M. 2000. "Reuniting children separated from their families after the Rwandan crisis of 1994: The relative value of a centralized database." *International Review of the Red Cross*, no. 838 (June 30): 351–67. Available on the icrc.org website.

Ressler, E. M., N. Boothby, and D. J. Steinbock, eds. 1988. *Unaccompanied children: Care and protection in wars, natural disasters, and refugee movements*. New York: Oxford Univ. Press.

Sprenkels, R. 2002. *Lives apart: Family separation and alternative care arrangements during El Salvador's civil war*. Stockholm: Save the Children Sweden.

Tolfree, D. 2003. *Community based care for separated children*. Stockholm: Save the Children Sweden.

4

GIRLHOODS STOLEN
*The plight of girl soldiers during
and after armed conflict*

Susan McKay

Introduction

The term *girlhood* typically summons images of girls growing and
healthfully developing, all the while encased within the protective
arms of families and kinship groups. In Western societies girlhood
may extend into the teen years, during which time girls often engage
in a range of exploratory behaviors that are not prototypically femi-
nine. Yet, in many cultures, girlhood can be a demanding time when
they participate in the heavy work expected of all females. At their
mothers' sides, girls learn gendered responsibilities—such as child
care, cooking, and domestic and agricultural work—and appropriate
behaviors toward men. Some girls may be so cloistered that they cannot move freely outside their homes or have interactions with boys
and men outside their families. At the end of girlhood, usually when
girls reach puberty, an initiation rite, marriage, or other celebratory
event may signify that they are now women. Notably, clear cultural
understandings exist about what constitutes girlhood and womanhood.

These distinct cultural notions of girlhood, although disparate,
represent situations in which girls are protected as they mature; they
contrast markedly with the adversity that many girls throughout the
world face. For girls who are physically and/or psychologically abused,

sexually exploited and/or trafficked, and forced into prostitution that results in HIV/AIDS and/or other sexually transmitted diseases (STDs), the demarcating line between girlhood and womanhood may become culturally blurred. Others experience unwanted pregnancies and unassisted childbirths, become de facto heads of households because caring adults do not exist, and/or participate in fighting forces as child soldiers.

This chapter examines girl soldiers' gendered experiences, which can lead to all of the above situations, among others. I adopt the following explanation of gender and gender roles drawn from *Women, Peace, and Security:*

> Gender refers to the socially constructed roles as ascribed to women and men, as opposed to biological and physical characteristics. Gender role vary according to socio-economic, political and cultural contexts, and are affected by other factors, including age, race, class and ethnicity. Gender roles are learned and are changeable. Gender equality is a goal to ensure equal rights, responsibilities and opportunities of women and men, and girls and boys, which has been accepted by governments and international organizations and is enshrined in international agreements and commitments. (UN 2002, 4)

Drawing upon recent studies, including my field research on girl soldiers (under eighteen years of age) in several sub-Saharan African civil wars, and reports from various parts of the world, I look at girls' roles and experiences as child soldiers and the physical, psychosocial, and economic impacts upon their lives when they return to civilian life. While recognizing that cultural meanings of girlhood may diverge from the following definition—for example, a girl may be considered a woman once she is sexually active or married—I define *girl soldiers* based on the Cape Town Principles, which explain child soldiers' age and the range of roles they perform:

> "Child soldier" . . . means any person under 18 years of age who is part of any kind of regular or irregular armed force in any capacity, including but not limited to cooks, porters, messengers, and those accompanying such groups, other than purely as family members. Girls recruited for sexual purposes and forced marriage are included in this definition. It does not, therefore,

only refer to a child who is carrying or has carried arms. (UNICEF 1997)

Although NGO, IGO, and UN organizations increasingly are working with former girl soldiers, their fledgling efforts fall far short of what is needed because most girls do not receive focused assistance. One reason is that child-protection workers often lack gender perspectives and do not think about girls being associated with fighting forces, accepting instead the dichotomy of boys as combatants and girls as victims of sexual assault (Kays 2005). Also, because only recently have more program initiatives been directed toward these girls, little is yet known about their experiences in fighting forces and during reintegration, and how to work best with them (see, e.g., Denov and Maclure 2006a; Denov and Maclure forthcoming; Fox 2004; Kays 2005; Keairns 2002; Mazurana et al. 2002; McKay 1998; McKay 2005a; McKay 2005b; McKay 2005c; McKay 2005d; McKay and Mazurana 2004; Nordstrom 1999; Save the Children 2005a; Save the Children 2005b; Save the Children 2005c; Temmerman 2001; UNICEF 2005; Verhey 2004).

Noteworthy, too, is that feminist scholars, who long ago could and should have shed light on the phenomenon of girl soldiers, have rarely mentioned girl soldiers or analyzed their situations (Fox 2004). Fox asserts that the issue of girl soldiers is "first and foremost a child-protection issue, and perhaps can and should only be linked to feminist theories on women and conflict in limited ways" (Fox 2004, 469). However, I suggest that girl soldiers not be categorized as the province of any particular group because the potential exists that others will abdicate responsibility to act. Rather, a broad approach involving an international array of actors that includes child-protection workers *and* specialists in gender and armed conflict; maternal, child, and public-health personnel; developmental psychologists; educators; human rights workers; policy makers; and those who fund programs for demilitarization, demobilization, and reintegration (DDR) processes can lead to more holistic responses, programming, and solutions.

Girls' experiences in armed conflicts as distinct from women's

As noted by Denov and Maclure, "Because of the gendered nature of society and the tendency to exclude girls and women from realms of social, political and economic power, significant attention needs to be placed on war-affected girls" (2006, 75). Since the early 1990s increased recognition has been accorded to how armed conflicts affect women and girls as a cohort—both as civilians who protect their homes and families and as females within fighting forces. The UN *Platform for Action* (McKay and Winter 1998; UN 1995), the Graça Machel report on the impacts upon children from armed conflict (UN 1996), and writings about the effects of war upon women and girls (see, e.g., Bennett, Bexley, and Warnock 1995, Enloe 2000; Jacobs, Jacobson, and Marchbank 2000; Lorentzen and Turpin 1998; Sajor 1998; Turshen and Twagiramariya 1998) reveal how profoundly women and children are affected by armed conflicts and that rates of civilian casualties are far greater than those of soldiers (Garfield and Neugut 1997; Roberts et al. 2004). In October 2000, the UN Security Council adopted resolution 1325 on women, peace, and security and highlighted the "importance of bringing gender perspectives to the centre of all UN conflict prevention and resolution, peacebuilding, peacekeeping, rehabilitation and reconstruction efforts." In response to the resolution, a study was undertaken that identified gender differences and inequalities during and after war (UN 2002).

Yet, although these pivotal works bring to light war's effects on girls and women, girls have been inappropriately grouped under the larger rubric of women because distinctions in girls' and women's experiences are not yet well understood and also because many girls transition into womanhood during armed conflicts. Noting this phenomenon, Stavrou observes that girls' experiences as soldiers within war and postwar societies must *not* be generically considered as "women's experiences of war" but understood within a particular conflict and context (Stavrou 2005a).

Despite the present limited ability to articulate distinct experiences between girls and women as distinguished by conflict and context, throughout the world a key gender-based experience of both women and girls during armed conflicts is sexual violence, including torture, rape, mass rape, sexual slavery, enforced prostitution, forced sterilization, forced termination of pregnancies, and mutilation (UN 2002). Although increased international attention calls for intervention and international advocacy that sexual violence—whether occurring within or outside a force (sexual violence may be perpetrated against female targets of military actions but not permitted internally within a force)—constitutes a war crime, rape and sexual torture continue to routinely occur (see Amnesty International 2004; Ben-Ari and Harsch 2005; McKay 1998a; McKay 1998b; McKay and Mazurana 2004; Sajor 1998; UN 1996; UN 2002). For example, in Darfur in western Sudan, women and girls have been subjected to rape and other forms of sexual violence during Sudanese government attacks on villages. Girls as young as seven and eight years old have been raped, and some women have been both raped and genitally mutilated (Human Rights Watch 2005). Therefore, a pivotal issue for girls (and women) is gender-based violence and its aftermath, including physical and psychological harm and the present lack of justice for this war crime (McKay 2000). Although boys, too, experience sexual violence, the frequency is comparatively low (McKay and Mazurana 2004).

Girls, girl soldiers, and gender

Understanding gender within any culture is complex because gender construction is a process, not an end point. Few common understandings exist about the meanings of gender within a particular society or about how armed conflicts affect girls and gender construction. Further, the influence of gender is often shrouded in the gender-neutral language of local, regional, and international organizations. As observed by Stavrou:

> Current semantics do injustice to the role played and the work done by girl and women soldiers. The fuzzy language of '*vulnerable groups associated with armed movements,*' . . . *women and children involved with armed forces or groups,*' . . . *women working in support function to armed groups and forces*' . . . needs to give way to the clear and functional work-related concepts of engineering, logistics, health corps, combat and service support. . . . Not labeling the work of non-combatant women [and girl] soldiers continues the gender discrimination of the division of labor whereby critical work that is essential for survival is simply considered a natural extension of women's domestic obligations and hence neither worthy of remuneration nor significant enough for women to qualify for training and livelihoods programs. (Stavrou 2005b)

Analyzing gendered girlhood within a particular cultural context and its alterations, even transformation, within fighting forces can provide fuller insights into girls' experiences during and after conflict. Such analysis draws attention to gender-specific needs of girls and contributes to improved responses for them within programs developed by grassroots groups, NGOs, and IGOs. As an example, gender analysis of formerly abducted girl soldiers in several African civil wars revealed key roles girls played within forces. In Angola, gender-based labor exploitation, including sex labor, was a significant factor in facilitating guerrilla wars (Stavrou 2005a). In Northern Uganda, Sierra Leone, and Mozambique, the productive and reproductive labor of girls has been a foundation upon which fighting forces have relied. Consequently, girls and women have been among the last released by forces, if they are released at all; this information is of key importance in developing demobilization programs to better reach girls (McKay and Mazurana 2004).

Girls' participation in fighting forces

Most people are surprised to learn that girls are widely used as child soldiers. Because few accurate estimates exist of girl soldiers' numbers within specific country contexts, figures not based upon careful analysis should be considered specious. Also, although girls' participation in the past has been widely under-reported, some figures presently appearing in child-protection literature appear to inflate estimated girls' numbers—possibly in an effort to raise international concern and advocacy for them. In considering estimates of global involvement of girls, the extent of girls' participation must be understood as context specific, with some fighting forces using girls extensively while others do not.

Between the years 1990 and 2003, girls were present in fighting forces (government forces, paramilitary/militia, and armed opposition groups) in fifty-five countries; in thirty-eight of these countries they were involved in situations of armed conflict (Mazurana and McKay 2001; McKay and Mazurana 2004). How do they enter these forces? Like boys, some girls join with their families and friends—because of family expectations, for ideological reasons, and/or in response to state violence. Others become part of fighting forces to escape physical and psychological abuse and sexual violence at home; because they perceive that they have few or no choices about their own futures; and/or to seek lives at variance with traditional societal expectations (Brett and Specht 2004; Paez 2001; McKay and Mazurana 2004). They may join to gain education and improve career opportunities, and/or because they imagine they will find greater gender equality, such as occurred widely in Peru when an estimated 40 percent of guerrillas in the Shining Path were female (Kirk 1997). Many were girls or college students when they joined, recruited by their professors.[1] The notion of girls freely joining, however, is a contested one, because these girls usually lack quality choices.

Children may be taken as orphans, as in Sri Lanka, or be born into a force. Many girls and boys are abducted or otherwise forced to join. Between 1990 and 2003, girls were abducted into armed forces and groups in eleven countries in Africa, four in the Americas, eight in Asia, three in Europe, and two in the Middle East. Many abducted children are also transported across international borders, especially in Africa (McKay and Mazurana 2004). In a study of forty Sierra Leonean girls, it was discovered that all were abducted by the Revolutionary United Front (RUF). They reported extreme coercion, violence, and fear, usually under the threat of a gun, and being forcibly separated from loved ones (Denov and Maclure forthcoming).

Girls' roles typically overlap and include working as spies and informants, in intelligence and communications, and as military trainers and combatants. They are health workers and mine sweepers, and they conduct suicide missions. Other support roles include raising crops, selling goods, preparing food, carrying loot and weapons, and stealing food, livestock, and seed stock. Important to understand is that, underlying these various roles and activities, girls' participation is central to sustaining a force because of their productive and reproductive labor. As such, they replicate traditional societal gender roles and patriarchal privilege, whereby girls (and women) serve men and boys. Their labor is a foundation upon which fighting forces throughout the world rely (McKay and Mazurana 2004).

Girls in fighting forces, especially when they have been abducted, often experience physical and psychological abuse, including sexual violence—although its occurrence varies by context, because some fighting forces eschew forced sex. Between 1990 and 2003, girls provided sexual services to boys and men in fighting forces in nine African countries, three countries in the Americas, five in Asia, and two in Europe. Again, depending on the context, when they reach puberty, girls may supply reproductive labor by giving birth to and rearing children who will become members of the force. For example, in the Lord's Resistance Army (LRA) fighting force in Northern Uganda, the leader, Joseph Kony, has fathered large numbers of children, who have grown up in his force. Girls in fighting forces in Mozambique, Northern Uganda, and Sierra Leone reported sexual violence, and abducted girls were almost universally raped—often by many men during a single day (McKay and Mazurana 2004). As in Sierra Leone, sex labor was integral to the function of girl soldiers in Angola (Stavrou 2005a). In contrast, within forces in Colombia, Sri Lanka, and the Philippines, sexual violence toward girl combatants in rebel forces is not common (Keairns 2002; Jareg 2005).

As yet, we know little about distinctions between girls and women in terms of psychological effects of sexual violence and how identity and self-esteem may be affected, although lifelong effects can be expected. We do know that throughout the world girls (and women) are stigmatized and marginalized when they experience sexual violence. Girls feel shame, and their communities may consider them to be morally compromised (Finnström 2003) and not marriageable (McKay and Mazurana 2004). With their bodies still developing, girls who are subjected to repeated sexual violence experience genital damage such as vaginal lacerations, which in turn make them more vulnerable to STDs. Sterility may also result. Although most data are anecdotal because of a lack of systematic epidemiologic studies, many girls purportedly die during pregnancy and childbirth because of immature bodies, unsafe conditions, and lack of health care.

How girl soldiers' experiences affect their lives

It is important to reiterate that, within fighting forces, girls' experiences are multifaceted, complex, and context specific. Thus, a girl soldier in a Colombian rebel force may have distinctly different experiences from a girl in Angola or Indonesia. Yet, they share commonalities such as altered identity and changed human networks, behaviors, and relationships. Physically, they are challenged to survive as they cope with illnesses, exhaustion, wounds, menstrual difficulties, complications from pregnancy and birth, STDs, and a host of other maladies such as malaria, intestinal parasites, tuberculosis, anemia, diarrhea, malnutrition, disabilities, scars, and burns (McKay and Mazurana 2004; Stavrou 2005a).

Exposed daily to a culture of violence and themselves perpetrators in acts of terror such as attacking their own families and neighbors, abducting other children, and killing civilians, they are no longer normal girls either in their own eyes or in the eyes of those who know them. Instead, girlhood is inverted and distorted. They have experienced what most of us never imagine, and they can never go back to girlhood innocence (McKay 2005a). Relationships and networks also are altered drastically. For girls, being apart from their mothers is one of their greatest hardships. They may also be forbidden to spend time with other girls because they might conspire to escape. Consequently, friendships may develop in secrecy. In Angola, some girls reported solidarity and friendship with other girls (Stavrou 2005a). Similarly, in Sierra Leone girls formed close relationships with other girls and women, which reduced their fear and brought solace, comfort, and solidarity. Also, older women sometimes offered protection to them (Denov and Maclure forthcoming).

Although still limited, we now have greater understanding about how girls' experiences change them psychologically and how identities may or may not be transformed within fighting forces. For example, some young girls who were abducted into the RUF but only stayed a short time were not subjected to sexual violence and were welcomed home; their identities appeared to remain reasonably intact (McKay and Mazurana 2004). In contrast, during the forty-year war in Angola, girls in the forces underwent deliberate suppression of their identities that resulted in diminished memories of relationships, place, and community. Their constant movement from place to place across the countryside led to their losing a sense of time, sequencing of events, and parts of their own identity (Stavrou 2005a). Such girls may find it difficult to recall their ages or how long they were in a force, or to retain identities that link them with civilian life.

Other girls have profound transformations in their identities because they become mothers, often from forced sex. They no longer view themselves as girls—despite their chronological age—because girlhood may be perceived to end when marriage and motherhood begin, as is true in many cultures. Because we presently know little about these mothers, critical questions remain to be asked, for example: In societies where being unmarried is tantamount to social exclusion, and marriage and motherhood convey womanhood, how do girls negotiate identity when they return with children fathered by unidentifiable males? What does it mean to a girl's identity when she returns from a fighting force and is called a "rebel wife" and her baby a "rebel baby," born of an unsanctioned marriage?

Another identity change that can occur for girls is developing a sense of self as efficacious. Many girls brutalized by violence found their identities changed, often gradually, from being victims of violence to perpetrators. Although most Sierra Leonean girl soldiers were abducted and subjected to continual violence, over time some girls gained power. For example, some girl soldiers in Sierra Leone were empowered because they resisted sexual violence, rebelled against authority and command structure (Denov and Maclure 2006) and participated in violent acts (McKay 2005a). Some girls who carried and used light weapons felt a sense of power and control, which, at the time, they relished (Denov and Maclure forthcoming). Others girls aligned themselves with commanders as "wives" and thereby gained protection, power, and status (McKay and Mazurana 2004).

Notably, however, many—probably most—girls are not empowered because they are not fighters, do not possess weapons, or are not privileged by their position within a force. In Angola, for example, of a group of forty girl soldiers only three reported that they worked as soldiers per se, whereas the rest worked in logistics and support (Stavrou 2005b). As observed by child psychiatrist Elizabeth Jareg, a program adviser to Save the Children Norway:

> Many [girls] experience front-line service and not infrequently express satisfaction that for the first time in their lives they have power and an equal status with men. Others have years-long experiences of being continually abused and forced to bear children with men who treat them brutally. (Jareg 2005)

Therefore, recognizing how varied girls' experiences are is critical to better understanding how identity may be shaped in fighting forces. Similarly, we can expect that in the post-conflict aftermath girls' identities will vary according to age when enlisted, length of time in a force, experiences, and roles.

Demilitarization, demobilization, and reintegration (DDR)

Gender disparities that privilege boy soldiers over girls mean that few girls enter or benefit from formal DDR programs, in which the readjustment process can be fostered. These programs are mainly designed to restore security, and as female combatants are not seen as a major security threat, they are insufficiently targeted (Bouta 2005). And, because these girl soldiers have been seen as less of a threat, "they have experienced threat from their own states and communities, from the armed groups they belonged to and then, upon reintegration, from their own states, communities, and the international community" (Fox 2004, 477).

In Sierra Leone, only 506 girls, compared to 6,052 boys, went through a DDR program. This is despite an estimated 25 percent of the child soldiers being girls (McKay and Mazurana 2004). Similarly, a study of forty former girl soldiers in Angola found that only one was recognized as a girl soldier and given limited benefits (Stavrou 2005b). In a study conducted in five provinces of eastern Democratic Republic of Congo, twenty-three girls, as compared with 1,718 boys, were demobilized by four international NGOs, despite girls being recruited or abducted as extensively as boys and estimated to make up 30 to 40 percent of the children in fighting units (Verhey 2004).

Jareg advocates that some children should be prioritized for rehabilitation because of the experiences they have had; these include those who have been severely abused and girls who have become mothers in fighting forces. Although rehabilitation does not guarantee successful reintegration, it suggests a better outcome (see, e.g., MacMullin and Loughry 2002). However, a study in Liberia found no significant difference to exist between ex-combatants who demobilized themselves and those who spent between one month and one year in interim care centers receiving training and support (cited in Peters, Richards, and Vlassenroot 2003).

These discrepant perspectives suggest that we have much to learn about what successful rehabilitation and reintegration mean and how to best promote these processes. A critical gender question to ask is, How can DDR be inclusive of and appropriate for girls? For example, should DDR for girls be community based rather than situated in venues with high-profile public processes?

Reintegration: Returned and neglected

Having experienced what is unimaginable for most people, girls now face reconstructing fragile lives as civilians (McKay 2004; McKay

2005b; McKay 2005c), a process about which we have limited under-standing. As observed by Jareg, "We need more long-term research into the factors influencing the process of becoming once more a member of one's family and community after years of exposure to unspeakable experiences. There is no doubt that many children will remain vulnerable for life" (Jareg 2005, 9). Girls, particularly those who have been gone a long time or return as mothers, face special challenges in reintegrating. One of these is that most girls "sponta-neously" reintegrate—meaning they find their own way back and quietly find a place to live, perhaps with family members, friends, or sympathetic adults. Though secrecy in "slipping back" protects them in some ways, they do not experience DDR program benefits and must depend upon their communities for help. Yet, because of gen-der discrimination and lack of community support, they are consis-tently neglected, which is amplified because communities know that girls have violated gender and societal norms—even though they were forced. A study of 111 girls and young women in postwar Sierra Leone concluded that community initiatives that lack local support have not been very effective in promoting girls' acceptance, protection, and reintegration; further, local communities were perceived as one of the biggest obstacles to girls' reintegration (Coulter 2003).

A key gender issue, therefore, is to understand better how girls are challenged when they confront often hostile and unwelcoming communities. What psychosocial supports exist within communities, both urban and rural, to assist girls? If they cannot return to their communities and families, where do they go, and how do they sur-vive? Also, how can grassroots groups or NGOs work with commu-nities to reach these girls in order to promote their healing and reintegration?

Children's views of reintegration

How do children view successful reintegration, and what are the re-alities of what they experience? In a Save the Children study of 211 Sierra Leonean children, the children "defined reintegration as be-ing loved and cared for by their families, being accepted and wel-comed by the community, and living in peace and unity with others" (Save the Children 2004, 5). They identified the importance of meet-ing their basic needs such as food, shelter, and water. Also, these re-turned children wanted to make productive contributions through schooling, work, and skills training. Yet, girls face special barriers. They are typically urged to resume traditional gender roles, returning to traditional societal structures and patriarchal practices instead of using strengths they may have developed (McKay and Mazurana 2004). Because in many cases they have missed years of formal schooling and less cultural value is placed upon girls attending school, they are expected to take up domestic and child-care responsibilities. Yet, to sustain themselves and provide for their children if they are mothers, they must learn skills and be educated for economic self-sufficiency. This may require that cultural expectations be reconciled with whether girls can choose to learn a nontraditional skill, such as welding or construction, that has more economic value. Unfortunately, girls themselves may avoid these nontraditional skills because of the cultural expectations for gender-appropriate behavior.

Almost all of a subgroup of forty children who shared ideas about successful reintegration in the study complained of neglect or abuse and identified this as one of their most significant problems (Save the Children 2004; see also Save the Children 2005c). Another problem the children faced was that the community encouraged early marriage. The children felt that NGOs and UN agencies should play a stronger protection role by convincing chiefs and community members of the importance of children's rights (Save the Children 2004). Also, girls who continued to live with commanders from their "bush" marriages reported physical and sexual harm. Alarmingly high numbers of these girls were supporting themselves by prostitution, propelled by lack of extended family care and their single-parent status.

Rituals that foster reintegration

In some communities, rituals to welcome and cleanse these girls are an important way to begin the reintegration and healing process (see, e.g., Wessells and Monteiro 2001; Wessells forthcoming). Although girls, in some instances, benefit from community rituals (McKay and Mazurana 2004), they also are often neglected—as occurred in Angola where welcoming and reintegrating rituals were aimed at men because it was assumed that women [and girls] did not kill (Stavrou 2005a). Some rituals may be required if a girl is to become part of the community. For example, in Sierra Leone, girls who did not go through the traditional rituals to excise their genitalia must undergo this ritual as part of reintegration so that they are acceptable to the community and then may become marriageable.

Leaving again

Despite rituals and community initiatives, because of their "second rate reintegration" many girls are unable to reintegrate successfully and therefore leave the communities to which they had returned. This may occur, in part, because they may use foul language, abuse drugs, smoke, and act in aggressive and quarrelsome ways. These behaviors are better tolerated in boys, who are not seen as so fully violating gender norms.

Girls also leave because they are not accepted by communities and/ or are stigmatized due to the children they bring with them. Such girls may be viewed with special contempt by communities (Jareg 2005). An investigation in Northern Uganda of twenty girl mothers concluded that girl mothers are excited when they return but then shocked when communities do not reciprocate their feelings, call them degrading names ("killers," "demon possessed," "bush behavior"), and treat them as second-class citizens (Uganda Team 2005). In Sierra Leone three-hundred girl mothers who were abducted into the RUF and did not go through DDR experienced family and community resentment when they returned with fatherless babies. Further, as they now attempt to organize themselves and participate in economic activities, the majority of these girl mothers (70 percent) are required to carry their babies everywhere and do not have anyone else to care for their babies; those children left behind with caretakers are poorly cared for and fed (Christian Children's Fund 2005). Girl mothers, their children, and their communities need support to reduce stig-matizing behaviors and to make sure these mothers are not denied training or access to school, which commonly occurs because they lack child care (McKay and Mazurana 2004). They must have liveli-hood options to avert their entry into prostitution (Save the Children 2004), especially because they often have sole responsibility for the support of their children and yet lack parenting, literacy, and eco-nomic skills. Also, they and their children must have access to and the means to obtain primary health care.

Girl mothers continue to experience extreme marginalization, which carries a high price because some girls may resort to prostitu-tion and/or to violence in response to their frustration and anger

(Denov and Maclure forthcoming; Burman and McKay 2006), or they leave communities entirely (Save the Children 2003; Stavrou 2005a; Stavrou 2005b). In Angola ex-soldier mothers increasingly prefer to live apart from their families or to develop nontraditional family forms. Of forty former girl soldiers, 53 percent lived in female-headed households —almost double the national average of 27 percent (Stavrou 2005b). Thus, instead of reintegration, former girl soldiers in Angola are "leaving" to establish new family forms, relationships, and kinship networks that are altering the sociocultural milieu of war-torn societies.

Integration of children born within fighting forces

Another important consideration should be for the children born of girl soldiers who come home with them. We need to understand what happens to these children, who may be viewed as "rebel children" because they were born in a fighting force and often do not have an identifiable father. Also, we have limited understanding of how girls' social reintegration affects their identity and their parenting—which, in turn, affects the emotional and psychological development of their children. Their children, who should experience love and protection, may be highly vulnerable because of the parenting they receive as well as the circumstances of their conception and early childhood years spent in the bush. Some promising research is now looking at the issues surrounding war babies, including issues of identity and long-term outcomes (see, e.g., Carpenter forthcoming).

Program priorities in working with girl soldiers in communities

The onus is upon communities to come to terms with what has happened, to heal, and to develop programs for returning girls as well as returning boys. Yet, communities are also devastated by armed conflict and must be supported through programs that enable them to respond to the needs of returning girls while still considering the needs of all war-affected children in the community. Child-protection organizations, therefore, must work closely with communities to support girls' successful integration so they can live useful lives and once again establish trusting relationships with adults. It is important that girls be consulted in developing programs to best address their needs.

To facilitate former child soldiers' reintegration and to reduce stigma and discrimination, UNICEF Child Protection Officer Abubacar Sultan advocates that relatives and communities take responsibility for them right at the beginning (McKay and Mazurana 2004). The primary approach, therefore, for psychosocial intervention is to support reestablishing children's primary relationships with parents, family, and communities (Arnston and Boothby 2002). This may mean tackling discrimination by chiefs and/or other community leaders, because their leadership can be pivotal in smoothing the way (Save the Children 2005b). Importantly, women leaders can play pivotal roles in supporting and working with returning girls, but they must be recognized and enabled to do so.

A critical issue for girls is promoting their self-esteem and reacceptance into the community and helping them to develop a positive perception about their futures and those of their children. To accomplish this goal, their resilience and agency must be fostered through very practical approaches, such as finding ways to enroll them in school, gain economic skills, and access primary health care. The latter is of great importance because of the diseases and injuries most suffer and due to the high incidence of STDs such as HIV/AIDS.

As previously discussed, some girls do not remain in communities. They may return to "bush husbands," live alone or with other girls, leave to escape discriminatory treatment, or seek more independent and egalitarian lives that defy cultural gender norms. Innovative programmatic initiatives should be developed to reach these girls—such as community-based approaches that address their long-term reintegration needs.

Community-based programs also must take into account sexual violence and find ways to discuss it within communities. This is necessary because sexual violence is not limited to experiences in fighting forces but also occurs to girls within communities (McKay and Mazurana 2004). Consequently, public discourse should be encouraged "to increase awareness of sexual violence, women's and girls' rights to personal security, and to reduce persistent taboos" (McKay and Mazurana 2004). Importantly, girls should be educated about their rights and encouraged to participate in actions to increase their sexual protection.

Since few rape-prevention programs or support services exist, local and international NGOs and IGOs should prioritize their development. In offering programs for girls who have experienced sexual violence, all affected girls should be eligible to participate. An example of how to organize this occurred in Sierra Leone where, with the help of an NGO, community members identified a cohort of sexually abused girls but did not single out those who had been associated with fighting forces. Also, in another program for abducted girls with small children, other high-risk, war-affected girl mothers from the community were included, although they had not been abducted (McKay and Mazurana 2004).

Forging girl-sensitive gender justice

Perpetrators of gender-based crimes and sexual violence against girls and women in situations of armed conflict must be prosecuted, with national and international legal systems providing accessible and gender-sensitive redress. However, prosecution of a small number of high-profile war criminals at the level of the International Criminal Court (ICC) or war tribunals fails to answer the need for gender justice for returning girl soldiers. Interestingly, concerning justice at the level of the ICC, former girl soldiers in Northern Uganda viewed justice as "getting us rehabilitated," not "tit for tat" (Uganda Team 2005). By implication, this means that gender discrimination must be eliminated by providing equitable treatment for girl soldiers within DDR processes and within communities, among other measures. In any war-torn country or region training about girls' and women's rights should be initiated both during and after armed conflict within government forces, security forces, peace-keeping forces, and personnel within DDR programs, interim-care-center staff, and other front-line groups. Such training should be based upon national policies and international standards that lay down principles for addressing sexual violence.

In resolution 1325 on women, peace, and security, the UN Security Council formally recognized that achieving gender justice is as central to social transformation as any other form of reparations after war (UN 2002). For former girl soldiers, although the injustice surrounding their inverted girlhoods can never be remedied, gender justice located in their own communities and countries can be instrumental in restoring dignity and hope to their lives.

Note

[1] Robin Kirk, personal communication, September 5, 2005.

References

Amnesty International. 2004. *Lives blown apart: Crimes against women in time of conflict*. New York: Amnesty International. December 8.

Arnston, L., and N. Boothby. 2002. *"A world turned upside down." Child soldiers in Mozambique: A case study of their reintegration*. Washington, DC: Save the Children.

Ben-Ari, Nirit, and Ernest Harsch. 2005. Sexual violence, an "invisible war crime:" Sierra Leone Truth Commission condemns abuse, discrimination. *Africa Renewal* 18 (4) :1–7. January.

Bennett, O., J. Bexley, and K. Warnock, eds. 1995. *Arms to fight, arms to protect: Women speak out about conflict*. London: Panos.

Bouta, T. 2005. *Gender and disarmament, demobilization and reintegration: Building blocs for Dutch policy*. The Hague: Netherlands Institute of International Relations "Clingendael." March.

Brett, R., and I. Specht. 2004. *Young soldiers: Why they choose to fight*. Boulder, CO: Lynne Rienner.

Burman, M., and S. McKay. 2006. Girls in fighting forces in Sierra Leone: Marginalization and health.

Carpenter, R. C. Forthcoming. War's impact on children born of rape and sexual exploitation: Physical, economic, and psychosocial dimensions. In *Children and war: Impact*, ed. W. Andy Knight. Alberta: Univ. of Alberta Press.

Christian Children's Fund. 2005. Presentation from Christian Children's Fund, Sierra Leone Programme on Girl Mothers in the Northern and Eastern Regions of Sierra Leone. *Conference on girl mothers in western and southern Africa*, Bellagio, Italy. April 12–18.

Coulter, C. 2003. *Assessment of the "girls left behind" project for girls and young women who did not enter DDR*. Evaluation conducted for UNICEF Child Protection, Freetown, Sierra Leone. July-August.

Denov, M., and R. Maclure. 2006. Engaging the voices of girls in the aftermath of Sierra Leone's conflict: Experiences and perspectives in a culture of violence. *Anthropologica* 48: 73–85.

———. Forthcoming. Girls and small arms in Sierra Leone: Victimization, participation, and resistance. In *Gender perspectives on small arms and light weapons*, ed. A. Schnabel and V. Farr. Tokyo: United Nations Univ. Press.

Enloe, C. 2000. *Maneuvers: The international politics of militarizing women's lives*. Berkeley and Los Angeles: Univ. of California Press.

Finnström, S. 2003. Living with bad surroundings: War and existential uncertainty in Acholiland, Northern Uganda. *Uppsala Studies in Cultural Anthropology* 35. Uppsala: Uppsala Univ. Press.

Fox, M. 2004. Girl soldiers: Human security and gendered insecurity. *Security Dialogue* 35 (4): 465–79.

Garfield, R., and A. Neugut. 1997. The human consequences of war. In *War and Public Health*, ed. Barry Levy and Victor Sidel, 27–38. New York: Oxford Univ. Press.

Human Rights Watch. 2005, April. *Sexual violence and its consequences among displaced persons in Darfur and Chad*. New York: Human Rights Watch.

Jacobs, S., R. Jacobson, and J. Marchbank, eds. 2000. *States of conflict: Gender, violence, and resistance*. London: Zed Books.

Jareg, E. 2005. *Crossing bridges and negotiating rivers—rehabilitation and reintegration of children associated with armed forces*. Available on the child-soldiers.org website.

Kays, L. 2005, January. Why we cannot find the hidden girl soldier: A study of professional attitudes towards gender analysis in international conflict and development work. *Peace, Conflict, and Development* 6: 1–26.

Keairns, Y. 2002. *The voices of girl child soldiers*. New York: Quaker United Nations Office. October.

Kirk, R. 1997. *The monkey's paw: New chronicles from Peru*. Amherst: Univ. of Massachusetts Press.

Lorentzen, L. A., and J. Turpin. 1998. *The women and war reader*. New York: New York Univ. Press.

MacMullin, C., and M. Loughry. 2002, April. *An investigation into the psychosocial adjustment of former abducted child soldiers in Northern Uganda*. Field report submitted to International Rescue Committee.

Mazurana, D., and S. McKay. 2001. Child soldiers: What about the girls? *Bulletin of Atomic Scientists* 57 (5) (September-October): 30–35.

Mazurana, D., S. McKay, K. Carlson, and J. Kasper. 2002. Girls in fighting forces and groups: Their recruitment, participation, demobilization, and reintegration. *Peace and Conflict: Journal of Peace Psychology* 8 (2): 97–123.

McKay, S. 1998a. The effects of armed conflict on girls and women. *Peace and Conflict: Journal of Peace Psychology* 4: 381–92.

———. 1998b. The psychology of societal reconstruction and peace: A gendered perspective. In Lorentzen and Turpin, *The women and war reader*, 348–62.

———. 2000. Gender justice and reconciliation. *Women's Studies International Forum* 23 (5): 561–70.

———. 2004. Reconstructing fragile lives: Girls' social reintegration in Northern Uganda and Sierra Leone. *Gender and Development, Peacebuilding, and Reconstruction* 12 (3): 19–30.

———. 2005a. Girls as "weapons of terror." *Studies in Conflict and Terrorism*, special issue, ed. Cindy Ness, 359–71. UK: Taylor and Francis.

———. 2005b. Girl soldiers' social reintegration in Northern Uganda and Sierra Leone. In *Post-Conflict reconstruction in Africa*, ed. Ahmed Sikainga and Ousseina Alidou. Trenton, NJ: Africa World Press.

———. 2005c. How do you mend broken hearts? Gender, war, and impacts on girls in fighting forces. In *The Handbook of International Disaster Psychology*, ed. Gill Reyes. Westport, CT: Praeger Publishing Company.

———. 2005d. Researching war's impacts: What about girls in fighting forces? In *Impact of war on children*, ed. W. Andy Knight. Alberta: Univ. of Alberta Press.

McKay, S., and D. D. Winter. 1998. The United Nations Platform for Action: Critique and implications. *Peace and Conflict: Journal of Peace Psychology* 4: 167–78.

McKay, S., and D. Mazurana. 2004. *Where are the girls? Girls in fighting forces in Northern Uganda, Sierra Leone and Mozambique: Their lives during and after war*. Montreal: Rights and Democracy.

Nordstrom, C. 1999. Visible wars and invisible girls, shadow industries and the politics of not knowing. *International Feminist Journal of Politics* 1 (1): 14–33.

Paez, E. 2001. *Girls in the Colombian armed groups: A diagnosis briefing*. Germany: Terre de Hommes. September.

Peters, K., P. Richards, and K. Vlassenroot. 2003. *What happens to youth during and after wars? A preliminary review of literature on Africa and an assessment of the debate*. RAWOO working paper. Amsterdam, Netherlands: Development Assistance Council. October.

Roberts, L., R. Lafta, R. Garfield, J. Khudhairi, and G. Burnham. 2004. Mortality before and after the 2003 invasion of Iraq: Cluster sample survey. *The Lancet* 364, 1857–64.

Sajor, I. 1998. *Common grounds: Violence against women in war and armed conflict situations*. Quezon City: Asian Center for Women's Human Rights.

Save the Children. 2003. *A study on the views, perspectives and experiences of "social integration" among formerly abducted girls in Gulu, Northern Uganda*. Gulu, Uganda: Save the Children. November.

———. 2004. *No place like home? Children's experiences of reintegration in the Kailahun District of Sierra Leone*. London: Save the Children.

———. 2005a. *Forgotten casualties of war: Girls in armed conflict*. London: Save the Children.

———. 2005b. *Girls formerly associated with armed groups and armed forces who did not go through formal demobilization: Save the Children UK's experience in Western Africa*. London: Save the Children.

———. 2005c. *No more faded cotton*. London: Save the Children.

Stavrou, V. 2005a. *Breaking the silence: Girls forcibly involved in the armed struggle in Angola*. Richmond, VA: Christian Children's Fund; Ottawa: Canadian International Development Agency.

———. 2005b. *Executive summary: Breaking the silence*. Richmond, VA: Christian Children's Fund; Ottawa: Canadian International Development Agency.

Temmerman, E. 2001. *Aboke girls: Children abducted in northern Uganda*. Kampala: Fountain Publishers.

Turshen, M., and C. Twagiramariya, eds. 1998. *What women do in wartime: Gender and conflict in Africa*. London: Zed Books.

Uganda Team. 2005. Presentation on girl mothers in Northern Uganda. *Conference on girl mothers in western and southern Africa*. Bellagio, Italy. April 12–18.

UN (United Nations). 1995. *Beijing Platform for Action*. New York: UN.

———. 1996. *Report of the expert of the secretary-general, Ms. Graça Machel: Impact of armed conflict on children*. New York: UN.

———. 2002. *Women, peace, and security*. Study submitted by the secretary-general pursuant to Security Council resolution 1325. New York: UN.

UNICEF (United Nations Children's Fund). 1997. *Cape Town annotated principles and best practices*. Adopted by the participants in the Symposium on the Prevention of Recruitment of Children into the Armed Forces and Demobilization and Social Reintegration of Child Soldiers in Africa. Cape Town, South Africa. April 30.

———. 2005. *The impact of conflict on women and girls in west and central Africa and the UNICEF response*. New York: UNICEF. February.

Verhey, B. 2004. *Reaching the girls: Study on girls' association with armed forces and groups in the DRC*. Save the Children UK/the NGO Group: CARE, IFESH, and IRC. November.

Wessells, M. G. Forthcoming. *Child soldiers: Stolen childhoods*. Cambridge: Harvard Univ. Press.

Wessells, M. G., and C. Monteiro. 2001. Psychosocial interventions and postwar reconstruction in Angola: Interweaving Western and traditional approaches. In *Peace, conflict, and violence*, ed. D. Christie, R. V. Wagner, and D. Winter, 262–75. Upper Saddle River, NJ: Prentice-Hall.

5

EDUCATION AND HOPE

A psychosocial assessment
of Palestinian children

Cairo Arafat and Thahabieh Musleh

Introduction

A considerable amount of literature deals with the impact of war and other traumatic events on child development. It is widely acknowledged that for children to develop "normally" and be "psychosocially healthy," a number of their basic needs must be met. Children who undergo traumatic experiences of war and conflict usually develop special needs, including understanding, emotional resolution, security, a sense of belonging, and self-worth (Ressler et al. 1993). Factors that determine how they cope with their ordeal include the type, degree, and duration of the stressful life events; their subjective understanding of them; and their stage of development. The social ecology of a child's life is also important. This includes parents, families, peers, schools, and religious and other community-based institutions.

Children's cognitive and affective processes can be damaged by conflict, imprinting emotional, psychological, and physiological scars. This may lead to distrustful and hostile behavior and can prevent the child from developing into a productive and social adult and citizen.

This chapter is reprinted, with slight adaptations, from Cairo Arafat, "A Psychosocial Assessment of Palestinian Children," The Secretariat of the National Plan of Action for Palestinian Children (July 2003). This research was supported by Save the Children and USAID.

111

However, under the right circumstances a child's cognitive and affective processes can also serve as a source of strength, building resilience and increasing the child's ability to bounce back from unusual stress or trauma. This is especially the case when a child can count on continuous support from parents, family, friends and/or other community members and social institutions.

Research into resilience has shown that most children can cope fairly well with low levels of risk. Most of the time their development and ability to reach their full potential will only be jeopardized when risk accumulates (Boothby 1996; Bracken and Petty 1998). The West Bank and Gaza represent such an environment.

Since the outbreak of the second Intifada in September 2000, injury and death have become part of children's daily lives in the West Bank and Gaza, affecting them directly or indirectly. According to the Palestinian Red Crescent Society, by April 2005 approximately 27,770 Palestinians had been injured and 3,602 had died since September 2000; approximately 18 percent of the deaths have been of children under eighteen years of age (PRCS 2005). Children have also been exposed to the destruction of homes, bombing and shelling raids, imprisonment, razing of agricultural property, uprooting of olive trees, construction of fences and barriers around or through their communities, as well as stringent curfews and closures confining them to their homes for prolonged periods. Economic decline, growing poverty, and the lack of financial and/or physical access to quality health care have had a further detrimental effect on the health and nutrition status of Palestinian children. A USAID-financed nutritional assessment in 2002 found that the incidence of acute malnutrition among children under five years old is 13 percent in Gaza and 4.3 percent in the West Bank (Abdeen et al. 2002). Finally, thousands of children have not had regular access to their schools due to closures, curfews, and destruction or confiscation of schools (Palestinian Ministry of Education 2003).

Following the Israeli military offensives in the spring of 2002, reports about increased trauma among Palestinian children multiplied. Watchlist, an international NGO, and the Women's Center for Legal Aid and Counselling (WCLAC), a Palestinian NGO, found increases in sleeping and eating disorders, concentration problems, crying, bedwetting, feelings of hopelessness, and preoccupation with death.

Against this background, Save the Children US and the Secretariat for the National Plan of Action for Palestinian Children (NPA), a Palestinian child-rights organization, decided in March 2002 to embark on an assessment of the psychosocial well-being of Palestinian children, in collaboration with Save the Children Sweden. The assessment was part of a USAID-financed project in which Save the Children-US and the NPA work together to provide support to Palestinian children through community-based psychosocial support programs. The West Bank and Gaza program highlights, among other things, the importance of self-esteem and coping skills in the lives of these children.

The main aim of this qualitative study was to learn what children have to say about their situations and to understand how they are dealing with the conflict that permeates their lives. Questions it sought to answer included the following: How do they perceive the situation? What does it mean to them? How are they coping with life events? To whom do they turn for help and support? What are their expectations for the future? The study was designed to provide children with an open forum in which to speak. To this end focus groups and open-ended questions were used to stimulate discussion. Additionally, researchers interviewed parents and teachers to obtain their views regarding children's psychosocial development and to gain insights into how they cope with their roles and responsibilities in the context of the prolonged conflict. The study was not designed to determine the prevalence of post traumatic stress disorder among Palestinian children or to project the long-term developmental consequences of the conflict on these children. Instead, it is hoped that by listening and learning from the children themselves, mental health professionals and community workers will be in a better position to design and implement programs in their behalf.

Methodology

For the study[1] three sets of focus group questions were developed targeting children, parents, and teachers. Each set of questions was divided into three sections. The first section focused on basic issues regarding health, nutrition, service availability, educational practices, housing, and information on types of trauma that had been experienced within the last year. The second and third sections included questions that were more open ended. The second section focused on the respondents' understanding of the situation, and their feelings and beliefs. The third section focused on factors within the respondents' lives that they perceived to be protective, including the availability of social support networks and the importance of maintaining routine in their lives.

A representative, stratified, random sample of 1,266 children aged between five and seventeen years from the West Bank and Gaza was selected to participate in the study. The sites selected included both areas that had suffered high levels of conflict—the Israeli military incursions of March and April 2002—and areas that had not. Additionally, a total of 449 parents (representing at least 270 households) were selected, the majority of whom were parents of children who took part in focus-group discussions. In approximately 60 percent of cases, both parents participated. Finally, seventy teachers were selected from the five participating school districts. Teachers were randomly selected from the government, the United Nations Relief and Works Agency, and private schools. Male and female teachers jointly participated in focus-group discussions.

This chapter discusses children's and teachers' views related to the role of schools in the psychosocial well-being of Palestinian children.

Children's perspective

The primary objective of the study was to gain a more precise understanding of how Palestinian children view their life situation and how they are coping with these life events. To this end, a total of 95 children's focus-group discussions were organized throughout the West Bank and Gaza. Moderators reported that the children were articulate in expressing their views. They also appeared to enjoy the opportunity to reflect openly and freely on their futures and to find the sessions informative and engaging. Many said they felt relieved to know that others thought and felt as they did; others were somewhat surprised to learn about some of their peers' experiences. The participants' enthusiasm was particularly evidenced by the eagerness with which they spoke out about their problems and their repeatedly expressed desire for more such sessions, voiced especially by the older children.

Risk factors

In focus-group discussions Palestinian children identified a number of issues that constitute risk factors in their lives. Broadly, the responses can be grouped as describing problems deriving from socioeconomic difficulties and problems associated with conflict-related violence.

Life is hard

Children's comments clearly indicated that economic and social conditions have deteriorated since the beginning of the second Intifada and that they continue to do so. Generally, the participants were open to discussing these changes, clearly identifying the kinds of problems that have emerged and what this has meant to them. The picture that emerged is largely consistent with the prevailing socioeconomic reality in the West Bank and Gaza, which is characterized by high and rising unemployment and poverty rates and concomitantly deteriorating living conditions.

Thirty-two percent of the children reported that their father was unemployed, while 11 percent said their father worked only part time. Of those fathers who were still working full time, the vast majority were civil servants employed by the Palestinian Authority. Eighty-five percent of the children indicated that their mothers were housewives without access to an external source of income. The remaining 15 percent of mothers held jobs as schoolteachers, cleaners, dressmakers, or (part-time) secretaries. Children reported that they themselves had less pocket money, that their parents had limited resources, and that they had observed changes in how family members interacted with one another.

Having to move is another phenomenon widely reported in the focus groups. One out of five children reported having had to relocate either permanently or temporarily for conflict-related reasons. Data from previous studies indicate that such relocations were not common before the Intifada. The problem is more pronounced in Gaza than in the West Bank, and it is also more prevalent in urban and camp settings than in rural areas. This trend of relocation is exacerbating the difficulty of overcrowding: 16 percent of the sampled children reported living in households with eleven or more people, 51 percent lived with seven to ten household members, and the remaining one-third lived in households with six members or fewer. Eighteen percent of the children reported living in homes with two or fewer rooms, whereas 35 percent lived in three-room homes, and 47 percent lived in homes with four or more rooms. Based on information provided by the 1997 PCBS Census and Housing Survey, overcrowding is a growing problem in the West Bank and Gaza.

Life is not safe

Focus-group discussions revealed the extent to which Palestinian children are aware of the danger and violence permeating their daily lives. The overwhelming majority of children (93 percent) reported not feeling safe in general and feeling vulnerable to attack, injury, house demolition or arrest. They not only fear for themselves but also for their family and friends. This is not surprising, given the extent to which the children interviewed had come in direct contact with conflict-related violence.

Almost half of the children reported witnessing and/or experiencing one or more conflict-related events. These events included home demolitions; shooting and shelling; closures and barriers on their way to and from school or surrounding areas; having parents, siblings, or friends imprisoned, injured or killed; and being under curfew. Most children involved in the study reported that they had not left their village, camp or city since the start of the Intifada. This supports comments made by parents that they keep travel with children to a minimum to avoid the hazards of closures and blockades.

•Intifada-related injuries

One out of every six children interviewed reported having been physically injured during the last two years. One out of five children reported having a family member who was injured or disabled, and almost one-third of the children reported having a friend or classmate who had been physically injured.

•Intifada-related death

Almost one out of ten children reported losing a family member through military actions, bombing attacks, or assassination attempts, while 16 percent had friends or classmates who had been killed during military operations.

TABLE 5–1. SOURCES OF INSECURITY AMONG PALESTINIAN CHILDREN
(numbers are in percents)

Life is not safe	OPT*	West Bank**	Gaza	5–12 years	13–17 years
Perception: Our parents cannot protect us	52	48	59	43	59
Witnessing/experiencing Intifada-related violence	48	40	61	40	54
Total destruction/sealing of the home	10	7	14	—	—
Suffering physical injury	18	15	22	15	20
Intifada-related death of a family member	9	9	9	—	—
Arrest (minimum of three hours)	5	7	1	1	7

*OPT (Occupied Palestinian Territory) represents the full sample of the study.
**West Bank includes East Jerusalem.

•Arrest

By the same token, 20 percent of the children had experienced the arrest of one or more family members, while 12 percent knew of friends or classmates who had been arrested. Sixty-three participants (5 percent of the total sample), all boys, reported that they had themselves been arrested since September 2000. Among them, forty-seven reported being arrested without charge, eight were arrested while participating in demonstrations, and the remaining eight were arrested for other reasons, including being related to someone who was wanted by the Israeli army or being in an area where the army was conducting mass arrests.

While six of the sixty-three boys arrested were immediately released, the remaining fifty-seven were detained for varying lengths of time—the minimum being three hours. The majority (forty-nine) were over thirteen years old, eight were between five and twelve years old. Of the fifty-seven, forty-four were released after a few hours; the rest were detained or imprisoned for at least one day. Two boys between ages five and twelve were detained for more than a week, and three reported being sentenced to prison for more than one year by Israeli military courts, during which time they were kept in Israeli jails.

All of the fifty-seven boys described their arrest and eventual interrogation and imprisonment as humiliating. Many said they had been submitted to psychological and physical pressure, including sleep denial. Twenty-nine said they had being subjected to a range of humiliating experiences, including having their clothes stripped off of them, having canvas bags tied around their heads, and being tied to poles. Twenty-five children said that they had suffered physical violence during imprisonment, while three reported being subjected to sexual abuse.

•Home demolition/sealing

In principle, the home functions as and is perceived as a safe haven for children. However, this is no longer true for Palestinian children. One out of three participants had seen his or her house damaged during the Intifada, and one out of ten had seen his or her house totally destroyed or sealed by Israeli forces. These homes were either located close to Israeli settlements, near checkpoints, or in areas frequently bombed and shelled. The children's reports are consistent with information that emerged from the parental focus-group discussions:

only 12 percent of all parents interviewed considered their homes to be safe, and 24 percent said that they had been forced to move out of their homes.

In this context it is not surprising that less than half of all children interviewed felt that their parents were capable of protecting them. This sentiment was especially prevalent among older children. Only 41 percent of the thirteen to seventeen year olds believed that their parents were capable of protecting them, compared to 57 percent of the younger children. Parents echoed these feelings. They lamented their limited ability to provide for and protect their children, and all those interviewed felt that their ability to do so had eroded since the start of the second Intifada.

Protective factors

The focus-group discussions allowed for the identification of several active coping strategies that the children use, as well as key resources in the community that support children's resiliency.

Self-efficacy and guarded optimism

Palestinian children are pessimistic about the future in general, as illustrated by their responses to a series of open-ended questions regarding issues that affect them negatively. However, they remain optimistic about their own personal growth and development, both in terms of maintaining ambitions to undertake professional careers and in their confidence of being able to cope under trying circumstances. Of the 1,266 children sampled, 85 percent felt that the dire situation would remain "as is" or worsen; only 15 percent were optimistic that the situation would improve. However, when asked about their own future, that is, their future at school or within the family, children displayed a more positive and hopeful attitude. This was most evident in their replies to the question, "What do you think will happen in the future? . . . What are your expectations?" Seventy percent indicated that they could do something to improve their situation. The remaining 30 percent reported that they were either unsure of their own capacity to improve the situation or were unable to improve the situation.

Children identified several strategies they use to cope with their situation.

The overwhelming majority of sampled children (90 percent) identified self-improvement efforts as their primary means of coping with life events. They indicated that they would continue to work on developing themselves personally and/or academically in order to be able to meet the needs of the future.

A majority of children wanted to play an active role in resisting the occupation; 71 percent reported that they could improve their situation by taking active measures against the occupation. The actions mentioned included partaking in awareness-raising activities regarding the situation in the West Bank and Gaza, refusing to purchase Israeli goods, helping families in need, and participating in peaceful demonstrations. Continuing their education was another action children identified as an important means available to them in resisting occupation. Some mentioned writing slogans on walls.

A smaller group of children (14 percent) were less interested in active resistance and preferred to participate in activities, such as sports, arts, and family events, as a means to "keep busy" or "to keep their mind off the reality." To a certain extent these children are seeking to make the situation better by withdrawing from it.

Approximately 7 percent were focused on learning to better protect themselves when in danger. It is striking that the strategy of protecting themselves when in danger was accorded little value or attention during focus-group discussions, despite the pervasive feeling of insecurity reported above. One possible explanation is that most children interviewed view the broader state of affairs as intractable and therefore focus on aspects of their personal lives over which they can still exercise a measure of control.

Finally, 7 percent of the children noted the importance of making themselves "fearless" and reported wanting to be soldiers in the future and/or develop "weapons, like firebombs." Some mentioned throwing stones at tanks or at soldiers. Though a few expressed the wish to become a martyr, there was little evidence in the discussions that these children had a true death wish; for instance, a number of them believed that after being a martyr they could come back and do other things. These responses are consistent with the general literature on children in conflict areas, which indicates that minors who are exposed to armed conflict can internalize the "culture of violence" (Dyregrov and Raundalen 1987).

Overall, the above findings indicate a high degree of self-efficacy[2] among Palestinian children; that is, they believe that they can achieve a degree of success through their own efforts, at least in the personal, academic, and social domains of their lives. This self-efficacy is key to the Palestinian children's generally positive outlook on their own futures. Their belief that they can do something about their futures is premised on their belief and interest in self-improvement. Self-efficacy has been highly correlated with resiliency in studies of other children growing up in adverse environments, including war zones (Haggerty et al. 1996; Macksoud, Aber, and Cohn 1996; Apfel and Simon 1996; Punamaki and Suleiman 1990).

School as a vital social and academic arena

The focus-group discussions illustrated the extent to which school plays a pivotal role in children's lives and is valued as such. In many ways responses indicated that children believe school provides them with the opportunity to work concretely toward improving themselves and ensuring a better future. This is not surprising, given that elders in Palestinian society traditionally stress the value of education as a tool for self-improvement. The majority of the children interviewed (96 percent) noted that schooling was an essential aspect of their lives. Only 4 percent did not share the view that schooling is important for them.

Similarly, most of the children reported that they were likely to continue their education, despite the difficulties in their lives. When asked about their motivation to continue school, children referred first to the desire for more information and knowledge; second, to ensuring a good livelihood; third, to building a solid and valuable social setting for themselves and their families; fourth, to education as a means of resisting ongoing occupation; and finally, to building their community. Only 6 percent of the children—including those who do acknowledge the value of school and those who don't—said they did not like school and did not want to return but knew their parents would insist. Approximately 3 percent of the children interviewed reported that they had dropped out of school, either to join the labor force or because they had difficulty completing their studies when invasions, curfews, and closures caused continuous disruption.

In addition to emphasizing the importance of school as an academic forum, the children also appreciate school as a place where they meet with their friends and enjoy the company and support of peers and teachers. When the children are at school, they have a chance to share the experiences that have occurred in their lives, listen to other children's stories, and learn better ways of coping. School thus serves to ameliorate the sense of isolation that many children living in conflict situations experience due to the breakdown of other systems in their lives and the prolonged times of closure and curfew.

The children generally expected schools to remain open. Their sense of security that each day they will still have somewhere to go, to learn, and to meet with their peers is noteworthy, given that children's education has been severely affected since the beginning of the Intifada. For example, according to the Palestinian Ministry of Education, 498 schools were disrupted and/or closed because of curfews and closures during 2002. Additionally, 269 school buildings were damaged by rockets and tank shelling since the beginning of the second Intifada, and 9 schools have been permanently closed, of which 3 have been turned into military bases (Palestinian Ministry of Education 2003).

Recreational activities

Recreational activities are important to children because they provide an informal, non-structured environment in which they can comfortably express their feelings and thoughts among peers. This can serve as an important source of strength and support in conflict situations. Yet, as revealed by the focus-group discussion, children's recreational activities clearly have been affected by the current crisis.

Approximately half of the children interviewed claimed that they no longer spend as much time on recreational activities. Activities mentioned include sports, reading and writing, computer games/ Internet activities, watching television, listening to music, drawing, playing outdoors, and going on small trips with parents to visit relatives or friends. A small group of children (6 percent) mentioned playing Intifada-related games, including playing "martyr" or "Israelis versus Palestinians."

When asked why they no longer pursued recreational activities, 53 percent of the children responded that they had insufficient time available, for a variety of reasons, including having to help parents more or needing more time for homework. From the discussions it also became clear that a significant part of children's free time is spent watching television, leaving less time for recreational activities outside the home. Eighteen percent explicitly attributed their decreased participation to the Intifada-related closures and curfews and lack of access to activity sites. Others (8 percent) reported that their parents did not allow them to go out after school to participate in activities because they feared for their well-being. Six percent noted that they had no place to go to, even if they wanted to participate in out-of-school activities. An even smaller percentage (3 percent) reported not participating in any activities because they did not have the funds or did not want to.

These reports by the children were partially confirmed by findings from the parents' group discussions. Half of the parents reported that children were still engaged in recreational activities one to three times a week. According to parental reports, at least one out of three of their children spends considerable time doing extracurricular activities or participating in summer-camp activities. Parents did not go into detail about how their boys and girls spend their time differently; however, traditionally, boys are more likely to be involved in outdoor activities, while girls tend to be more involved in home-based activities. The parents' group discussion focused more on play at home, and in particular on the so-called Intifada-related games.

Parents acknowledge the importance of providing guidance for their children and also of recognizing their need for recreation. However, they feel stretched in their ability to meet these needs. At least one-quarter of the parents admitted to not spending time with their children because they are stressed or burdened by other concerns. Most feel incapable of effectively ensuring their children's long-term psychosocial well-being while the current conflict prevails.

Friendships

As noted above, positive peer relationships are a potential source of resiliency, especially for children growing up in adverse settings. In light of this, the study also attempted to gather information about friendship formation and quality of peer interaction through its group discussions.

The findings show that most Palestinian children establish and maintain friendships within the school environment. Other sources of friendship are neighbors, relatives, and persons from clubs and community institutions like the mosque, church, or library. As revealed in the interviews, children spend most of their time at school; then in their homes, neighborhoods, and with members of their extended family; and last, in children's clubs. These findings are largely consistent with the life patterns of children in other countries. One exception is that the school is playing a more prominent socializing role in the West Bank and Gaza, as noted above. Another exception is that most children did not report spending considerable time with their friends within a home setting, possibly because many live in crowded domiciles.

Sharing feelings and thoughts with their peers emerged as an important coping strategy for Palestinian children. Study participants widely report spending less time playing with their friends and more time talking about recent events, primarily related to the conflict, exchanging views on such topics as what happened the night before, what was likely to occur, what they should be doing, and so forth. Politics ranked first as a conversation topic, while play and school were a distant second and third, respectively. Peer discourse can often provide children with important information about current events and can ease feelings of isolation in an insecure environment. As such, it is an important coping mechanism.

Role models

When asked about their role models, children ranked their fathers first, followed by "educated and cultured persons." Mothers were ranked third. It is likely that these responses reflect in part the patriarchal aspects of Palestinian society: Fathers, and males in general, are widely seen as decision makers and as exercising control and having access to resources—including access to education. According to national data, men in the West Bank and Gaza tend to be more literate than women, and in 90 percent of cases, fathers tend to be the major breadwinner for the family. When parents were asked about the role models of their children, they did not mention themselves. Instead, they put national Intifada figures and leaders at the top of the list and "martyrs" second. Israeli Prime Minister Sharon and President Bush took joint third place as role models. These responses indicate that parents are not picking up on the importance and influence of their own behavior on their children. It may also reflect parental insecurity, due to their perceived inability to provide for and protect their children.

Teachers' perspective

Teachers are traditionally highly respected members of Palestinian society, which values education as a means of obtaining employment and signaling social status. Prior to the Intifada, approximately 95 percent of Palestinian children under the age of sixteen attended school, typically spending four to five hours a day in class, six days a week. By interviewing a small sample of teachers, the study sought to gain further insight into the behavior and psychosocial well-being of these children, and to learn how teachers were helping them cope with the current situation.

The first part of the discussion focused on obtaining information about teaching conditions, including the time that participants spend traveling to and from schools, their salaries, and problems encountered inside and outside the classroom. Open-ended questions subsequently explored a broader range of issues, soliciting teachers' assessment of their students, their attitudes, the nature of activities undertaken in the classroom, and students' expectations for the future.

First and foremost, the discussions illustrated the extent to which teachers themselves currently feel stressed. They cited as sources of frustration and strain low salaries and difficult working conditions, including large class sizes, one- to five-hour commutes to and from school, and a lack of routine and structure in educational programming. Such concerns were particularly prevalent among teachers in public schools, as well as male teachers acting as the primary breadwinners in their families.

As a result, teachers said they felt less motivated, were more anxious in dealing with students, more hurried in their teaching, and less willing to spend time explaining lessons. While they understood the importance of adapting in the current crisis and could clearly identify the negative impact of their behavior, they could not identify ways to overcome it. It is important to keep this in mind when assessing their perspectives on the psychosocial well-being of their students and also when designing comprehensive, community-focused psychosocial support programs for Palestinian children.

Children in the classroom

Teacher discussions illustrated the extent to which the current crisis was affecting students. Nine out of ten teachers noted that the students' attitudes and behavior in class had undergone changes, generally resulting in a drop in academic performance. The changes identified ranged from increased absentmindedness and lack of concentration to increased aggression and anxiety, less attention to follow up and homework after school, and increased absenteeism. Teachers generally worked with more than one grade and tended to provide only general information about their students, not making distinctions on the basis of age or gender.

Like parents, teachers indicated that the dangers associated with the journey to and from school help explain declining academic performance and increased absentmindedness among many Palestinian students. Eighty-two percent of teachers reported that the commute weighed on their own minds when in the classroom, and that this interfered both with their ability to teach effectively and students' ability to concentrate.

Teachers also believed that aggressive behavior among Palestinian children was becoming more prevalent. Fifty-nine percent observed higher levels of irritation and stress in students. This was especially the case for students coming from broken or dysfunctional families. Teachers reported that children also tended to be more aggressive and disruptive in class following periods of closures, curfews, and bombings and shelling. They said such behavior was observed at all grade levels.

One-quarter of teachers interviewed were alarmed about increasing absenteeism and rising dropout rates. They said that most students drop out because either they or their parents fear for their safety going to or returning from school. Teachers reported that they were working with parents to encourage them to keep students in school but that they were unwilling to pressure reluctant parents too hard in this regard, since they themselves cannot guarantee the safety of the children. It should be noted that though schooling is compulsory in the West Bank and Gaza and all children are guaranteed a place, responsibility for ensuring continuing attendance largely rests with parents, not school administrations. This is especially the case since the outbreak of the current crisis.

Interaction and guidance

Teachers were clearly aware that they needed to help students cope with the current crisis, and described several strategies that they had adopted. Over 90 percent had allocated more time in class for discussions in which children could speak out about their feelings and difficult experiences in their lives. They had also allotted more time to drawing, creative writing, and physical exercise. Teachers said that they believe these types of activities were important avenues for self-expression and improved the students' ability to concentrate and perform in the classroom. They also felt it was important that parents allow their children to express their feelings and thoughts. Accordingly, those children who had open relations with parents and teachers were said to be more likely to cope better. However, many teachers also cited obstacles to focusing time on these strategies targeting students' well-being. Making time for supportive class exercises is not easy when under constant pressure to make up for class time lost to closures and curfews. In this context remedial education was widely viewed as important.

Over half of the teachers (57 percent) said relations with their students had improved over the past two years. Most of them reported feeling more sympathetic and in tune with their students and being more accessible and sensitive to their needs for love, care, and guidance. Only 12 percent of teachers reported that relations with their students had worsened during the past two years, mainly due to increased student anxiety and aggressiveness. These teachers noted that students were more disobedient in class and were challenging their authority. The remaining one-third of the teachers reported either minimal or no changes in their relations with students. It is worth highlighting that this closely matches the findings of the children's focus-group discussions. Over 60 percent of the students sampled indicated that their relations with teachers had improved during the last year, while only 10 percent of the students reported that their relationships had deteriorated. The remaining 30 percent did not notice any change in teacher-student relations.

Conclusions and recommendations

Conclusions

Palestinian children are under significant psychosocial strain, mainly due to the violence that currently permeates their lives, inducing pervasive feelings of insecurity. Their precarious situation is aggravated by the widespread feeling that neither parents nor teachers can fully care for or protect them. Under such circumstances it is difficult to remain a carefree child. Parents and teachers observe widespread trauma-related behavior, ranging from nightmares and bedwetting to increased aggressiveness and hyperactivity, as well as decreasing attention spans and capacity to concentrate. They report that a minority of children have become fixated on thoughts of death and revenge.

Nevertheless, Palestinian children continue to exhibit resilience, as evidenced by their enduring sense of self-efficacy and optimism about their own futures. A majority of them continue to feel that they can improve their own lives by developing academically, personally, and socially. Indeed, it is striking that they continue to channel their energy into positive, constructive, and peaceful activities, and that only a small minority drift toward violent ideation. While supporting the personal, academic, and social development of the general population of Palestinian children, it is also important to identify and assist the much smaller percentage of these children who are vulnerable to violent ideation. As Graça Machel notes, "War affects the psychological and social well-being of adolescents at a time of life when they are deeply focused on establishing their identity. In the aftermath of war, many adolescents have great difficulty imagining a future that holds a meaningful place for them" (Machel 2001). One means of assisting the psychosocial recovery of such children is to encourage positive social interactions with caring adults and to facilitate participation in activities that encourage them to express themselves and to act as "helpers" within society. This is particularly important insofar as it strengthens children's self-image and esteem.

School plays an essential role in the lives of Palestinian children. Although both parents and teachers were concerned about children's eroding ability to concentrate in class, as well as rising absenteeism and dropout rates, the children themselves clearly continue to value their education. They see it as their primary means of improving their present and future situations. As such, it is also viewed as a key way for them to resist the occupation peacefully.

The importance of school as a social arena and source of support for Palestinian children has grown during the Intifada. Considerable national-level and community-level effort has been devoted to keeping schools open and supporting remedial education programs to help children to catch up with their studies following forced absences—

despite curfews, closures, and violence that prompt parents to keep their children at home as much as possible. The school is, therefore, one of the few consistent venues where children can regularly enjoy and express themselves in a peer setting. Talking with friends is particularly important; increasingly, children use recreational time to share feelings and talk about the current crisis rather than to play. Critically, school attendance also provides a stabilizing routine and reassuring reference point in the increasingly chaotic lives of Palestinian children. Predictability, academic achievement, and positive peer relationships are highly correlated with childhood resiliency (Boothby 1996; Apfel and Simon 1996; Braken and Petty 1998; Haggerty et al. 1996).

The nurture and care that Palestinian children receive from parents and teachers is compromised by the fact that the adults are stressed and frustrated. Many struggle to cope with loss of incomes and rising violence. Parents, in particular, feel unable to protect and provide for their children adequately and feel that this has undermined their authority. Teachers feel challenged by difficult work conditions: low salaries, long and dangerous commutes to and from school, interruptions due to curfew and closures, lack of structure in educational programming, and problems in the classroom, including rising absenteeism and dropout rates.

Despite their own difficulties, parents remain focused on the importance of supporting their children. They attach great importance to their children's need to continue their education, and they are aware of the need to prevent them from developing long-term psychological problems. However, while the majority of parents reported significant interaction with their children, the number of those who do not interact with their children or provide them with guidance remains significant. For their part, teachers remain focused on helping their students cope in the conflict. To this end, most try to allocate extra time for classroom activities that allow students to express themselves and talk about their problems. They are also focused on ensuring the children's safety while at school.

Recommendations

Based on the findings of this assessment, it is suggested that a three-pronged, interactive intervention strategy be adopted to help Palestinian children and families cope with the current conflict.

Children

Programs should be supported that channel children's resilience, encourage positive aspects of their outlook on the future, and empower them to take control of their lives. This includes giving them opportunities to participate in regular recreational, cultural, sport, and other nonformal activities that provide them with life skills for the present as well as the future and also support their physical, psychological, cognitive, social, and behavioral development. A special emphasis should be placed on activities that allow children to express themselves; resolve psychological, social, and behavioral problems; and encourage their desire to become positive and supportive members of their community. As much as possible, these activities should seek to inject "normalcy" into children's lives, especially for those who repeatedly suffer distressing or traumatic experiences. This will require establishing more centers and spaces for children's play and recreational activities, subject to proper adult supervision.

Schools

Building on ongoing initiatives, teachers and school counselors should be provided with guides to classroom psychosocial exercises that allow children to express themselves and improve their ability to concentrate and be attentive in class. Furthermore, the school's capacity to serve as a multi-functional center should be bolstered, allowing children to study, play, and socialize throughout the day. This will require improvements in physical infrastructure designed to make schools more child friendly; the training of psychosocial facilitators who can support children in the context of both in-school and out-of-school activities; and programs that train teachers to deploy proper psychosocial methods in dealing with children in conflict. Last, teachers should be provided with psychosocial services, including counseling and debriefing. Like Palestinian parents and children, they are under considerable strain.

It is outside the scope of this research project to assess the psychosocial damage that may ultimately befall either the children who participated in this study or Palestinian children in general.

Children's ability to cope with the stresses of the current crisis is to a large extent contingent on the kind of support they receive, including the closeness of their relationships with parents and teachers, their

primary caregivers. Children who are not secure in their environment and do not enjoy sufficient support are more likely to be overcome by the strains of the conflict. In this context it is hoped that the
kinds of interventions suggested can help safeguard the children's
overall well-being. It is also hoped that they will be particularly targeted at those children who have been most affected by the conflict.

If Palestinian children are to be afforded their right to develop to
their full potential, they must be able to enjoy safety in their homes,
schools, and communities and be able to continue aspiring to a future
very different from their present.

Notes

[1] For a more comprehensive explanation of the methodology, see Cairo
Arafat, "A Psychosocial Assessment of Palestinian Children," The Secretariat of the National Plan of Action for Palestinian Children (July 2003). A
total of forty-nine facilitators and forty-nine moderators were trained to
conduct the focus-group discussions. All the moderators were qualified school
counselors familiar with the communities in which they worked. Data collection took place in July and August 2002.

[2] Coping with self-efficacy is defined as a person's subjective appraisal of
his or her ability to cope with the environmental demands of the stressful
situation and has been correlated with better psychological adjustment following severe environmental stressors and military combat (American Psychiatric Association, *Diagnostic and Statistical Manual of Mental Disorders*, 3rd
ed. rev. [Washington, DC: American Psychiatric Association, 1987]).

References

Abdeen, Z., G. Greenough, M. Shahin, and M. Tayback. 2002. *Nutritional
    assessment of the West Bank and Gaza Strip, 2003*. Funded by USAID
    through CARE International. Available on the usaid.gov website.
Apfel, R., and B. Simon, eds. 1996. *Minefields in their hearts: The mental health
    of children in war and communal violence*. New Haven, CT: Yale Univ. Press.
Boothby, N. 1996. Mobilizing communities to meet the psychosocial needs
    of children in war and refugee crises. In Apfel and Simon, *Minefields in
    their hearts*, 149–64.
Bracken, P. J., and C. Petty, eds. 1998. *Rethinking the trauma of war*. London:
    Free Association Books.

Dyregrov, A., and M. Raundalen. 1987. Children and the stresses of war: A review of the literature. In *War, violence, and children in Uganda*, ed. C. P. Dodge and M. Raundelen. Oslo: Norwegian Univ. Press.

Haggerty, R., L. Sherrod, N. Garmezy, and M. Rutter. 1996. *Stress, risk and resilience in children and adolescents: Processes, mechanisms, and interventions*. Cambridge: Cambridge Univ. Press.

Machel, G. 2001. *The impact of war on children*. UNICEF. Malaysia: C. Hurst and Co.

Macksoud M., L. Aber, and I. Cohn. 1990. Assessing the impact of war on children. In Apfel and Simon, *Minefields in their hearts*, 219–30.

PRCS (Palestinian Red Crescent Society). Tables of deaths and injuries. Available on the palestinercs.org website.

Palestinian Ministry of Education. 2003. Report on conditions within the educational sector. January. Available online.

Punamaki, R., and R. Suleiman. 1990. Predictors and effectiveness of coping with political violence among Palestinian children. *British Journal of Social Psychology* 29: 67–77.

Ressler, E., J. Tortorici, and A. Marcelino. 1993. *Children in war: A guide to the provision of services*. New York: UNICEF.

6

SILENCED VOICES?

Youth and peer relationships in armed conflict and its aftermath

Siobhán McEvoy-Levy

Introduction

In war and peace youth build relationships with their peers in multiple situations contained within larger social ecologies. Their peer interactions take place in a myriad of settings—on the streets; in schools, churches, and military and political organizations; in refugee camps; in work places (official and unofficial); in law and order institutions; in the arts; and in sports and other leisure activities. These interconnected spaces of youth interaction, in turn, shape and are shaped by families; communal, racial, and ethnic groups; nations; and even global communities. As part of a large web of interactions, youth affect processes of war and peace.

The central question addressed in this chapter is how the peer relationships of youth influence the trajectories of armed conflict and the reconstruction of postwar societies. This chapter uses a global framework to explore the breadth and complexity of youth contributions to processes of war and peace. After discussing the actions and interactions of youth in a variety of social spheres, we turn to the seemingly silenced voices therein, and to a consideration of the roles youth play in constructing war-supporting narratives. The chapter argues that the agency of youth in war and postwar situations is multidimensional and extremely influential. Young people's actions, and their collective narrations of those actions, influence how conflicts

133

are experienced, understood, remembered, transmitted across generations, and, potentially, transformed. For reasons of space the chapter gives significantly more attention to the conflict-reproduction roles of youth. However, it also highlights young people's peace-building roles by noting that rarely is conflict solely viewed as valorous, as opposed to peace, in spaces where youth interact. Moreover, discrete peace communities also exist, within which youth are central actors. In the chapter's conclusion the implications of these findings for peace building interventions are considered.

Who are youth? This chapter employs a global framework and therefore uses the twelve to thirty age range to define youth. While there are significant differences among people within this age range, there are several reasons for using this framework. First, it better reflects the global reality of the cultural differences that exist in the definition of youth. In the West, and in international law, children are those under eighteen, and youth are either adolescents or those under twenty-five. But in many African countries, the term *youth* may apply up to age thirty-five or forty. The second reason for using the age twelve to thirty framework is that many human beings who are defined as children in international law are in fact household heads, combatants, and laborers crucial to their economies. At the same time, they are not politically enfranchised. But they may have specific needs, interests, and identities, rights to voice, and contributions to make. Third, the twelve to thirty framework allows consideration of a larger body of militarized people in their twenties who are central to the dynamics of war and peace. People of this age range are often involved in peace activism as well as in political and socioeconomic violence. Particularly in war-torn societies, and especially where conflict has been protracted, this group is distinct from the rest of the population in that it often contains those who are economically marginal and politically franchised, but who have very little real decision-making power. Their apathy can be powerfully facilitating to war, but at the same time they are often idealistic, change-oriented, and have a desire to make a societal contribution. Those who are war survivors have special skills, knowledge, needs—and, perhaps, traumas.

Spaces of youth interaction

Using the age twelve to thirty framework, this section examines eight spaces of youth interaction—armed groups, postwar gangs and militia, refugee camps, schools, the streets, economies of war and postwar, religious communities, and communities of peace. This is not an exhaustive list of the spaces where youth interact with their peers, but it includes some of the most significant spaces. The aim is to establish the breadth and complexity of youth involvement on the continuum of armed conflict and peace building and to identify the specific dimensions that appear to be peer driven and/or that establish new constructs of the peer group in relation to war and peace.

Armed groups

The forcible recruitment of children and young people into armed groups is well documented (Cohn and Goodwin-Gill 1994; Brett and McCallin 1996; Boothby and Knudsen 2000). While youth are frequently the victims of these processes of imposed militarization, they are also their perpetrators. It is often youth who socialize the new recruits and who sometimes identify which youth are to be abducted. Having themselves been inducted in this manner, they reproduce the conflict both by brutalizing their peers and by creating supportive "family." Indeed, it is often the promise of new family or community that attracts youth to armed groups, particularly youth who have been displaced by war. Youth also may enter armed groups simply for a meal or shelter or clothing. Or, asserting their own power, they may enter as substitutes for peers, siblings, and adult family members, or to save whole communities from attack (Brett and McCallin 1996).

Peers also influence the voluntary enlistment of youth in armed groups. Numerous cases show that the influential motivations of prestige, belonging, and popularity are shaped by interactions with peers (Brett and McCallin 1996; Cohn and Goodwin-Gill 1994). Youth are also reported to join armed groups for "fun" or because "my friends are joining" (Cohn and Goodwin-Gill 1994). Some Palestinian youth involved in stone throwing were reported to have done so for protection against accusations of collaboration from their peers (Brett and McCallin 1996; Cohn and Goodwin-Gill 1994). Yet explanations of youth involvement in armed conflict cannot be reduced to peer pressure alone. Young people conceptualize their involvement as a duty to the wider community or nation in a struggle spearheaded by youth. Finally, some evidence also suggests that people receive a moral education in some armed groups and develop social loyalties (see Cairns 1996) that, in fact, can translate into active engagement in civic life, community development, and peace building later on. While it has become quite well accepted that child soldiers make wars more lethal and harder to end (Singer 2005), we know that children sometimes also mitigate violence against their peers at discrete moments within armed groups (see "Communities of peace," below).

In general, the complexity of the roles of youth in armed groups requires further study and creates numerous dilemmas related to the protection of youth in war zones, acknowledgment of their rights, and the larger projects of conflict resolution. Peer interaction in armed groups involves numerous asymmetries of power and the creation of new social categories (blurred victim-perpetrators, for example, or youth-elders) and new conflicts (particularly intergenerational ones).

Postwar gangs and militia

When wars end, an enormous vacuum develops into which the youth combatant falls—his or her livelihood, survival, and identity are re-cast or even threatened by peace. One of the challenges of recon-structing war-torn societies is the reintegration of ex-combatant youth into society, a complicated task that in best practice addresses the many dimensions of a young person's economic, psychosocial, physi-cal, spiritual, and (less commonly) political needs. A fundamental challenge after combat is that the young people involved may no longer see themselves as children or want to return to schooling or other age-appropriate roles. Intergenerational conflict is likely, as has been evident in South Africa, where the anti-apartheid activist generation was encouraged to return to "normal" pursuits and marginalized from the new government. After the first Intifada, Palestinian girls, in par-ticular, experienced difficulties readjusting to the traditional and sub-ordinate roles their families expected (Barber 1999).

A common feature of the postwar landscape is the evolution of gangs, community-defense organizations, and vigilante groups made up of marginalized youth, many transitioning en masse into these groups from military and rebel groups or returning from exile. In Guatemala, for example, youth returning after war were denied their ancestral rights to land and instead "claimed public parks through thievery, defaced municipal buildings and terrorized local markets in a language of refusal, creating a place for themselves even where one was not available" (Olson 2004). Military intervention against the youth was the state response in 2000. In South Africa youth gangs and rising crime levels were among the most noticeable features of the post-apartheid period (CSVR 1998, Simpson 1992, Dissel 1997). Youth gangs not only replicated the "family" of the political struggle, helped meet economic survival needs, and reflected the masculinism and militarism idealized during the struggle, but they also reflected the needs of post-combatant youth for positive community roles (Marks and McKenzie 1995, Dissel 1997). Many of the members of anti-apartheid movements developed alternative police forces, self-defense units, and self-protection units to protect their communities from crime and vigilantism (even while they were accused of both themselves) (Marks and McKenzie 1995). Yet they did not want to remain on the margins; instead, these youth demanded integration into the new South African police force. After threats of violence in Gauteng in 1995, youth were incorporated into the local police, encouraging youth in other areas to demand similar treatment. Violent conflict also resulted between those youth eventually chosen and those not selected in given communities, and between the youth and existing police over operating modes and command structures (Marks 1999). These youth rejected notions of their traditional roles. Instead, they reconstructed their peer group as nation/community defenders, roles they wished to extend into the post-struggle period.

While the strategies of the state in Guatemala and South Africa have been different—with the South African government at least making efforts to address youth demands—it is clear that conflict occurred in both cases because youth perceived themselves in one way while society and the state perceived them in another. Although a certain dimension of young people's destabilizing power exists as a result of their economic marginalization, their political marginalization and lack of voice are also potent factors. Marginal youth are often officially silenced at precisely the moment when they have earned and expect inclusion in the social life and institutions of their reconstructing societies. The end goals that political elites term *democracy* and *peace* are learned by the next generation in contexts that seem to model exclusionary practices, and militarized peer groups may offer more compellingly authentic and inclusive alternatives. Youth continue to be potent sources of instability in post-conflict scenarios, involved in actual crime and also partially construed as threats by fearful publics (including other youth). All of these narratives—whether of youth, the state, or the general public—create complex and competing understandings of war and peace.

Refugee camps

The long-term implications of war are also symbolized by the ago-
nies of the displaced; here, peer relationships of youth are also significant. For youth in refugee camps the loss of friends is cited as one
of the main sufferings of displacement (Swaine and Feeny 2004). Similarly, these authors report that youth who are not displaced but who
lost friends in wartime also experience a form of dislocation. They
experience emotional rather than physical displacement without a
supportive community of friends and confidants. On the other hand,
the experience of war and displacement may also affect the ability to
trust and make close friends, as Boothby found among Cambodian
refugees (Boothby 1983). And the congregation of youth may mark
not a community of choice but one of alienation and conflict. In a
study of displaced youth returning to parts of post-genocide Rwanda
that have received little development aid, Sommers notes that it was
common to find groups of "frustrated" and "agitated" young males
drinking in bars or in their homes (Sommers 2006). Land shortages
trapped them in a state of social immaturity and uncertain identity
because they were prevented from building a house and farming, both
prerequisites for marriage and family. Youth relationships, then, often revolved around conflict over scarce resources.

For young people displaced by war, their peers may be a symbol of
loss, a source of support, and a source of competition. They may also
be a source of threat and exploitation. Kosovar girls in refugee camps
were protected from sexual trafficking by male peers of their own
ethnic group. Yet these were the same young men who otherwise
facilitated the trafficking (Swaine and Feeny 2004). They made certain exceptions, demonstrating their relative power to oppress women,
while consigned to the voiceless fate of being refugees.

When young victims and perpetrators mingle and overlap in the
same space, an idealized notion of the peer group as source of belonging, comfort, and support seems misplaced. Yet, Gillian Mann
finds that the roles that separated children, particularly girls, play in
"delegated parenting" teach "important survival skills, as well as how
to relate to one another, to lead and follow others, to agree and dis-
agree, to negotiate with one another and to support one another in
achievement of shared tasks" (Mann 2004, 12). Jason Hart's study of
young Palestinians growing up in a Jordanian refugee camp shows
that children can creatively build culture (2004). Boothby's work with

displaced Cambodians records how many "adolescents speak passion-
ately, and at times with almost premature wisdom, about the nature
of good and evil." While expressing anger about the horrors of the
past, and distrust for those responsible, they were also able to view
the enemy—especially other adolescents—as having "suffered too."
Boothby notes that this may perhaps be a demonstration of "tolerance for the kind of ambiguity found in a world where circumstances
often come full circle" (Boothby 1983, 67–68). The meanings contained in these peer-group encounters of displaced youth—the personal and collective memories and the ideas that they construct—affect
gender relations, societal reconstruction, and reconciliation in the
long term. Yet, such youth narratives remain virtually untapped as a
policy-relevant source of knowledge about war and peace.

Schools

Along with armed groups, post-conflict gangs, and refugee camps,
schools are an important space of youth interaction. As Andoni notes
about Palestinians involved in both the first and second Intifadas: "It
[the conflict] is transmitted to younger generations both experien-
tially, through living it, and theoretically, through formal and informal education" (Andoni 2001, 214). Some attention has been given
to formal education as a militarizing mechanism. The use of educational institutions and orphanages specifically for "warehousing" children for future military use has been found in numerous cases
(Boothby and Knudsen 2000; Brett and McCallin 1996, 56). Governments and armed groups use ready-made youth groups—scout
troops, summer schools, and youth movements—as sites for the militarization of youth, understanding well that beyond composing cap-
tive audiences, young people's peer groups are potent socializers,
mediums that not only transmit but enhance the desired message.

On the other hand, schools are also the sites of peace-building
programs, ranging from projects to revise textbooks, inter-communal encounters, human rights and peace education, and citizenship
training. Schools can actively counter cultures of violence through
formal curricula, informal student interactions, and friendships forged
across conflict groups. Schools also can function as safe havens, perhaps the only safe havens for war-affected youth, when conflicts are
ongoing. However, the protection and peace-building roles of schools
confront significant barriers. In many cases schools cease to function

during war and are reconstructed slowly afterward. Even after ceasefires, the continuing threat of gender-based violence means that girls are less likely to attend school in many war-affected regions (Sommers 2002). Material resources, the morale of teachers, and competence in dealing with contentious issues may be lacking. Schools may remain segregated by conflict group. The resistance of parents and communities as well as children to perceived "reeducation" poses another barrier. So, the peer interaction of youth within schools occurs in simultaneous and cacophonous competition with external and internal politics and tensions. On the positive side, students also shape schools by challenging teacher apathy. As a collective, Bosnian students wore down teacher skepticism and even some teachers' active obstructionism to build a cross-ethnic youth group (Helsing et al. 2006). Still, not enough is known about the ways in which youth collectively process and share the war and peace teachings they receive in schools or informally, at home or on the street. Since formal schooling may not reach (or be attractive to) many older militarized or marginal youth, the informal spaces of their peer interaction and peer education are sources of further information—and these are especially neglected. Therefore, the next sections examine the interactions of youth on the streets, in work places, in religious communities, and in peace groups.

On the streets

Many contemporary armed conflicts, whether in their hot or post-conflict phases, are intimately conducted among local factions that live in close quarters. The interaction of rival youth on the streets is often central to how these conflicts evolve. For example, student demonstrations in Kosovo in 1981 had an important effect on Albanian and Serbian relations that helped shape later conflict. Not only did the demonstrations mean that Serbian children were discouraged from socializing with Albanians but, as Mertus notes: "The extreme youth of those arrested after the demonstrations had a tremendous influence on Kosovar Albanians, shaping the future of not only the arrested but also their relatives and friends, who were forever to mark time in relation to the 1981 demonstrations." She goes on to note that these same arrests also became a rallying point for their Serb rivals: "The age of the arrested would also become an issue for Serbian nationalists who would argue that the state had intentionally failed to arrest the real leaders" (Mertus 1999, 43).

Ceasefires and peace agreements rarely mean an end to inter-communal and/or ethnic street violence and demonstrations. In postwar Kosovo mass riots have been triggered by the ethnically motivated killings of youth by other youth, and by young people generating (later unsubstantiated) rumors of such killings (BBC 2004a; BBC 2004b; BBC 2001). Youth in Kosovo have also protested against the United Nations in response to war crimes prosecutions (BBC 2002). In Northern Ireland small-group encounters and assaults, rumors spread by youth, fights outside bars on weekends and after sporting events can all spiral into widespread riots involving adults. As with the presence of postwar gangs and militia, the impact that these activities have on conflict trajectories and post-conflict peace are both immediate and lasting, creating general skepticism about the value of an accord and leading to destabilizing escalations of conflict.

However, youth also may restrain their peers in some of these situations. Groups of youth also organize in many situations to take back the streets, to repaint murals and write counter-violence graffiti, and to participate in organized marches and peace vigils (see below, "Communities of peace").

Economies of war and postwar

Another space of youth interaction is in the economies of war and postwar. It is well known that youth are integral to local economies, involved in all sorts of trade, barter, and production to support themselves and whole households, and also are the shock absorbers of economic crisis. War usually threatens education, job training, and basic livelihood, while at the same time opening up opportunities for involvement in criminal enterprises, sexual exploitation, and also creative cooperation. Some of the different ways in which young people's peer relationships both construct and are constructed by these activities have already been discussed. Humanitarian intervention and peace-building strategies also transform economies, and this creates a kind of paradox, because new opportunities for some as a result of such interventions create new conflicts, even while they contribute to reconstruction (Sommers 2006; Wessells and Jonah 2006). Mertus takes a quite critical position on the impact of donor funds on civil society in Kosovo, noting that youth are lured away from civic and political participation by short-term aid-related employment:

> The flood of donor dollars into Kosovo has created an imbalance in the labor market and altered social values that once promoted community involvement. With the promise of making ten times the amount of their parents, young English-speaking students have abandoned their studies and accepted dead-end, short-term jobs with international agencies. With local government positions paying one-tenth the salary of parallel international positions, one-half the amount of a UN driver, and one-third the amount of a translator, talented local professionals have little incentive to work in government. (Mertus 2004, 342–43)

Mertus writes that the provision of public services by international agencies has "destroyed any sense of volunteerism and reduced the Albanians' sense of group solidarity" (Mertus 2004, 343). Again, while the specifics of various cases will undoubtedly be different, it is clear that within this space of youth interaction, new notions of belonging and citizenship are constructed that will have implications for sustainable peace.

Religious communities

Especially compelling in Brett and Sprecht's analysis of the narrative of a young Afghan recruited into a militant group at age fifteen is the detailed interplay of events involved in his evolution into a fighter (Brett and Sprecht 2004). Certainly, Afghan youth, displaced by war and educated in Pakistani *madrassahs* later became Taliban recruits (Rashied 2001). But according to Brett and Sprecht's research it was the young fighter's inability to pay for his religious education that propelled him into a displacement experience and then into armed conflict. These authors' findings provide a caution in that they destabilize the notion that religious schools are the primary gateways into child soldiering or terrorism, rather than one of a number of influential interacting social spaces.

Nevertheless, religious identity and aspiration, as well as cultural identification infused with religious symbol and story, appear to be some of the most powerful motivators for children in armed conflict.

In Uganda spiritual rituals are used to control child soldiers (Anderson, Sewankambo, and Vandergrift 2004). In other conflicts religious segregation, whether in housing or schooling, is a factor in perpetuating mistrust and stereotypes of the "other," as it is, for example, in Northern Ireland. Young people also interact with their peers in religious settings that not only include religious schools or religiously based neighborhoods, but social clubs, Internet websites, and discussion boards.

In many intractable conflicts the street is also a religious space. Prior to the 1998 peace agreement, religious images such as the Madonna or the crucifixion of Christ were mingled with political statements on buildings in Belfast. Names of martyrs and Qur'anic verses are inscribed on walls in Gaza. Children on the streets experience these communications as part of their everyday socialization, but they also interact with them, adding their own pieces of graffiti in support or opposition. Children also participate in celebration parties for martyrs, take school trips to sites of assassination, and watch television programs that blend sacred injunctions to armed violence with puppetry and song (Oliver and Steinberg 2005). In many of these activities the religious and the recreational lives of youth blend.

Most analyses of religious recruitment to political violence emphasize the indoctrination of children by adults. Very little systematic research has been done on whether and, if so, how children influence, adapt, or transmit sacred narratives, or how they see their own spirituality in combination with a political or armed struggle. But perhaps just as frequently as religious teaching inspires activism, youth become involved in armed conflict in spite of, and even because of, the apolitical, nonviolent, or accommodationist stance of religious organizations. For example, young Republican activists in Northern Ireland, particularly those recruited in urban environments, often criticized the Catholic Church on these grounds, even though they were supported by a popular culture that identified with the Catholic martyrological tradition. The "bland, sterilised sermons of most imams post 9/11" has been one reason for radicalism of young British Muslims, according to a recent report (Malik 2004). Young Israeli Jews protesting the Gaza withdrawal in 2005 seemed both motivated by religious conviction and strategic in their manipulation of religious symbolism. Traditionally dressed girls deliberately tangled with police in a manner they knew would inflame conservative religious opinion, which views such male-female contact as improper

(King 2005). These young activists used Internet chat rooms and cell phone text-messaging to organize, creating another (virtual) space of religious/political peer interaction.

Finally, religious spaces of interaction also have fostered young peace builders. Interfaith youth groups and religious peace-building initiatives proliferate in conflict zones. One example is the Muslim/Christian Youth Dialogue Forum, created by ex-combatant youth in Nigeria (Smock 2004). The Canada-based Youth in Peace Education project, which is "an international, interfaith, and intergenerational project that aims to assist peace educators worldwide by providing online resources for interfaith curriculum development" is another example (Smock 2005, 9). There is no doubt that religion gives meaning to some children's lives as it does to some adults' lives, and can be an inspiration for both violent and peaceful action. Robert Coles broke new ground with his study of the spiritual lives of children (Coles 1990). But research on the religious lives of children has not kept pace with the evolution of contemporary warfare, and much more work needs to be done.

Communities of peace

There are also many examples of alternative communities and grassroots networks that evolve in war zones and promote peace. Often these overlap or are contained within other spaces of youth interaction, as discussed above. In Angola, Nordstrom finds that street children created supportive communities in the storm drains beneath the streets. They shared limited resources and created their own system of ideas to govern their community. She shows how youth provided each other with physical, emotional, and economic nurturing (Nordstrom 2006). In Sierra Leone, Wessells and Jonah found that a dominant girl soldier, nicknamed "Mommy Queen," protected younger girls in her armed group. She reported reuniting 130 children with their families after the fighting was over (Wessells and Jonah 2006). Youth in Bosnia rebuilt a fountain to re-create a historic meeting place for youth of their deeply divided communities (Helsing et al. 2006). In these cases the tragedy of war is recast for some in ethical communities that emerge in spite of, and through, memories of trauma, and are often manifested in the literal occupation of space. This territorialism may be seen as a practical and moral counterweight to the heavy hand of war. Where groups of youth support and protect one another in opposition to, or subversion of, the adult world of armed competition, there is much to be learned about the values and dynamics supporting peace.

Moreover, it is evident that youth are at the forefront of a myriad of more conventional organizations and movements that promote peace (see McEvoy-Levy 2006a). Youth are involved in social development, capacity building, peace education, and micro-level networks for resolving conflicts, including (as mentioned) religious dialogue groups and many activist groups, both secular and religious, against social injustice or direct violence. As well as the established bridge-building activities in which youth are always central participants, young people are involved in informal friendships and cross-communal dating. They attempt to build peace by resisting stereotypes, breaking through conflict barriers, and asserting their own power to define and engage with the "other." But of all the roles of youth in war zones, their participation in formal and informal peace communities is the least documented and analyzed.

Narrating war and peace

The active agency of youth in a variety of military, economic, and social arenas should by now be apparent. They help create and sustain war, and they create and act for peace. Yet they are much less influential in conventional political arenas. In general, youth are subordinate to adult elites who make political decisions, sign peace accords, write history, and distribute aid. So, all of these spaces of youth interaction are also spaces of marginalized voices. And it is particularly the political voice of youth that is silenced. However, youth also actively construct their own identities, create "imagined" peer groups, and construct narratives in their everyday interactions that involve themselves in and create politics.

The interactions of youth in all these spaces discussed above, and more, are accompanied by rich narrations of their motives, as a few examples will illustrate:

The French destroyed our air force, they took our airport, they fired on the presidential palace in Yamoussoukro, they put their tanks right next to the president's residence. When they attacked those symbols of the republic, we knew they were trying to depose the president. . . . I am nearly 22 and I haven't yet worked. Our economy is in a mess and it's all in French hands. I must defend my future. (Copnall 2005)

In this interview one of the young patriots involved in recent violence in Cote d'Ivoire develops a narrative of involvement based on military, political, and economic motives, and describes how "we," youth as a group, came to a collective understanding of the nature of the threat.

For youth involved in the anti-apartheid struggle, the conflict created with the older generation is evident in the following testimony:

Our parents still have that old image they grew up under. They tell us that the white man is a white man and what he says is final. . . . We are caught in a trap. What our parents don't seem to have is a desire for us to be better people. . . . So now we do everything for ourselves without consulting our parents because it is useless to talk to a stone. (Lambert and Webster 1988)

This testimony does more than state the fact of intergenerational tension. It encapsulates conflict as a "trap" and parents as "stone[s]." It contains a critique and a longing for a different outcome. Again, the tension is conceptualized as "our," that is, youth's, conflict with adults.

Another way in which youth construct their own peer group is in the identifications they describe with figures from global popular culture and other international actors. For example, Sommers describes the "defiant outcast" image that is embraced by Sierra Leonean youth who model themselves on Tupac Shakur and Tanzanian youth who revered Saddam Hussein (after the first Gulf War), creating a new nickname based on the scud missile called "Scudi ya Bongo," meaning "a fearless, unsinkable urban youth" (Sommers 2003). They critique their current situations by adapting the identities of outsiders and international pariahs. Similarly, a young man from Northern Ireland critiques the peace process with this analysis:

Oh, it'll be what *you'll* call peace. But at the same time the drug trade will go up, there'll be more cocaine, heroin and harder drugs on the street. Northern Ireland already has a lot of ecstasy. There'll be more cases of AIDS. (McEvoy-Levy 2006b, 155)

He rejects what he perceives to be an adult, middle-class, narrow, and vague notion of peace and identifies more pressing real-life problems, which will particularly affect young people like himself.

A testimony from a young Bosnian refugee in London takes us into a more overtly personal evaluation of the cost of war:

> As much as I want to go back, the idea of returning scares me. That would again be a new beginning, a painful and ruthless step that I have already made once. Besides, I wonder if I would be able to face my friends again. A lot of them have been killed, many of them have been wounded, others might not understand me. We do not share the same destiny anymore. (Lesic 1995, 62)

Even for a young refugee living in relative comfort, the trauma of initial displacement is compounded by the painful prospect of later being judged by one's peers, of not being properly understood, and of being unable to maintain one's new identity. Hard-won independence and personal sovereignty and, at the same time, the prospect of loneliness, become the lenses through which war (and peace) are understood.

Finally, the narrative from an Internet discussion board sponsored by the UK-based wing of the international political organization Hizb ut-Tahrir (Party of Liberation) in 2005 demonstrates that while a religious narrative may be central to a group's ideology, less visible—but also powerful—are the surrounding narratives. On the group's discussion board the contributors (all different individuals) offer postings of links to recent news articles that demonstrate the "decadent West." They highlight acts of sexual violence and murder, particularly against children. One contributor to the discussion board suggests that these crimes should be called "terrorist acts" and prosecuted in anti-terrorism courts.

Much attention has focused on the appeal of Hizb ut-Tahrir for young Muslims, particularly in the wake of the July 7, 2005, terrorist bombings in London. As the Internet postings suggest, at least part of the appeal lies in the channel that membership in this organization can offer to complex feelings of injustice, social concern, and, perhaps, sexual threat. The war in Iraq, economic exclusion, and the compelling idea of global Islamic community may be primary motivators. But the participants in these narratives also collectively develop a narrative of political violence that includes violence against women and children in general (and not just Muslims).

All of these narratives show how young people's involvement in and attitudes toward armed conflict and peace are influenced by structures and factors beyond their control—military action, economic instability, political exclusion, displacement, and peace processes. But within those constraints youth engage in collective processes of deliberation and knowledge creation with their peers, and they seek to transmit those meanings to a wider audience. In telling their stories they also assert their own individuality as witnesses, recording and sharing knowledge. "A person's identity is defined in frames constructed or operationalized for rhetorical purposes during specific social interactions" (Buckley and Kenney 1995, 39). Marc Ross demonstrates that "cultural communities" are defined by "shared systems of meaning and identity" that are created through "psychocultural interpretations" and, at moments of crisis or conflict, "psychocultural dramas" (Ross 2001; Ross 1995). George Lakoff has argued that "how we talk, how we frame things, tells a lot about how we think" and shape actions: "It's always important to have a good story, whether in trying to persuade others or in thinking things through for yourself. When the question arises as to whether to go to war, you can't justify your decision, either to others or to yourself, without a good story" (Lakoff 1999, 24).

Therefore, the narratives of youth in conflict are likely to provide valuable information about how conflicts are reproduced, because they point us to the places where the personal and the collective interact, where memories and identities are made, and where the meanings that affect attitudes toward war and peace are crystallized.

Conclusion

What is the importance of the findings of this research for peace-promoting interventions in general? This chapter provides insights that are perhaps most relevant for peace building in postwar periods

with a view toward preventing renewed violence and creating legiti-
mate and sustainable peace.

The breadth of youth involvement in the many overlapping spaces
of war and peace argues for an intentional and genuine inclusion of
youth in any peace process or peace-building project. The actions of
youth have important impacts at every stage of the armed-conflict
and peace-building continuum. Their roles in militaries, rebel groups,
militias, and gangs influence armed conflict and post-conflict reconstruction. At the same time, many young people work against war
norms and values and create alternative communities out of both con-
tingency and conviction. The contours of postwar society are influenced by the roles of these youth in social and economic life—their
crime, poverty, homelessness, labor, fulfillment of the routine tasks
of caring for others and traveling to school, and formal and informal
peace-building work. As social, political, and economic agents, then,
youth are a multidimensional force. But the roles that youth play in
creating social understandings of conflict, through their actions and
through their narrations of their actions, are not well understood.

In intractable conflicts all of the spaces where youth interact are
heavily intersected and influenced by the "war system." But elements
of a nascent "peace system" are also found in most of these spheres
(Irwin 1989). An interesting finding is that while the war and peace
systems compete in these spheres of youth interaction, there also seems
to be a synergy between them, and it may be that this synergy is particularly strong in spaces where youth are central actors. The synergy between war and peace meanings and actions seems to be
facilitated both by the vulnerable and precarious situation of youth,
who must be creative to survive, and by their natural idealism and
innovation. Combatants turn or return to community development,
children paint war-supporting graffiti, and their narratives explaining conflict highlight an ambiguity of loyalties, emotions, and interests. Almost all frame war within a far more complex context than
official political platforms, flags, and slogans communicate. So, while
it is clear that much of the fate of children and youth in contemporary armed conflict lies in manipulation and exploitation by adults,
youth also influence armed conflict and postwar society with the
knowledge they create. Their narrative-creation and peer-education
roles, if better understood, could be utilized as peace-building mechanisms. Youth narratives provide useful, nuanced, and new knowledge

about conflict and peace that could inform and authenticate peace-education programs. They provide information on the experience of war and fuller explanations of the needs entailed in peace.

Moreover, a range of psychosocial interventions may benefit from the understanding that the narrative construction that creates political or conflict meaning is organic to the everyday interactions of youth. The findings suggest that the capabilities and needs of youth in creating political meaning ought to be clearly and intentionally integrated into holistic interventions. Politics (in its micro and macro manifestations) should be recognized along with the security, economic, health, cultural, and spiritual needs of ex-combatant youth and war-affected youth as a whole. Trauma does not lead directly to the reproduction of violence but is mediated by a variety of belief systems, which are shaped by core institutions of society, by war and peace systems and processes, and informally at the grassroots level by the actions and narrations of people (and significantly, by youth). This understanding may open up new avenues for thinking about actively promoting resilience, which seems to be quite contingent on future events, through inclusion of youth in postwar politics. Along with early memories of love and nurturing and the coping skills of parents, active political participation is believed to enhance resilience for war-affected children (see, e.g., Boothby 1983; Cairns 1996). This is where psychosocial, peace-education, and elite political initiatives might usefully intersect. The active and genuine inclusion of young people and their ideas in aid and education programs, policy plans, and national narratives might constitute an empowering practice for youth. Such an experience of inclusion could help prevent renewed violence and also provide information vital for postwar reconstruction. The multidimensionality of youth interaction with society (in war and peace) offers enormous potential for more widely utilizing their roles in generating new knowledge and in informally educating not only their peers but also the wider society.

References

Anderson, R. E., F. Sewankambo, and K. Vandergrift. 2004. *Pawns of politics: Children, conflict, and peace in Northern Uganda*. World Vision Report. AfricaFocus Bulletin, September 30. Available online.

Andoni, G. 2001. A comparative study of Intifada 1987 and Intifada 2000. In *The new Intifada. Resisting Israel's apartheid*, ed. R. Carey, 209–18. New York: Verso.

Barber, B. K. 1999. Political violence, family relations, and Palestinian youth functioning. *Journal of Adolescent Research* 14 (2) (April): 206–31.

BBC. 2001. "Second day of Mitrovica clashes." *BBC News*. UK edition online. January 31.

———. 2002. "Kosovo anti-UN protests turn violent." *BBC News*, UK edition online. February 8.

———. 2004a. "Serb teenager shot dead in Kosovo." *BBC News*, UK edition online. June 6.

———. 2004b. "Six die in riot-hit Kosovo town. *BBC News*, UK edition online. March 17.

Boothby, N. 1983. The horror, the hope. *Natural History* 1: 64–71.

Boothby, N., and C. Knudsen. 2000. Children of the gun. *Scientific American* 282 (6): 6–66.

Boyden, J., and J. de Berry, eds. 2004. *Children and youth on the frontline: Ethnography, armed conflict and displacement*. Studies in Forced Migration 14. New York: Berghahn Books.

Brett, R., and M. McCallin. 1996. *Children: The invisible soldiers*. Vaxjo: Rädda Barnen.

Brett, R., and I. Sprecht. 2004. *Young soldiers: Why they choose to fight*. Boulder, CO: Lynne Rienner.

Buckley, A. D., and M. C. Kenney. 1995. *Negotiating identity: Rhetoric, metaphor, and social drama in Northern Ireland*. Washington, DC: Smithsonian Institution Press.

Cairns, E. 1996. *Children and political violence*. Oxford: Blackwell.

Cohn, I., and G. Goodwin-Gill. 1994. *Child soldiers: The role of children in armed conflicts*. New York: Oxford Clarendon Press/Henry Dunant Institute.

Coles, R. 1990. *The spiritual life of children*. Boston: Houghton Mifflin.

Copnall, B. 2005. A young patriot's conviction and anger. *BBC Focus on Africa Magazine Online*. January 4.

CSVR (Center for the Study of Violence and Reconciliation). 1998. *Into the heart of darkness: Journeys of the amagents in crime, violence, and death*. Paper prepared as part of research conducted by the Centre for the Study of Violence and Reconciliation for the Council for Scientific and Industrial Research. Johannesburg: CSVR.

Dissel, A. 1997. Youth, street gangs, and violence in South Africa. In *Youth, street culture, and urban violence in Africa*. Proceedings of the international symposium held in Abidjan, May 5–7. Johannesburg: CSVR.

Hart, J. 2004. Beyond struggle and aid: Children's identities in a Palestinian refugee camp. In Boyden and de Berry, *Children and youth on the frontline*, 167–88.

Helsing, J., N. Kirlic, N. McMaster, and N. Sonnenschein. 2006. Young people's activism and the transition to peace: Bosnia, Northern Ireland, and Israel. In McEvoy-Levy, *Troublemakers or peacemakers?*, 195–216.

King, L. 2005. The fresh new face of Israeli defiance. *Los Angeles Times*, 1. June 28.

Irwin, R. A. 1989. *Building a peace system*. Washington, DC: ExPro Press.

Lakoff, G. 1999. *Metaphorical thought in foreign policy: Why strategic framing matters*. Washington, DC: The Frameworks Institute.

Lambert, R., and E. Webster. 1988. The reemergence of political unionism in contemporary South Africa. In *Popular struggles in South Africa*, ed. W. Cobbett and R. Cohen, 20–41. London: James Currey.

Lesic, Z. 1995. *Children of Atlantis: Voices from the former Yugoslavia*. Budapest: Central European Univ. Press.

Malik, S. 2004. For Allah and the Caliphate. *New Statesman*, 27–29, September 13.

Marks, M. 1999. South Africa's transition and the emergence of new roles and identities. Paper written for Northern Ireland Council for Voluntary Action Conference, June 24.

Marks, M., and P. McKenzie. 1995. *Political pawns or social agents? A look at militarized youth in South Africa*. Paper presented at Confronting Crime Conference, Cape Town, South Africa. September.

Mann, G. 2004. Separated children: Care and support in context. In Boyden and de Berry, *Children and youth on the frontline*, 3–22.

Mertus, J. 1999. *Kosovo. How myths and truths started a war*. Berkeley and Los Angeles: Univ. of California Press.

———. 2004. Improving international peacebuilding efforts: The example of human rights culture in Kosovo. *Global Governance* 10: 333–51.

McEvoy-Levy, S. 2006a. Introduction: Youth and the post-accord environment. In McEvoy-Levy, *Troublemakers or peacemakers?*, 1–26.

———. 2006b. Politics, protest, and local "power-sharing" in North Belfast. In McEvoy-Levy, *Troublemakers or peacemakers?*, 139–72.

———. 2006c. *Troublemakers or peacemakers? Youth and post-accord peace building*. Notre Dame, IN: Univ. of Notre Dame Press.

Nordstrom, C. 2006. The jagged edge of peace: The creation of culture and war orphans in Angola. In McEvoy-Levy, *Troublemakers or peacemakers?*, 96–116.

Oliver, A. M., and P. F. Steinberg. 2005. *The road to martyr's square: A journey into the world of the suicide bomber*. New York: Oxford Univ. Press.

Olson, K. R. 2004. Children: The grey spaces between war and peace: The uncertain truth of memory acts. In Boyden and de Berry, *Children and youth on the frontline*, 145–66.

Rashied, A. 2001. *Taliban: Militant Islam, oil, and fundamentalism in Central Asia*. New Haven, CT: Yale Univ. Press.

Ross, M. H. 1995. Psychocultural interpretation theory and peacemaking in ethnic conflict. *Political Psychology* 16 (September): 523–44.

———. 2001. Psychocultural interpretations and dramas: Identity dynamics in ethnic conflict. *Political Psychology* 22 (Spring): 157–78.

Simpson, G. 1992. *Jack-asses and Jackrollers: Rediscovering gender in understanding violence*. Occasional paper written for the Centre for the Study of Violence and Reconciliation. Johannesburg: CSVR.

Singer, P. W. 2005. *Children at war*. New York: Pantheon.

Smock, D. 2004. Divine intervention: Regional reconciliation through faith. *International Review: Issue on "Religion—Beyond Harvard Beliefs"* 25 (4).

———. 2005. Teaching about the religious other. United States Institute of Peace Special Report 143. July. Available on the usip.org website.

Sommers, M. 2002. *Children, education, and war: Reaching education for all (EFA) objectives in countries affected by conflict*. World Bank Conflict Prevention and Reconstruction Unit, Working Paper 1. Washington, DC: World Bank.

———. 2003. *Urbanization, war, and Africa's youth at risk: Towards understanding and addressing future challenges*. Basic Education and Support Policy (BEPS) Activity. Washington, DC: US Agency for International Development.

———. 2006. In the shadow of genocide. Rwanda's youth challenge. In McEvoy-Levy, *Troublemakers or peacemakers?*, 81–98.

Swaine, A., and T. Feeny. 2004. A neglected perspective: Adolescent girls' experiences of the Kosovo conflict of 1999. In Boyden and de Berry, *Children and youth on the frontline*, 63–86.

Wessells, M. G., and D. Jonah. 2006. Recruitment and reintegration of former youth soldiers in Sierra Leone: Challenges of reconciliation and post-accord peace building. In McEvoy-Levy, *Troublemakers or peacemakers?*, 27–48.

7

WHEN FORMER CHILD SOLDIERS GROW UP

The keys to reintegration and reconciliation

Neil Boothby

Introduction

Every day, all around the world, children are abducted and forced
into armed service. An estimated 300,000 children are actively participating in more than thirty-six ongoing conflicts in Asia, Africa,
Europe, the Americas, and the former Soviet Union. In the recent
Sierra Leone conflict, approximately 80 percent of all rebel soldiers
were seven to fourteen years old. During the Liberian Civil War,
from 1989 to 1997, children as young as seven took part in combat.
In the hostilities in Cambodia that nominally ended in the early 1980s,
one-fifth of wounded soldiers were between the ages of ten and fourteen. Yet, despite the widespread use of children as soldiers—and recent advances in international law to prohibit the practice—no one
has ever carefully documented how these young people fare over time.

This chapter offers initial findings from a longitudinal study of
thirty-nine former child soldiers in Mozambique. Over sixteen years
(1988 to 2004) information was collected on these former child soldiers, beginning at the Lhanguene (lang-ay-nee) Rehabilitation Center
in Maputo, and continuing after they were reintegrated into families
and communities. The study was designed to shed light on three basic questions: How have former child soldiers fared as adults? Are
there similarities and differences in their adult life outcomes and, if

155

so, how might they be explained? What organized efforts work best in assisting young combatants returning to civilian life?

Background

Mozambique's armed conflict lasted for almost thirty years. In 1964, Frelimo (the Mozambique Liberation Front) launched an armed insurgency for national liberation from the Portuguese colonists. Portugal bitterly resisted liberation efforts but acquiesced after a ten-year war. In 1975 the minority regimes in South Africa and Rhodesia looked on in alarm when Mozambique declared itself an independent nation. Rhodesia, in particular, viewed this as a threat because it shared its eastern border with Mozambique and feared its own indigenous population also would fight for independence (Vines 1991). The Rhodesian secret police organized, trained, and armed anti-Frelimo groups and disgruntled ex-Frelimo soldiers into an organization called the Mozambique National Resistance, which became known as Renamo (Hanlon 1984). In 1977, after Mozambique gave sanctuary and support to guerrillas fighting the Rhodesian regime, Renamo infiltrated Mozambique and began its own brutal guerrilla operations.

In 1980 Renamo lost its sponsorship in Rhodesia after the minority regime fell and the country became Zimbabwe. South Africa then intervened and offered its territory as a sanctuary and training ground. With South African support Renamo returned to Mozambique and continued to wage a guerrilla campaign to undermine the country's infrastructure and government by destroying factories, schools, health clinics, and stores (Morgan 1990).

Mozambican children in war

Mozambique's conflict had a devastating impact on its youngest citizens. Surveys conducted during this time revealed that one-third of Mozambique's children died before they reached the age of five from starvation, malnutrition, and preventable illnesses related to the continuing conflict (UNICEF 1987).

What happened to Mozambican children who did survive beyond age five? In an effort to answer this question, in 1989 members of our initial research team interviewed 504 children from seven of

Mozambique's ten provinces, stretching across a broad geographical area from Maputo in the south to Nampula in the north. Mozambican nationals asked a randomly selected sample of 252 boys and 252 girls between the ages of six and fifteen to describe their war-related experiences in detail. The results were staggering:

- Seventy-seven percent had witnessed murders, often in large numbers.
- Eighty-eight percent had witnessed physical abuse and/or torture.
- Fifty-one percent had been physically abused or tortured.
- Sixty-three percent had witnessed rape and/or sexual abuse.
- Sixty-four percent had been abducted from their families.
- Seventy-five percent of the abducted children had been forced to serve as porters or human cargo carriers.
- Twenty-eight percent of the abducted children (all boys) had been trained for combat.

In addition to the above statistics, children's descriptive accounts provided considerable insight into how Renamo socialized children into violence. Adults relied on physical abuse and humiliation as the main tools of indoctrination. In the first phase of indoctrination, Renamo members attempted to harden the children emotionally by punishing anyone who offered help or displayed feelings for others, thus conditioning them not to conspire to question the group's authority. Children were then encouraged to become abusers themselves. A progressive series of tasks—taking the gun apart and putting it back together, shooting rifles next to their ears to get them used to the sound, killing cows—culminated in requests to kill unarmed human beings. Children were expected to assist adult soldiers without question or emotion. Those that resisted were often killed. Those that did well became junior "chiefs" or garnered other rewards such as extra food or more comfortable housing. Upon reaching the final stages of training, normally after their first murder, Renamo marked the occasion with ceremonies that resembled traditional rites of passage. This process of mimicking traditional ceremonies appeared to be aimed at usurping children's ties to their families, communities, and traditional ideas of right and wrong.

In 1988 Save the Children began its Children and War Program in Mozambique. The program's initial focus was on thirty-nine boy soldiers (between six and sixteen years old) at the Lhanguene Center in Maputo who had escaped or been liberated from rebel strongholds. All of these boys had been abducted from their families by Renamo, taken to base camps, trained as combatants, and, in many instances, encouraged to kill people. After brief stays in prisoner of war camps, the government decided to place them at the Maputo Center, and Save the Children was asked to provide psychological and social assistance.

A team of Mozambican and international staff was assembled to develop the psychosocial program. The team began by learning what it could about the ways in which Mozambican communities might respond on their own to boys and girls who had been victims as well as victimizers. As a result of these investigations, rehabilitation efforts at the Lhanguene Center focused on four interrelated components:

1. *Establish safety and appropriate codes of conduct.* The baseline requirements of rehabilitation efforts were deemed to be a safe place and appropriate behavioral norms. The former soldiers participated with the center's staff in setting these norms and a peer-and-adult monitoring system (including rewards and punishments). Daily, structured activities were also key to this component.

2. *Reestablish self-regulatory processes.* An assumption was made that problematic behavior exhibited by former child soldiers (whether passive-withdrawn or aggressive-violent) was in part the result of coping and survival strategies learned during the war. An "activities package" was developed to enable former child soldiers to regain proper impulse control and modulate aggressive as well as withdrawn behavior. Activities ranged from team sports to choreographed dance, music, and group art. All required cooperative, synchronized, and group-oriented behaviors in order to "win" or be "successful."

3. *Promote security-seeking versus survival-seeking appraisal and behavior.* Initially, the majority of former child soldiers continued to appraise events and human interactions from a survival perspective. Along with the activities package mentioned above, adult-child relations were also seen as a way to promote security-seeking versus survival-seeking appraisal and behavior. Pro-

gram staff supported the efforts of the Mozambican Women's Organization volunteer caretakers, who were key actors in this effort to reestablish a sense of security and trust.

4. *Support meaning-making.* Personal narratives, drawing, and child-adult discussions were employed to explore objective and subjective aspects of their child soldiering experiences. Traditional healers and religious leaders also provided ceremonies and services to help the boys come to terms with their past deeds and lost loved ones. Work in this domain also focused on efforts to reconnect former child soldiers to their national, family, and community identities. This occurred through ritualistic song-dance activities, as well as through socio-drama and theater performances. Three common themes were integrated and repeated in all these later activities: renouncement of Renamo, devotion to government, and love of family and community.

The Mozambican government established the Lhanguene Center in part as a political tool to publicize the atrocities committed by Renamo. Maputo-based government officials also perpetuated the belief that the boys' families would never accept their return because of the crimes they had committed. As part of their long-term planning, Save the Children staff undertook investigative trips to rural communities to see if these government reports were accurate. They were not. Overwhelmingly, family and community members who had lost their children to Renamo wanted them back. This was also true of community-level political leaders, but less so for senior district and provincial leaders. A family tracing and reunification program was developed, and relatives for all thirty-nine of the Lhanguene boys were eventually located.

Family reunions took place between December 1988 and May 1989. At the time of reunification, families were provided a one-time assistance package to help relieve the extra economic burden another person would create on already strained families. These packages consisted of foodstuffs and clothing for all family members, as well as school-fee and health-care vouchers for the returning former child soldiers. All of these former child soldiers went through traditional cleansing ceremonies to facilitate their personal recovery and reintegration into families and communities. Sensitization campaigns, targeted at local military, police, teachers, and community leaders, were also initiated to encourage receiving community members to support the reintegration of former child soldiers. Apprenticeships with local carpenters, masons, and other skilled laborers were established for older boys so they could learn basic employment and business skills. Most of the boys also received seeds and tools. Community projects—such as repairing hospitals and water systems—were undertaken as part of this reconciliation program, which emphasized forgiveness and collective responsibility for the fate of child soldiers and other orphans and separated children in need of care and placement. Finally, Save the Children staff and government social workers continued to visit these former child soldiers on an annual basis.

Methods

Any research done in a war-torn setting is difficult and fraught with practical and ethical constraints (Jensen 1996). Such is the case here. The thirty-nine boy soldiers in this study were not randomly selected; rather, they were chosen by the Mozambican government from among many former child soldiers to draw international attention to Renamo's abuse of children. Save the Children was asked to assist these boys, and it was agreed that the best course of action would be to return them to their families as soon as possible.

Between 1989 and 1990 three members of our research team undertook a parallel study of 504 war-affected boys and girls. The results from this study reveal that the Lhanguene child soldiers' experiences were similar to those of other abducted children in Renamo base camps. Unfortunately, although girls were also abducted and forced to take on different roles with Renamo, the government selected only boys for the Lhanguene Center.

When the Lhanguene Center opened in 1988, culturally sensitive assessments were conducted to guide the rehabilitation and reintegration efforts. War-related experiences (events, severity, and duration) were recorded using a life events profile. Children's ecologies were assessed using a documentation, tracing, and reunification protocol. A child behavior inventory was also established to assess aggression, traumatic symptoms, and high-risk versus positive social behavior. After reunification with families, follow-up assessments were conducted in 1988, 1989, and 1990 in the boys' communities. A number of these visits were videotaped.

For the 2003–4 phase of our research, former Lhanguene staff led research teams and conducted interviews, as it was not possible to gain access to rural communities without the presence of these trusted individuals. We believe that establishing this safe space for them ensured that no former child soldiers or family members declined to be interviewed; nor did any terminate the interview once it had started. Through one-on-one interviews, free-listing and pile-sorting activities, and focus groups, social functioning was determined using several indicators: household income, housing and food security, children's health status, and educational status. The former child soldiers' household income, housing ownership, and their children's educational status were compared to means for Mozambique, and their children's health status was measured by the WHO/NCHS normalized, referenced weight-for-height scale (WHO 2000). Food security was qualified by the self-reporting of having to miss meals because of lack of access to food.

To triangulate the data, we conducted additional focus groups with families, community members, and community leaders. Our aim was to gain as accurate a picture as possible of how the former child soldiers have adapted over time, paying particular attention to their psychosocial well-being and their roles as husbands, fathers, economic providers, and neighbors.

Throughout this chapter the statistics should not be considered statistically significant because our small sample size precluded sufficient power. An increase in sample size was impossible due to the specificity of the former child soldiers we worked with through the Lhanguene Center.

Findings

The Lhanguene boys

The Lhanguene Center boys' Renamo experiences were similar to those reported by other abducted boys. The length of time spent in base camps ranged from two months to three years, and their functional roles varied from spies, cooks, cleaners, and porters to combatants and leaders of combatants. During this time the boys experienced or witnessed firsthand virtually every known type of violence or cruelty. Their survival depended on Renamo leaders, who were impulsive, unpredictable, suspicious, and quick to react to the slightest provocation. According to the boys, the leaders boasted of their sexual prowess and their power over life and death. Simultaneously, the leaders practiced a hybrid religiosity. Several Renamo leaders referred to their guns as "enforcers" and "guardian angels." Others made pacts with a "devil spirit" in order to attain fortune, invulnerability to bullets, and invisibility from their enemies.

One of the program team's most striking initial observations was the range of behaviors the boys exhibited when they first arrived at the Lhanguene Center in Maputo. Some appeared listless and numbed, unable or unwilling to talk or engage in organized activities. Others were talkative, anxious, and active. A number of younger boys interacted with adult caretakers as soon as they entered the center; many older ones avoided contact or communication with others altogether. Some did not interact with peers, others engaged openly with one another, a few older boys bullied younger ones, and some engaged in fights and high-risk behavior.

Mozambican volunteer caretakers recorded their observations of the boys' behavior while they were at the Lhanguene Center. The following synthesizes one volunteer's observations during the first three months at the Center:

"[When they first arrived] there was fighting between the different groups of boys from Inhambane, Gaza, and Maputo provinces. Three boys continued to act like the [Renamo] leaders, ordering other boys to obey or steal things for them. A lot of the boys lied to get their way and stole whatever they could. They did not think if something was right or wrong; they just took what they wanted. At night when the lights went out, several boys pulled out homemade knives to protect themselves. The fighting lasted until the boys went to [the local] school where neighborhood students called them *banditos*. Then they stopped fighting each other and joined together to defend themselves against other students.

"We [the caretakers] were frightened of the boys, too. None of us wanted to work with them at first. We thought they were going to hurt us. But day by day, each side began to get to know the other better. After about a month, the situation improved. I think the boys realized that we were different from Renamo. I guess we realized they weren't going to hurt us either. After a while we just started treating them like our own children. We joked with them, watched their football games, encouraged them to do their homework, made the younger ones sit on our lap. It was difficult because some of them insulted us at first, and argued when they did not get what they wanted."

Save the Children program staff used the child behavior inventory protocol to record observations of the boys' behavior at the center at one- and three-month time intervals. These observations roughly parallel the descriptive account provided above.

Considerable "normalization" of individuals' behavior took place during the initial three months of intervention at the Lhanguene Center. The boys also became more cohesive as a group, demonstrating increasingly supportive and cooperative attitudes and behavior toward one another. Leadership dynamics shifted as well: The three former Renamo youth leaders were increasingly marginalized, no longer able to dominate younger boys, who increasingly turned to other older boys for direction and advice. Some program staff reported that overall aggressive behaviors subsided and positive social behaviors increased as the boys became increasingly comfortable and attached to their adult caretakers.

The length of time spent with Renamo was a factor related to these boys' adjustments at the center. In general, boys who spent six months or less with Renamo (72 percent) appeared to emerge with their basic trust in human beings and social values more or less intact. Although all of these boys had been exposed to severe trauma, and some also had participated in abuse and violence, members of this group described themselves as victims rather than members of Renamo. The following comments are indicative of these boys' accounts of their relationship with Renamo:

"We were forced to do it."
"We did not have a choice."
"They would have killed me if I refused to obey."
"I never would have done any of this if I did not have to."

A different picture emerged for boys who had spent longer than six months with Renamo (28 percent). They continued to exhibit disobedient and uncooperative behaviors during the first three months at the center. Despite their ability to articulate the belief that violence was wrong, these boys continued to use aggression as a principal means of exerting control and social influence. One thirteen-year-old Lhanguene boy, for example, told a center staffer that Renamo was not concerned about people's well-being; instead, it used them "like animals" to achieve its objectives. He stated that he thought this was wrong. The next afternoon, however, this same boy was observed beating up a smaller child because this child refused to steal food for him.

These boys' self-images appeared to be bound up with the persona of their captors. They rarely described themselves as victims; rather, they tended to identify themselves as members of Renamo:

"I could have escaped but didn't because I had a good position."
"I was a leader and others respected me."
"I first served as his [a base camp leader] personal servant. Then he made me chief of a group of other boys. I had power."
"They used to follow my orders. Now [at the Lhanguene Center] they don't."

Traumatic symptoms over time

The 2003 phase of our study found that a number of the post traumatic stress symptoms that were prevalent while the boys were at the Lhanguene Center continued to be problematic into their adult lives. All of these boys experienced recurrent thoughts or memories of traumatic events while at the Lhanguene Center, for example, and still did sixteen years later. While other symptoms also persist, the number of former child soldiers experiencing them as adults is considerably less than those who experienced them as children (see Table 7–1).

To date, we have identified two variables that are linked to decreases in post traumatic stress symptoms over time: shorter duration of time with Renamo and use of cognitive strategies to manage symptoms. As noted above, former child soldiers who spent six months or less with Renamo exhibited less severe symptoms and behavioral problems at the Lhanguene Center than those who spent over six months with the guerrilla group. This trend continues into adulthood: adults who spent six months or less with Renamo scored much lower on the TSCL than those that spent one year or longer. Moreover, the three former child soldiers who were with Renamo for two

TABLE 7–1. POST TRAUMATIC SHOCK SYMPTOMS[1]

Question	Percentage that responded either "Sometimes" or "Frequently"	
	Lhanguene CBI 1988	TSCL 2003
Recurrent thoughts or memories of the most hurtful or traumatic events	100%	100%
Feeling as though the event is happening again	63%	45%
Recurrent nightmares	52%	36%
Sudden emotional or physical reaction when reminded of the most hurtful or traumatic moments	48%	36%
Inability to remember parts of the most hurtful or traumatic events	61%	45%
Avoid activities that remind you of the most hurtful or traumatic events	35%	63%

[1] On the TSCL, the scores ranged from 32 to 77 with a mean score of 47 out of a possible range of 28 to 112 for twenty-eight questions. Chronbach's alpha coefficient was .8849. Statistical significance for all tests, including logistic regression analyses, was set at $p<.05$, and were two tailed without adjustment for multiple comparisons. Boys who spent fewer than six months with Renamo scored between 32 and 40 on the TSCL, while those who spent over six months scored between 42 and 77, with only five exceptions.

years or longer continue to suffer significantly as young men. There appears to be a child soldiering duration-of-time threshold that is correlated with individual well-being and social functioning outcomes.

As adults, former child soldiers are managing their post traumatic stress symptoms differently. Those who actively work at identifying their triggers and avoiding them scored lower on the TSCL and appear to be managing their symptoms more effectively than those who do not employ these same strategies.

Frequency of symptoms is reduced first by cognitively identifying social situations, physical locations, or activities that have triggered an emergence of post traumatic stress symptoms in the past, and second by actively avoiding them in the future. One traumatic reexperience trigger is physical location: Some former child soldiers avoid places where they witnessed or participated in violent and inhumane events. For one former child soldier it is a large tree in his village where Renamo thugs killed his father and abducted him. For another, it is a village footpath where, as a twelve-year-old boy, he came across a row of decapitated heads (all facing the same direction) impaled on poles. Four former child soldiers cited social drinking with other male companions as a traumatic reexperience trigger. Boisterous drinking rekindled memories of rowdy, drug and alcohol induced Renamo base-camp experiences. All four of these former child soldiers now actively avoid social drinking. Routine activities are also associated with traumatic reexperiencing. Two young men reported that they no longer slaughter animals; they report that this routine chore "reminds me of the war." Their wives now assume this function. Another former child soldier no longer uses a hoe. Still another finds it difficult to use a machete. Both of these tools were instruments of torture and death during Renamo's reign of terror.

Moreover, severity of post traumatic stress symptoms is reduced by conscious efforts to not dwell on troubling thoughts and feelings when they emerge in the course of day-to-day life. Former child soldiers with lower TSCL scores described a kind of cognitive "change of menu" strategy to ward off painful thoughts and memories. The following statements are indicative of this approach to managing post traumatic stress symptoms:

"Thinking about what I did in the war is wasting time because it [the war] helped nothing."
"When I start to think about the war, I go to church and read the bible. I keep reading until the bad thoughts disappear."
"I try to think about the present and the future, not the past."
"When bad thoughts enter my mind, I replace them as quickly as possible with better ones."
"I think about my children or my wife."

"I go straight to work [when war-related thoughts or feelings emerge]."

"Repairing my house, working the land, and making things help me forget what I don't want to remember."

Conversely, former child soldiers with higher TSCL scores do not actively use avoidance or employ other identifiable cognitive coping strategies to manage their troubling thoughts and feelings. Instead, when confronted with painful memories they tend to become consumed by them, often withdrawing from daily activities and routines. The following comments from these former child soldiers' family members are indicative of these less adaptive tendencies:

Wife: "Sometimes he is fine, and sometimes he is not. I can tell when things are bad for him because he stops working and spends time alone. Sometimes he tells me about what's bothering him, but most of the time he does not. I try to do my best to help him forget, like doing more work and selling things [normally the husband's responsibility] so when he returns from his bad thoughts things will be in order. Eventually, he goes to work, forgets, and gets better."

Mother: "He will suddenly get irritated and then very quiet. He'll go into the house and refuse to leave. We all know that his mind is back in the past. I tell everyone that we must be patient with him, but sometimes this is difficult. We all know he has suffered. We talk to him about the war, how it is over, and how he must also get over it. We try to do this with a good attitude and patience. Sometimes he threatens us when we talk to him this way, but so far nothing bad has happened. We will continue to live as we have and accept him as part of the family. He can change; it is just a matter of perseverance."

It is important to note that professional mental-health services are nonexistent in rural Mozambique. These findings are thus indicative of some of the ways these former child soldiers are coping with psychological distress on their own, within their own families and communities, and without the benefit of formal assistance or support. In this context better coping involves cognitively mapping out strategies to avoid trigger situations and making conscious efforts to replace troubling thoughts and feelings with positive thoughts or to engage quickly in the routines of work or other aspects of everyday life.

While all of these former child soldiers continue to experience post traumatic stress symptoms, only three suffered significantly impaired social functioning—and those three boys were deemed "troubled children" while at the center. Indeed, 1988 Lhanguene staff recorded they had significant difficulty adjusting to postwar life. All three had been with Renamo for two years or longer. Two were youth leaders, and one was only six years old when he was abducted.

Vasco, one of the boys who had been a Renamo youth leader, exhibited behavior at the Lhanguene Center that was disruptive, violent, and overly aggressive. During our follow-up work in 2003, we learned that he had been unable to curb his violent ways. He was reunited with his mother, but when she passed away, he went to live with his grandmother. He married, but his wife soon left him and moved back home with her parents. According to Vasco's grandmother:

> "He drinks a lot and then becomes very nasty. He threatens to kill everyone: the neighbors, his friends, and his relatives, including me. Sometimes he has used a machete. His violence and aggressiveness was the cause of the divorce."

Vasco has been unable to work on a regular basis. Last year he obtained a menial job on a farm in a neighboring village, but he continued to drink heavily, remained violent, and was finally let go. "We only talk to him when he is sober," reported his grandmother during a 2003 interview.

Fernando was fourteen when he joined Renamo; shortly thereafter he became leader of a Renamo youth brigade. He was sometimes aggressive while at Lhanguene and complained he was no longer "respected" by his peers at the center. For Fernando, return to civilian life involved a loss of status. His thoughts and behavior tended to be disorganized. He also had problems with physical coordination; his movements were stiff and awkward, although he had no visible signs of physical injury. Follow-up reports in 1989 and 1990 indicated that he had difficulties reintegrating into his family and daily life. He felt ostracized and isolated at school and quickly dropped out. Thereafter, he was neither employed nor actively sought any sort of cash-income labor. He minimally contributed to his family's welfare by repairing the house when needed. His older sister reported that he spent much of his time out with other male friends, drinking and rowdily reminiscing about "better times" with Renamo. Fernando was killed in 1999. Witnesses reported that he was shot late at night when, in the midst of a drunken rage, he threatened and attacked a police officer. A second officer shot and killed him.

Franisse also had significant difficulties at the Lhanguene Center. He was the youngest boy at the center, abducted at the age of six. At the center he was withdrawn and uncommunicative most of the time, and when he entered school he also became disruptive and was unable to concentrate. Franisse told gruesome stories about how his mother and father were murdered, as well as what he had been forced to do during the war. However, during a 1991 follow-up visit, it was discovered that his mother was still alive and that other aspects of what he had told workers at the Lhanguene Center were not true. Staff at Lhanguene also recorded concern that Franisse was unable to comprehend basic instructions required for play and learning and suggested that he might be cognitively impaired. Our 2003 follow-up interviews confirmed that he was still having significant difficulties. At twenty-three, Franisse had not married but instead had built himself a small hut next to his mother and stepfather's house. Periodically, he made and sold brooms from reeds he collected in the river, but otherwise did not contribute to the family's income or welfare. His parents reported that he spends most of his time alone and does not engage in life in the way that "normal or healthy" people do. They recited numerous accounts of violent mood swings and delusions. One day, for example, Franisse brought home some rice and oil as a gift for his mother. The next day he stormed into her house, accused her of stealing those items from him, and demanded to have them back. He even brought the police to the house to have her arrested. His mother was angry and shamed by her son's behavior but acknowledged that often he was not "in control of himself." She would like to help him more but does not know what to do other than being supportive and giving him her best advice. Neighbors also reported bizarre and unpredictable behavior. As one of them put it: "He never came home from the war. The fighting still continues in his mind."

Family reunions

All of the Lhanguene boys were reunited with relatives (parents, grand-parents, aunts, uncles, or older siblings) between December 1988 and April 1989. Assessment reports and videotapes of initial reunifications reveal overt and reserved joy and excitement, as well as tears and words of sorrow over time spent apart. Subsequent follow-up visits in 1989 and 1990 found that all of the Lhanguene boys continued to be well received by their relatives. Only one boy required an alternative place-ment. He was initially returned to an uncle who shortly thereafter went to South Africa to work in the mines. The boy's maternal aunt immediately came forward and took the boy into her family. The following recorded comments are indicative of how these boys viewed family acceptance a year after their reunifications:

> "I was well treated; no one ever said anything bad about my participation in the war."
> "I was well received by my family, they made me part of the family and they shared their food with me."
> "They were glad to see me because they knew that I had suf-fered."
> "They paid lots of attention to me."
> "I was well received. They made a traditional ceremony of wel-coming to inform and thank the ancestors for protecting me."

No negative comments were recorded at that time.

Community acceptance

In 1989 and 1990 all of these former child soldiers also reported be-ing accepted by their communities, with two exceptions. One boy reported that the community was not happy with his return and ac-cused him of having killed their relatives: "A few boys called me a *bandito* when I came home, but my family stood for me and soon they stopped saying those things." A second boy described how his lack of money led to a poor reception by his community: "People in my com-munity did not pay attention to me when I came back. I don't feel trusted because I am poor and have nothing to give to people when they ask or need things. They just say hello as they pass on the path." Here, the boy's sense of not being accepted was linked to his economic situation, which he blamed on the war, rather than on the specifics of his child-soldiering experiences. All other boys reported that they were received without problems or discrimination:

"I have been well received by the community."
"People came to speak with me and welcome me."
"They received me well because the government brought me and they respected me."
"The community treated me well. They even sacrificed a hen to commemorate my return and inform the spirits of my arrival."

Our 2003 follow-up research employed a "feeling of acceptance" scale on which the former child soldiers overwhelmingly reported that they had been accepted by members of their communities. As adults, they largely feel that their friends respect them, that their families care for them very much, and that their friends look out for them:

"I can rely on my friends."
"When I need something, I ask my neighbors and friends, and if they can help me, they will."
"If I died tomorrow, I think that people would miss me."
"Members of my community rely on me and I rely on them. It is how we live here."

Traditional ceremonies

All of the Lhanguene boys went through traditional ceremonies upon return to their villages. In Mozambique these ceremonies date from pre-colonial times and are believed to be especially important when events, such as war and population displacement, upset the normal course of life. It is thought that the spirits of the victims of war or those slighted will bring bad luck or death, not only to the perpetrator but also to members of his extended family or community. Ancestral rebuke might come from simply missing a social duty or obligation toward others or might be triggered by contentious relationships among the living. A person might unknowingly activate ancestor action against another by simply harboring hostile sentiments against that person. Within this belief system, atrocities committed during the course of a brutal war become imbued with layers of spiritual meaning, necessitating such traditional ceremonies. The traditional ceremonies afford individuals a chance to be cleansed of their acts during the war and provide protection for the community from ancestral rebuke that may be brought on because of what the child had done.

Interviews in 2003 found that most former child soldiers believed these ceremonies had helped them return to civilian life. Their comments indicated that these ceremonies focused on a range of reintegration concerns, including repairing social ills, cleansing those that came home contaminated from the atrocities of war, and resolving social conflict in cases where normal social roles had been perverted. Not only were these ceremonies important for these former child soldiers as individuals, but they were also reported by former child soldiers, family members, and neighbors to be vital for rebuilding community trust and cohesion. These former child soldiers reported that thanking the ancestors was important for community and family cohesion because ancestors have much power over the events of daily life. Because they were highly mobile during the war, moving from base camp to base camp, their protective spirits might become confused and not know they had returned. Thus, it was important to let the spirits know that the child had returned safely, ensuring his further protection. As one former child soldier described: "When something special happens, like in this case my return home, it is necessary to give thanks to the ancestors."

Traditional ceremonies also reportedly endow those returning from war with the ability to forget their experiences and begin a normal life again:

"Yes, it was helpful because today I am leading a normal life."
"There is a definite difference between before and after the ceremony."
"The war memories never came back after the ritual."
"Before there was something missing in my body and in my life, but after, I am OK. I came back to normal life and now I feel like the others."
"It was helpful because it removed the evil that I was bringing with me. I was able to forget easily all the evils that I had, even though I still dream about it."

While former child soldiers used the term *forgetting* to describe the benefits of traditional ceremonies, subsequent discussions revealed that they were referring to the shame associated with their war-related experiences rather than the actual experiences. Forgetting, in this case, was in reference to varying degrees of absolution of painful stigma associated with their participation in the war. Many reported that this internal transformation helped them to become "just like everyone else."

Family members and neighbors also reported that the traditional ceremonies were important because they gave the community a defense against problems that returning child soldiers could bring with them. During the war children were forced to violate social hierarchies, sometimes killing elders and commanding their peers into battle. The righting of these wrongs and the reestablishment of social hierarchies with deceased ancestors were priorities. While social stigma based on one's participation in the war appeared to be minimal, family and community members still were concerned that the Lhanguene boys might be disruptive due to their previous indoctrination into violence. Other researchers also found that purification ceremonies created a spirit of communal tranquility because community members see themselves as being protected and capable of confronting any situation that reintegration might bring about. Indeed, communities fulfill an important role in the reintegration of former child soldiers, as it is in the community that all social issues relating to the individual returnee are resolved.

Sensitization campaigns

In addition to traditional cleansing rituals, our research indicates that community sensitization campaigns also had a positive impact on community acceptance of former child soldiers. Sensitization campaigns were designed to enable community members to understand that former child soldiers were victims too, even though they may have perpetrated violence against that very community. During the course of our 2003 focus-group discussions, community members reported that they remembered government officials coming and talking to them about the children returning and that it made an impact on them:

> "I remember the government people coming to tell us that our sons were going to come home and that we should treat them like everyone else. That is what we have done."

"We listened to the advice of the people that came from Maputo. We have accepted these boys, and they live with us now. There is no difference."

"The big men came and told us what to expect from our boys. Now we eat what they eat, we live together. We are all the same."

"They are our sons; what they did they were forced to do, so we cannot blame them for such bad things."

Making up for lost time

To what extent has this group of former child soldiers been able to overcome the time spent away from fulfilling their normal life milestones and regain a foothold in the normative life cycle of rural Mozambique? As explained earlier, several indicators were employed to explore this question: household income, housing and food security, children's health status, and educational status.

Despite disruptions to their life trajectories, this group of former child soldiers is faring as well as, and often better than, national averages for these socioeconomic and child-welfare indicators. The national average for household ownership is 91.7 percent, which matches the average of the former child soldiers (91 percent).

While 100 percent of these former child soldiers are engaged in farming, 63 percent of them earn additional income from wage-labor endeavors. The national average for off-farm activities of rural inhabitants in Mozambique is estimated at 38 percent (Amimo et al. 2003). Off-farm wage labor for this population includes working in the mines in South Africa, working as guards, working on local construction projects, and doing odd jobs in their communities. Many also are engaged in other informal sector income activities, including making charcoal, cutting and selling reeds from the river for cash, and running small kiosks to sell agricultural produce.

The central and southern provinces of Mozambique, where this study took place, have an ongoing food crisis. The low availability of food and the lack of access to food result in food insecurity and hunger (WFP 2006). All of these former child soldiers and their families are affected by this crisis. Eighty percent reported that they are not always able to eat or provide their children with balanced meals. A vast majority also said that the adults in their households have reduced portion sizes or skipped meals almost every month during the past year. Despite this food shortage, the weight-for-height of their children (under five years old) is above the national average. All scored above the median using the WHO/NCHS normalized referenced weight-for-height scale (WHO 2000). Most of the former child soldiers or their spouses reported their children to be in either good or excellent health. In the context of Mozambique's chronic food shortage, these findings bode quite well for the resiliency of the Lhanguene boys following their harrowing experiences with Renamo.

While the former child soldiers seem to be doing well, all reported that their daily economic situation has been, and continues to be, one of the major obstacles in their transition to civilian life. Historically in Mozambique, individual welfare has been linked to informal sector enterprise and collective help networks. The extended family normally provides a form of "social security" to its members, which follows longstanding patterns of personal and kinship relationships. Indeed, many former child soldiers indicated that obstacles to reintegration often stemmed from economic difficulties and their inability to help others when asked for money or other necessities.

When asked what external assistance could have been provided by the Lhanguene initiative, most reported that they wished they had received a professional skill set that would have made them viable contributors to their family's economy. As stated above, apprenticeships were highly successful for the few boys who were able to take part; however, apprenticeships and targeted vocational training are not feasible on a national or regional level. Ultimately, field practitioners must model economic interventions along the lines of the various livelihood or microcredit programs in place around the world in order to reach the number of young people that need assistance while remaining cognizant of the limits of local economies.

One of the most devastating legacies of child soldiering was the years of lost economic opportunity that, in turn, made difficult the key life cycle tasks of choosing a wife and building a family. Many of these former child soldiers reported these challenges to be more problematic than the actual experiences of the war:

"I had no problems choosing a wife, but I have had problems because of a lack of money."
"I had no resources; I had to begin everything from the beginning."

"Those who did not go to the war had the time to earn some money, but I had nothing after the war."

Discussion

Journalistic accounts labeled Mozambique's children a "lost generation" and "future barbarians." Our research suggests that this is not the case. To the contrary, the vast majority of the group of former child soldiers we followed for sixteen years have become productive, capable, and caring adults. Most have regained a foothold in the economic life of rural Mozambique, are perceived by their spouses to be good husbands, are taking active steps to ensure their own children's welfare, and are engaged in the collective affairs of their communities. Only a few continued their violent ways or are so dysfunctional that they have been unable to take hold of their lives.

At the same time, none of these child soldiers is truly free from his past. All continue to struggle with psychological distress that is linked to their child-soldiering experiences. There are no mental-health professionals in rural Mozambique. When troubling memories from the past reappear—as they sometimes do—these former child soldiers rely solely on themselves, their families, and their friends for comfort and support. Many have managed to reduce the frequency of post traumatic distress by identifying situations that have promoted painful thoughts and feelings in the past and avoiding them. They try not to dwell on troubling memories when they do emerge; rather, they consciously think about more positive aspects of their lives, re-engage in day-to-day work activities, or seek solace in religious institutions, prayers, rituals, and texts. Wives, for the most part, are aware of their husbands' struggles. They tend to encourage their husbands not to become overwhelmed by their thoughts and feelings and compensate in other ways when their husbands do become despondent. Extended family members and neighbors also are aware of these tendencies and typically respond with patience, advice, or support.

The next phase of our research in Mozambique is focusing on the adult outcomes of a similar group of child soldiers who were not provided organized assistance. Until the research is complete, we are not in a position to comment on the efficacy of particular interventions. Nonetheless, we do believe it useful to offer some preliminary findings based on these young men's self-reports and the observations of their wives and neighbors.

Neither the hybrid approach developed at the Lhanguene Center nor the work of traditional healers and spiritualists put an end to the horrors of the past. Indeed, we must question if a "cure" is even possible in the aftermath of severe and chronic child-soldiering experiences. In either case, our findings do suggest that supporting and strengthening coping skills for anticipated trauma and grief responses need to be key intervention objectives. Moreover, in the absence of formal mental-health programs (the norm in most of today's war-affected countries), avoiding situations and activities that remind former child soldiers of troubling experiences may be among the adaptive coping skills they should be encouraged to employ.

A number of interventions aided these former child soldiers' transitions into society. Most of them described the time they spent with adult caretakers and other former child soldiers at the Lhanguene Center positively. Program efforts to promote safe codes of conduct, self-regulation, and security-seeking behavior also appear to have engendered a sense of social responsibility among these former child soldiers that is evident today.

Traditional cleansing ceremonies played key reconciliation roles. They helped to repair relationships with their families and communities and to realign the boys' well-being with the spirit world. The rituals enabled these boys to feel "like everyone else" and deepened their sense of acceptance. This, in turn, ameliorated degrees of guilt and shame over past misdeeds. Alerting ancestors and spirits to the boys' return further represented a form of protection for community members who worried about what these boys might do once they came home. Numerous community members also recalled the government-led sensitization campaigns organized sixteen years earlier by Save the Children. They, too, helped to foster community acceptance and forgiveness.

In general, other forms of assistance that supported normal, life-cycle milestones—such as employment, housing, farming, and marriage—were viewed as helpful by these former child soldiers. Apprenticeships, income-generation projects, seeds, and tools were cited as positive forms of support. In contrast, education stipends (for fees, books, and clothes) were not deemed helpful. They tended to cause tension in several families because they singled out one child for support over the others. Also, most of these boys were not motivated to stay in school. Instead, they felt compelled to earn money, find a wife, and build a house. In the end, understanding the normative life cycle, including key developmental milestones and how systems that support them have been affected (and can be assisted and realigned), emerged as a pragmatic framework for designing and evaluating reintegration programs.

References

Amimo, O., C. Delgado, D. Larson, M. Bittencourt, and D. Graham. 2003. The potential for financial savings in rural Mozambican households. 25th International Conference of Agricultural Economists, Durban, South Africa. Ohio State Univ.

Hanlon, J. 1984. *Mozambique: The revolution under fire*. London: Zed Books.

Jensen, P. 1996. Practical approaches to research with children in violent settings. In *Minefields in their hearts: The mental health of children in war and communal violence*, ed. R. J. Apfel and B. Simon, 149–64. New Haven, CT: Yale Univ. Press.

Morgan, G. 1990. Violence in Mozambique: Towards an understanding of Renamo. *The Journal of Modern African Studies* 28 (4): 603–19.

UNICEF. 1987. Children on the front line: The impact of apartheid, destabilization, and welfare on children in southern and South Africa. New York: UNICEF.

Vines, A. 1991. *Renamo: Terrorism in Mozambique*. London: Villiers Publications.

WHO. 2000. Management of the child with a serious infection or severe malnutrition. *Bulletin of the World Health Organization* 72: 273–83. Available online.

WFP. 2006. Draft country programme—Mozambique 10446.0 (2007-2009). Available online.

8

A LIVING WAGE

The importance of livelihood
in reintegrating former child soldiers

Michael Wessells

Introduction

Chronic poverty is among the most important and damaging aspects of the social ecologies of war zones. Poverty corrodes the health and well-being of all children and often obstructs positive options such as education or a means of earning a living. Although poverty does not cause armed conflict, its enabling role is visible in the disproportionate numbers of wars fought in developing countries, particularly those that have failing economies. Not infrequently, poverty sets the stage for political rebellion and the rise of rogue leaders promising a better life who use war to pursue their own political agendas.

The link between poverty and conflict is palpable among children, approximately 300,000 of whom are believed to be in armed groups (Machel 2001). Some children join these groups in hope of gaining otherwise unattainable wealth, often with the goal of sending money home to help support their families. Children's participation in armed groups violates their rights, exacts a tremendous physical and psychological toll, and ultimately damages many civilian children as well, because they are among the most vulnerable and often bear the brunt of attacks and war-associated deprivations (Machel 2001; Wessells, forthcoming).

If the poverty, conflict, and child-soldiering linkage is worrying from a child rights perspective, it is of equal concern from a peace perspective. In fact, child soldiering fuels armed conflict by enabling both the eruption and continuation of wars (Singer 2005; Wessells 2002). In the post-2002 fighting in Liberia, children made up nearly half of the soldiers (HRW 2004). Following the signing of the 1994 Lusaka Protocol, which brought about a temporary ceasefire in Angola, banditry became a major threat to peace—some of it committed by former child soldiers who viewed the gun as their best means of earning a living (Wessells and Monteiro 2001).

To protect children's rights and build peace, it is vital both to reintegrate former child soldiers into civilian life and to prevent their recruitment into armed groups. This chapter argues that efforts toward these ends require careful attention to the issue of livelihoods—including job and life skills, access to jobs, and participation in successful income-generating activities. This chapter presents a case study of Sierra Leone, illustrating the pivotal role of livelihoods in the reintegration process. Because children's perspectives have received insufficient attention in the literature on child soldiers, this study employs a narrative research methodology that validates children's voices and agency and also illuminates children's subjective understandings of their situations, including the social ecologies influencing them. The chapter concludes with an analysis of the value of integrating psychosocial and economic support in aiding former child soldiers' reintegration and the broader tasks of reconciliation and peace building.

Economics, livelihood, and recruitment

Worldwide, children join armed groups through both forced recruitment and nonforced recruitment. Children's decisions to join reflect diverse motives such as revenge, a desire to escape abusive family situations, a quest for power and excitement, protection and survival, and to help free their people from oppression (Brett and McCallin 1996; Brett and Specht 2004; Wessells, forthcoming). Although children are politically active and make decisions to join without obvious external coercion, it is simplistic to attribute these decisions unilaterally to free choice. The desperation and paucity of options in war zones beg the term *voluntary recruitment* and alternate terms such as *non-forced recruitment* may be more appropriate. Children may join because they have no other means of obtaining food or because they want protection or health care that's accessible only in armed groups. One of the most common motivations for non-forced recruitment is economic—the quest for money, material gain, and status.

Money and wealth

Children in war zones frequently seek money to acquire necessities such as food and medicine. Living in families besieged by economic hardship, some children view soldiering as a means of fulfilling their family responsibilities. A Cambodian boy who joined an armed group at age thirteen said:

"I send most of the money I am paid each month back home. To this day I have never admitted to my family that I am in the army—I am too afraid that they would force me to return home. How would I provide for them?" (UNICEF 2003, 31)

Aside from the sense of family responsibility, some children join armed groups in hope of a better life. A Colombian boy who had joined a paramilitary group said:

"After school I was a baker's assistant. It was hard work and paid badly. I went to work on a farm, but the work was hard too, so finally I joined the paras. I had friends inside. It paid 300,000 [US$100] a month. It seemed like an easier life." (HRW 2003, 41)

Children's need for money is not lost on troop-hungry commanders, who lure children into armed groups with the promise of wealth, though they typically never deliver. An East Timorese boy who had joined an armed group at age seventeen stated: "I was paid once, when I first joined the militia. I got 25,000 rupiah [about US$3–$5]. After that I was never paid again" (UNICEF 2003, 49). The lure of money is also evident in words of a Liberian refugee boy who had joined the National Patriotic Front of Liberia:

"I joined the revolution in 1991 when I was 12, but I got fed up with the rebel life after being beaten by my commanders and decided to go to Sierra Leone where I ended up in Waterloo refugee camp. But I couldn't get away from the war life. At

Waterloo, when I was about 14, I was recruited to join the ULIMO's [United Liberation Movement of Liberia for Democracy] by a Mandingo named S. They promised us money and said we'd be able to take whatever we could manage. I fought with ULIMO from 1992 to 1995" (HRW 2004, 29–30)

Opportunities for looting—a common practice among armed groups—help to attract a ready pool of child recruits, some of whom become regional mercenaries (HRW 2005). The power of looting as an incentive to join indicates that having a livelihood is not equated with amassing money. In many developing countries wealth resides in one's possessions (even if stolen), livestock, and services useful in bartering.

It would be a mistake to view voluntary (non-forced) child soldiering for economic gain as a phenomenon unique to developing countries. In the United States and the United Kingdom, among other places, volunteer recruits come disproportionately from lower socioeconomic classes, for whom the military offers a way out of poverty and a gateway to opportunities. Poor, young Americans are often attracted by the lure of the US military because of its successful mixture of patriotic appeals and lucrative training and education opportunities. The US government continues to recruit seventeen year olds, who in 2002 composed 5 percent of new, active-duty recruits and 23 percent of new, reserve-duty recruits (CSC 2004). Although this practice is legal under the Optional Protocol of the CRC, of which the United States is a signatory, it propagates the global norm of child recruitment—and the harm caused by this norm is most conspicuous in war-torn countries, where large numbers of children are combatants.

Unemployment, lack of education, and political radicalization

Many war zones feature a combustible mixture of unemployment, lack of educational and training opportunities, and failed expectations. The resulting sense of hopelessness and futility, coupled with the desire to change a failed political system, can convert ordinary teenagers into activists who foment political rebellion. The radicalization of youth—those between fifteen and twenty-four years of age—has played a prominent role in political change throughout history (Goldstein 2001). Young people's engagement in political rebellion is likely to be a potent force in developing countries, where people under eighteen years of age constitute half the population, and economic pressures make livelihood issues a profound concern at progressively younger ages.

The very high levels of unemployment characteristic of war zones—up to 80 percent—create emotional burdens on young people. In most developing societies teenagers are regarded as adults and are at a developmental stage in which they seek to define their place in adult society. In rural areas young men do this by obtaining land, marrying, and starting a family, all of which are sustainable only with jobs and livelihood opportunities. The ravages of war, however, foreclose or sharply reduce these opportunities, casting many young men into a state of unemployment, idleness, and hopelessness. A youth from Sierra Leone summarized the impact of this situation:

"There is no job facility. You will see educated youths without jobs, just moving around. If at the end of the day that person hears about some rebels, he can join them, just to survive. That is why most of these guys decided to join the rebels, because they were not having jobs. Some were educated, but they decided to join the rebels instead of sitting down and waste their time. That is why most of the youths joined the rebels. That is the major reason. Because of lack of jobs." (Peters 2004, 15)

In addition, teenagers in many developing countries point to their lack of education and training as major life problems. In Sierra Leone lack of access to education sparked the discontent that fueled youths' desire to join the rebel group called the Revolutionary United Front (RUF) and overthrow the government (Richards 1996). Many Sierra Leonean teenagers claim they need training in order to have a positive future and enter adult roles in civilian society (Peters 2004). Citing lack of education as a reason for non-forced recruitment, one youth said:

"Well, it is obvious. Before the war we were attending school, right. But as soon as the war entered Sierra Leone everything went berserk, everything was destroyed. By then there was nothing to do for us, we were just wandering around, without going anywhere. So we decided to join the army because we were doing nothing, except going up and down the area. The school was closed, everything was closed. We were in the barracks and we knew all these things, the movement of the soldiers. Our parents were already there. There was no education, that made us join." (Peters 2004, 20)

By themselves, education and training probably will not allow young people to achieve positive roles and meaning in life. After all, education does not translate into livelihoods if few or no jobs are available. Indeed, high levels of educational attainment can result in severe frustration when no jobs are available following graduation. In addition, although education and training build the capacities for livelihoods, life skills are also needed to enable young people to make use of their training and earn a living.

Teenagers tend to blame the current government for their economic misfortunes, and as the system loses legitimacy, disaffected young people increasingly invest their hopes with a new order, ushered in by revolution (Braungart 1984). Teenagers' radicalization and alienation—and their desire to overthrow an oppressive system that has failed them and denied them opportunities—make them a highly fertile cohort for recruitment into armed groups. In Sierra Leone one sixteen-year-old girl who had been a commander said:

"I'm proud of what I learned—how to speak to groups, organize people, command, use weapons. I never got this from [the] government. How else am I supposed to have a future? If I had it to do again, I'd join again."[1]

In young people's eyes, learning skills is not only about economics but also the ability to find a place in society in the future.

This analysis sheds new light on the "youth bulges" hypothesis, which says that societies are at greater risk of armed conflict if a large percentage of their population is between fifteen and twenty-five years old (e.g., Goldstein 2001). Youth bulges alone do not cause armed conflict but become dangerous when coupled with factors such as high levels of unemployment (see Urdal 2004).

Present economic hardship and a lack of future economic alternatives alienate youth and children from the prevailing order, plant seeds for revolution, and propel children into armed groups. As was true in the French Revolution and even earlier, contemporary armed conflicts are in part fueled by radicalized youth who see no future in the current system and seek to overthrow it. This link indicates the importance of livelihoods for the reintegration of former child soldiers.

Pathway to reintegration

Following armed conflict, most countries initiate a process of disarmament, demobilization, and reintegration (DDR) as a means of standing down opposing armies, building confidence in the peace process, creating a unified national army, and enabling former soldiers to make the transition to civilian life. A central element of most reintegration programs is livelihoods support, an emphasis readily understood in economic and political terms. Without the means to earn a living, young people are likely to return to fighting or banditry to meet their basic needs. As said by one young Sierra Leonean who had joined the RUF at age sixteen:

> "When the war ended, people said we should come out of the bush. But I was not going to come out with no shirt on my back and people looking down on me because I have no shoes. . . . If there was no job and no money, no way would we come out— we would go back to the bush and fight again."

The prevalence of this sentiment in Sierra Leone indicated the need for large-scale DDR programs that included livelihood components. The following case involving the work of Christian Children's Fund (CCF)/Sierra Leone in the Northern Province in 2002 and 2003 illustrates the value of livelihood programs and provides a foundation for analyzing the psychosocial dimensions of livelihood interventions. The narrative research on this project included key informant interviews, focus-group discussions, and interviews with over one hundred former youth soldiers.

Post-conflict Sierra Leone

In January 2002, following the end of a decade-long war that was notorious for its mutilations and mass rapes, the situation was precarious.

The wounds of the war were fresh in people's minds. Over a million displaced people were returning to mostly destroyed villages and living in abject poverty. Local people feared former child soldiers, many of whom had attacked and looted their villages and abused people. One adult in the Northern Province, which was home to the RUF toward the end of the war, said:

> "We used to fear them and thought they would start fighting in our communities. When they came from the bush, we looked at them as animals."

Former child soldiers feared reprisal attacks, and village tensions ran high as former soldiers who had fought on opposite sides returned home.

The combination of stigmatization, fear, and lack of a livelihood left many former child soldiers in doubt over their ability to reintegrate into civilian society. Former boy soldiers wondered how they could find places in their villages and earn money to meet their basic needs and build positive futures. Former girl soldiers, most of whom had been sexually abused and forced to be "bush wives" or sex slaves for their captors, were particularly stigmatized. Having been raped, they were regarded locally as "damaged goods" and unmarriageable. In the view of many Sierra Leonean women, for a woman of marriageable age to be unmarried is tantamount to social death. Also, girl survivors of rape in the bush viewed themselves and were viewed by others as spiritually polluted or unclean (Kostelny 2004). This view, common in many rural areas of sub-Saharan Africa (Honwana 1997; Wessells and Monteiro 2004), led local people to describe the girls as having "unsteady minds" and therefore being unfit to interact fully with family members or to participate in community activities.

Linking stop-gap employment, skills training, and reconciliation

To support the reintegration and peace-building process, CCF/Sierra Leone implemented a DDR program for former youth soldiers in twenty-six communities of Koinadugu, Bombali, and Tonkolili. Districts in the Northern Province were selected because they exhibited high levels of need and had significant numbers of returning former soldiers. The program strategy was to link material improvements and economic recovery with processes of reconciliation and peace building (Wessells and Jonah 2005). Economically, the program engaged former youth soldiers in stop-gap employment, defined as temporary employment aiming to meet urgent needs for income, thereby enabling them to come out of the bush. Subsequently, the former soldiers would receive skills training in areas that could generate income on a sustainable basis. The strategy was also to implement the livelihood activities in ways promoting reconciliation between former soldiers and community members and between former soldiers from previously opposing groups. The program drew on the established social-psychology principle that cooperating to achieve a common goal is an effective means of reducing intergroup conflict (Sherif et al. 1961).

Each community engaged initially in a process of intensive consultation, facilitated by CCF staff, aimed at identifying the main needs of local children and choosing projects that would benefit the children most. Some communities selected the construction of a school or a health post as their project, whereas others elected to rebuild a bridge needed to transport farmers' goods to local markets. CCF supported the project by providing the construction materials and facilitating an inclusive planning process, but communities owned and managed the projects. With the planning and materials procurement under way, CCF staff conducted community psychosocial workshops to reduce child soldiers' stigma and promote reconciliation. These workshops emphasized that children had been exploited by adults and forced to do many things; pointed out the value of young people to the community; supported a discourse of unity; and awakened traditional modes of reconciliation through song, proverb, and dance.

As the time for construction approached, the communities selected work teams to do the building. To avoid benefits for former soldiers only, a problem discussed further below, the work teams consisted of former youth soldiers and civilian youth in a sixty-to-forty ratio. The selection criteria included high level of motivation, ability to do heavy labor, and willingness to stay in the community. Wherever possible, the work teams mixed former members of the RUF with members of the Civilian Defense Forces (CDF), local militias that had fought against the RUF. Following their selection, the work-team members participated in a two-day psychosocial workshop emphasizing reconciliation, putting the past behind, and the value of rekindling traditional systems of reconciliation and forgiveness.

In the construction phase communities implemented ninety-two civic works projects, employing 2,840 former soldiers and 2,160 civilians. Each team member worked for a minimum of twenty days and 160 hours, earning a stipend of 53,000 leones (US$27). Although small by international standards, the stipend enabled them to purchase basic items such as clothing and food. The participants also gained valuable experience regarding the kind of longer-term work they might want to pursue.

Following the completion of the civic-works projects, the participants had the opportunity to participate in skills training under the supervision of master artisans from the local community. The skills had been selected according to a market analysis identifying which activities the local economy would support. Over an eight-month period, participants learned skills such as carpentry, tailoring, gara tie-dying, and soap making, while receiving a monthly stipend of 60,000 leones (US$18). A common error in many livelihood programs is to assume that vocational training alone will prepare people to earn an income. However, skilled workers often fail to sustain an income due to their poor skills in handling money, tracking income and expenditures, and saving. Since most of the trainees in this program were illiterate but wanted to set up their own businesses, the skills training included basic skills of business literacy.

In year one of the program only former youth soldiers participated in the skills training. This practice, however, sparked considerable jealousy, with local people referring to the stipends for former youth soldiers as "blood money." Some former youth soldiers said they suffered reverse stigmatization because they were better off than the village youth whom they had attacked during the war. A nineteen-year-old man in Sierra Leone who had entered the RUF at age sixteen said:

"Because of the DDR, I wore nice shoes and new clothes. I was very grateful because I could never have come out of the bush in the state I was in. But other youth had no nice shoes and clothes. I became stigmatized for a different reason."

To correct this problem, subsequent phases of the program opened the skills training to civilian youth. This revision, which quieted local jealousies, led to equal participation by the two groups in year two of the program. In all, a total of 1,130 people participated in the skills training.

Microcredit and business activities

To enable the recipients of the skills training to start their own businesses, the program offered a microcredit loan and payback option to people who were selected according to criteria such as high levels of motivation and being trusted by others. Small solidarity groups of three to ten people who each agreed to be accountable for the others received an initial loan of 120,000 leones (US$60), which was to be repaid together with a small service fee over a six-month period. Loans were used to purchase capital items such as farming tools, sewing materials, fabric for dyeing, or other items for a small business. Successful repayment qualified groups for larger loans subsequently. CCF staff provided ongoing support and advice in regard to the participants' business activities.

Over the course of the project, 817 solidarity groups received loans. Remarkably, the loan repayment rate was 99 percent, which contrasts starkly with frequently heard comments in the field that soldiers are a bad investment for microcredit programs. The combination of mentoring by older master artisans, business training, and continuing staff support, along with the young people's determination to earn a living, probably contributed to the high repayment rates.

For former girl soldiers special steps were required to enable participation in skills training and business activity. To address their perceived spiritual contamination, CCF staff worked with traditional healers, who performed group cleansing rituals to undo the contamination (Kostelny 2004). Following the rituals, community members said it was safe to interact with the girls, and the girls, too, said they felt free to integrate with others. Also, local communities formed reconciliation committees that raised awareness of the need for tolerance, educated people about the girls' situations, and set rules against harassment. As a result, girls had relatively high levels of participation in both the skills training and income-generating activities. Of the 4,580 people who benefited from the income-generating activities, 2,567 were girls.

Program impacts

Youths' narratives consistently indicated the positive impact of their access to livelihoods as a result of the program. A former youth soldier who had joined the CDF at age fifteen said:

> "I fought with the CDF for eight years and believed all they told me. After the ceasefire, I had no gun and got no package [he did not qualify for the government benefits for former soldiers since he had no automatic weapon to turn in]. Now we are presentable and can survive. . . . Before we had only cassava, but now we have rice—this makes us believe in peace."

The powerful impact the access to livelihoods had on girls is visible in three testimonies, which were characteristic of the larger group:

> "I was called *kolonko* [prostitute] before. Now I am respected and held in high regard in my village because of my business accomplishments. I can buy food. I save money in my cash box."

> "We had been ashamed of what had been done to us. We arrived naked from the bush, without any means of support. Now we are respected members of the community."

> "In the bush we had not been treated as human. We ate anything . . . even dogs if we could find them. When we returned, we kept to ourselves because we were ashamed. But now I can mingle with everyone. I have respect because of my business." (Kostelny 2004, 511)

For these girls, having an income conferred not only purchasing power but also prestige and a powerful boost in self-esteem. If cleansing enabled them to reenter the social arena, having cash gave them status and a positive place in their villages. Some girls even reported being sought after as marriage partners due to their business success.

The program also enjoyed wider successes in regard to peace building. Having access to immediate income and livelihoods, most former youth soldiers came out of the bush, surrendered their weapons, and stayed in their communities. The program also succeeded in decreasing the stigmatization of former youth soldiers and in reconciling them with their communities. Former soldiers commented that they had come to see former opposing soldiers as human beings like themselves. This provided a welcome contrast with the dehumanizing images harbored previously on both sides. By the end of the program, community members said consistently that they saw the former soldiers not as troublemakers but as citizens having much to contribute to their communities.

The program also had a discernible impact on bringing communities into the peace process. Before the program many local people regarded peace as remote, despite the signing of the ceasefire. As one elder put it, "We were hungry before the war. We were hungry during the war. And now we are still hungry." Feeling excluded and abandoned by their government and denied basic necessities such as food and clean water, local people regarded terms such as *peace* and *reconciliation* as hollow unless accompanied by tangible, physical improvements in their lives. The material improvements achieved through the civic-works projects and the reestablishment of trade—and youths' participation in them—elevated the hopes of many community members, helping them believe peace was at hand. Overall, this program illustrates the centrality of livelihood in the reintegration of former child soldiers. Also, it points out the benefits of interweaving livelihood and psychosocial supports in a manner conducive to reconciliation.

Livelihood and psychosocial supports

In the humanitarian world livelihood and psychosocial interventions have coexisted as separate sectors, having little dialogue or cross-fertilization. This separation owes its existence in no small part to the fact that economists, the main architects of livelihood interventions, and psychologists, the principal architects of psychosocial interventions, typically have little contact or conceptual discourse and espouse very different theories. Fortunately, at field level, generalist practitioners cross the lines, exploring the intersections of livelihood and psychosocial supports. This section analyzes the rich interconnections between livelihood support and psychosocial support, which have not been outlined explicitly in the psychosocial literature but have significant implications for practice. It outlines how practice may be strengthened by intentionally designing programs exploiting synergies and building upon the complementary intersections of psychosocial and livelihood supports.

Livelihood supports contribute to psychosocial well-being

Although Western-trained psychologists frequently conceptualize psychosocial support in terms of counseling or related activities, a field perspective urges a more holistic, locally grounded approach. To begin with, lack of an income is one of the main sources of stress and suffering for former child soldiers. Analyzing the reactions of former child soldiers, Western-trained psychologists tend to emphasize issues such as trauma and post traumatic stress disorder associated with the experience of violence and life-threatening events. In contrast, much evidence from field settings indicates that for many former child soldiers, the greatest psychosocial impact comes not from the emotional residues of past violence but from current life stresses (McCallin 1998; Wessells, forthcoming), not least of which is lack of disposable income.

A sad illustration of this can be seen in the story of a girl from Sierra Leone who was abducted by the RUF at age twelve. She had been forced to carry heavy loads, was raped by her captor, and was forced to be his "bush wife." She also contracted HIV/AIDS, became pregnant, and transmitted the disease to her baby. Describing what she regarded as her biggest source of stress, she said: "Now I have AIDS and my baby too. . . . I'm too poor to buy medicine. . . . What will happen to me and my baby?" For this girl, economic problems created profound psychosocial stresses related to poor health, inability to care properly for her baby, and hopelessness. Her anguish over her poverty and her inability to fulfill her maternal role suggests the traumatic past is a less potent psychosocial issue than the economic stresses of her current living situation (see Bracken and Petty 1998), a point frequently overlooked by excessively clinical approaches.

To assist such girls, psychosocial support programs should include livelihood supports to relieve economic stresses. In fact, the provision of livelihood support is part of holistic psychosocial assistance. Since psychosocial well-being has many dimensions (Ahearn 2000; Dawes and Donald 1994; Williamson and Robinson 2006)—physical, cognitive, emotional, social, and spiritual—it can be improved in part through livelihood supports enabling physical and material well-being. In regard to the girl survivors of sexual violence in Sierra Leone, livelihood supports provided self-confidence and hope—and also increased protection by reducing their need to earn money through prostitution. These apparently individual effects were socially mediated, as outlined below.

Livelihood interventions have strong psychosocial impact, in part by changing people's social roles, status, and identity. For former child soldiers, having an income enables them to enter and to succeed in normal civilian roles such as husband, wife, mother, and worker. To take on such roles is to become functional in civilian life and to be seen as a responsible citizen rather than a troublemaker or misfit.

Effects on social identity and deportment

Having a positive social role not only gives a former soldier a sense of place in civilian society but also defines expected behaviors and attitudes, producing changes in social identity. To live as a mother, father, or worker requires civilian deportment and attitudes quite at odds with life as a soldier, where military swagger and aggressive behavior are acceptable. As former child soldiers perform civilian roles, they undergo changes in identity, which are fluid, constructed by situation, and constituted by multiple elements, any one of which may become active in a particular context. During the reintegration process former child soldiers begin to see themselves as civilians and to define their future in those terms. Community members, too, come to see the children as civilians and treat them with respect rather than fear or contempt. The views of others carry enormous weight in most developing countries, which tend to have collectivist views, defining *self* not as an autonomous individual but in terms of social relations and the groups one functions within (Triandis 2001). As former child soldiers redefine themselves as civilians, they become even more likely to continue in their nonmilitary social roles, progressively assimilating themselves into civilian life.

Effects on healing and reconciliation

Livelihoods also contribute to psychosocial processes of healing and reconciliation. Conceived broadly, healing is not only an individual process of coming to terms with painful experiences but also a social process. In collectivist societies healing is not something occurring "between one's ears" so much as it is a process of improving formerly damaged social relations such as those between a child soldier and the village he had attacked and looted. Livelihood supports have strong psychosocial impact by enabling former soldiers to enter new social roles and improve their family and community relations. In this respect community reconciliation is an integral part of the healing process rather than a separate element of peace building. Also, war-related stresses are communal, since communities experience the shattering of their infrastructures, public spaces, and practices that confer a sense of meaning and continuity. Appropriately designed livelihood supports can mitigate these stresses and enable the physical rebuilding and tangible communal improvements needed to give people a sense of recovery and hope (Wessells and Monteiro 2001).

Livelihood supports are also a vital component of reconciliation processes. Although empathy with and removal of stigmatization from former child soldiers were influential in the case of Sierra Leone, these processes alone cannot reconcile former child soldiers and communities. Lasting reconciliation and reintegration occur when local communities see young former soldiers earning a living and filling social roles, supporting family and community well-being. Dialogue alone will not bring peace to villages bearing the scars of political exclusion and harsh living conditions. People whose difficult life conditions are reminders and embodiments of the war system need to see material improvements and to have hopes of economic development. In these respects livelihoods are not only economic supports but are vital supports for reconciliation and peace building.

Toward an integrated approach to livelihood supports

Just as livelihoods complement psychosocial supports, so too can psychosocial supports enhance the impact of livelihood activities. In the Sierra Leone case study livelihood supports were important for economic reasons but achieved added value by being implemented in ways conducive to reconciliation. Similarly, the livelihood interventions with former girl soldiers gained traction when coupled with purification rituals designed to steady the girls' minds and rid them of spiritual pollution. These examples illustrate the value of interweaving livelihood and psychosocial supports. They also remind us that psychosocial assistance consists not only of stand-alone programs but also of integrated programs in which efforts related to livelihoods or even health and water/sanitation include psychosocial dimensions.

In the reintegration of former child soldiers a more thorough blending of psychosocial dimensions into livelihood programs is clearly warranted as a means of adhering to the "do no harm" principle. The literature on child soldiers is replete with evidence of the damage done through inattention to psychosocial dimensions. For example, the recent DDR program in Liberia extended cash payments meant as livelihood support for former child soldiers (CSC 2004). However, this practice privileges child soldiers and creates divisive jealousies at the village level just when social unity is needed most. Moreover, commanders tend to extort the money from the children, using it to recruit additional child soldiers (Wessells, forthcoming). Similarly, many DDR programs that include livelihood supports have discriminated against girls (McKay and Mazurana 2004). Also, programs too often enable former child soldiers to earn a living without probing whether they are likely to squander their profits on alcohol or other substances for abuse.

In assisting war-affected children, vertical or single-sector programs should give way to a new generation of integrated programs designed to build on inter-sectoral synergies. By integrating livelihood supports, psychosocial programs can become more comprehensive and address more effectively the holistic impacts of war. When livelihood supports are organized to protect the most vulnerable people, they contribute to protection in ways that strengthen psychosocial well-being. Conversely, by integrating psychosocial dimensions, livelihood programs can achieve greater impact and avoid causing unintended harm. The integration of psychosocial dimensions into livelihood programs, then, constitutes an important future direction for the enrichment of practice. Our success will be gauged by the voices of future generations of war-affected children.

Note

[1] Unless otherwise attributed, quotations from Sierra Leone youth are taken from my research.

References

Ahearn, F., ed. 2000. *Psychosocial wellness of refugees.* New York: Berghahn.

Bracken, P., and C. Petty, eds. 1998. *Rethinking the trauma of war.* London: Free Association Books.

Braungart, R. 1984. Historical and generational patterns of youth movements: A global perspective. *Comparative Social Research* 7 (1): 3–62.

Brett, R., and I. Specht. 2004. *Young soldiers: Why they choose to fight.* Boulder, CO: Lynne Rienner.

Brett, R., and M. McCallin. 1996. *Children: The invisible soldiers.* Vaxjo: Radda Barnen.

CSC (Coalition to Stop the Use of Child Soldiers). 2004. *Child soldiers global report 2004.* London: CSC.

Dawes, A., and D. Donald. 1994. *Childhood and adversity: Psychological perspectives from South African research.* Cape Town: David Philip.

Goldstein, J. 2001. Demography, environment, and security. In *Environmental conflict*, ed. P. Diehl and N. P. Gleiditsch, 84–108. Boulder, CO: Westview.

Honwana, A. 1997. Healing for peace: Traditional healers and post-war reconstruction in Southern Mozambique. *Peace and Conflict: Journal of Peace Psychology* 3 (3): 293–305.

HRW (Human Rights Watch). 2003. *You'll learn not to cry: Child combatants in Colombia.* New York: HRW.

———. 2004. *How to fight, how to kill: Child soldiers in Liberia.* New York: HRW.

———. 2005. *Youth, poverty and blood: The lethal legacy of West Africa's regional warriors.* New York: HRW.

Kostelny, K. 2004. What about the girls? *Cornell International Law Journal* 37 (3): 505–12.

Machel, G. 2001. *The impact of war on children.* London: Hurst and Company.

McCallin, M. 1998. Community involvement in the social reintegration of former child soldiers. In Bracken and Petty, *Rethinking the trauma of war,* 60–75.

McKay, S., and D. Mazurana. 2004. *Where are the girls? Girls in fighting forces in Northern Uganda, Sierra Leone, and Mozambique: Their lives during and after war.* Montreal: International Centre for Human Rights and Democratic Development.

Peters, K. 2004. *Re-examining volunteerism: Youth combatants in Sierra Leone.* Monograph no. 100. Pretoria: Institute for Security Studies.

Richards, P. 1996. *Fighting for the rain forest: War, youth, and resources in Sierra Leone.* Oxford: International Africa Institute.

Sherif, M., O. Harvey, B. White, W. Hood, and C. Sherif. 1961. *Intergroup cooperation and competition: The Robbers Cave experiment.* Norman, OK: Univ. Book Exchange.

Singer, P. 2005. *Children at war.* New York: Pantheon.

Triandis, H. 2001. Individualism and collectivism: Past, present, and future. In *The handbook of culture and psychology,* ed. D. Matsumoto, 35–50. New York: Oxford Univ. Press.

UNICEF. 2003. *Adult wars, child soldiers: Voices of children involved in armed conflict in the East Asia and Pacific region.* Bangkok: UNICEF.

Urdal, H. 2004. *The devil in the demographics: The effect of youth bulges on domestic armed conflict, 1950–2000.* Social Development Papers 14. Washington, DC: World Bank.

Wessells, M. G. 2002. Recruitment of children as soldiers in sub-Saharan Africa: An ecological analysis. In *The comparative study of conscription in the armed forces,* Comparative Social Research 20, ed. L. Mjoset and S. Van Holde, 237–54. Amsterdam: Elsevier.

———. Forthcoming. *Child soldiers: From violence to protection.* Cambridge, MA: Harvard Univ. Press.

Wessells, M. G., and D. Jonah. 2005. Reintegration of former youth soldiers in Sierra Leone: Challenges of reconciliation and post-accord peacebuilding. In *Youth and post-accord peacebuilding,* ed. S. McEvoy-Levy, 27–47. Notre Dame, IN: Univ. of Notre Dame Press.

Wessells, M. G., and C. Monteiro. 2001. Psychosocial interventions and post-war reconstruction in Angola: Interweaving Western and traditional approaches. In *Peace, conflict, and violence: Peace psychology for the 21st century,* ed. D. Christie, R. V. Wagner, and D. Winter, 262–75. Upper Saddle River, NJ: Prentice-Hall.

———. 2004. Psychosocial assistance to internally displaced people in Angola: A child focused, community-based approach. In *Refugee mental health: Ecological approaches to adaptation and recovery,* ed. K. Miller and L. Rasco, 67–94. Upper Saddle River, NJ: Erlbaum.

Williamson, J., and M. Robinson. 2006. Psychosocial interventions, or integrated programming for well-being? *Intervention* 4 (1): 4–25.

9

RELIGION AS RESOURCE AND RISK

The double-edged sword for children in situations of armed conflict

Michael Wessells and Alison Strang

Introduction

The human story is in no small part a story about people's quest for meaning. At the heart of the search for meaning is religion, defined broadly to include spiritual beliefs and practices and also religious institutions such as the church, the temple, or the mosque. Through religion, many people find answers to questions such as, Is there a supreme Being? Why are we here? Is there an afterlife? Why do people suffer? Is there justice? and What is the right way to live? Religion not only provides a sense of place in the cosmos but also offers moral guidance and practices that provide a higher sense of purpose, spiritual fulfillment, deliverance from suffering, and a means of achieving redemption and salvation.

Religion is a central part of people's culture and identity, and it has discernible positive impacts on children's lives (Coles 1991). Among Palestinian children, Islamic faith is a significant source of psychosocial well-being (Barber 2001). In Timor Leste (formerly East Timor), following the brutal attacks by Indonesian paramilitaries in 1999,

Catholic children reported that their faith had gotten them through difficult times. Religion is also a source of peace; many religious leaders encourage youth to pursue peace and to help end social injustice and promote reconciliation. In these respects religion is a positive feature of children's social ecologies, a macro-level layer above family and community.

However, religion is a source of hatred and violence as well as of love and peace. Some have argued that violence is intrinsic to religion, manifesting itself in the requirement for blood sacrifice for atonement or appeasement of a divine being or beings (Hall 2003). Whatever the validity of this claim, historically religion has been a major source of war and continues today to inflame bloody conflicts between Hindus and Muslims in India, Jews and Muslims in the Middle East, and Sunnis and Shiites in Iraq, to name only a few. Children suffer disproportionately in war owing to their special vulnerabilities (Machel 2001). They also become engaged as warriors who continue cycles of violence. The Crusades included children who wanted to fight against the infidel (Boothby and Knudsen 2000), just as in contemporary Palestine, Muslim youth fight Jewish troops and settlers they view as infidels who seek to dominate Muslim peoples (Rosen 2005). Children's participation in armed conflict exacts an enormous toll of physical, psychological, and social damage on children, not to mention their families, communities, and societies (Machel 2001; Wessells, forthcoming a). Also, religion animates terrorist actions viewed by perpetrators as divinely sanctioned religious struggles (Juergensmeyer 2003; Silberman 2005; Stern 2003). So prominent is religion as a source of conflict that some analysts have claimed that Islam versus the West defines the main fault lines along which contemporary global violence occurs (Huntington 2003; Lewis 2003).

Because religion is a double-edged sword, it is vital to avoid a polarized view of religion as either a wholly positive or a wholly negative influence on children's development and well-being. This chapter unearths the complexity of the relation between religion and children's well-being. The first section analyzes religious influences as highly contextual and owing extensively to local leadership, political ideology, and influences of the state and other vested power structures. Next we consider how religion supports children, advancing their spiritual life and coping under difficult circumstances. We then examine how religion can cause harm to children through, for example, supporting warrior identities and youth participation in organized violence. The chapter ends with a reflection on the implications for humanitarian practice.

Religion in the social context

Religion has been a contested issue in social science less because of concerns over the veracity of religious beliefs than because of the question of how to think of religion. Whereas some religious scholars have argued that religion transcends science, others have sought to bring religion into the house of social science, examining how it shapes beliefs, values, actions, and social systems. The latter view resonates with our perspective.

However, significant analytical questions remain. For example, is religious faith a cause unto itself or does its contribution to violence, suffering, or well-being depend on its interaction with historical, economic, and political factors, among others? Taking a multidisciplinary approach, this section suggests that religion is thoroughly interwoven with issues of social identity, political context, and power, cautioning against attempts to think of religion in isolated terms or as an unvarying universal. In the real world, religion exhibits the malleability, intermixing, and dynamism observable in other aspects of culture.

Social identity, ideology, and the radicalization of religion

All the great religions of the world espouse the value of peace and offer venues for individual and collective spiritual enlightenment. If the most dominant religions counsel peace, why, one might ask, is the world racked by so many wars, including wars having religious roots?

The short answer is that religion exists not in a vacuum but in a complex social context having diverse actors, political agendas, power brokers, and situations that individually or collectively may transform religion into an extreme, politicized instrument of war, hatred, and oppression. Even without going as far as Durkheim, who argued that religion is essentially and only an expression of social power (Durkheim 1912), religious beliefs exist in a system of vested power in which the church or the mosque, for example, wield considerable influence over believers' actions and are in turn shaped by political forces. In Catholicism, the church, with its powerful institutions such as the Vatican and actors such as the pope and cardinals, shapes beliefs through religious teachings and calls to action. Religious leaders do not exist apart from politics but are part of the global political system.

Although this linkage of religion and politics is perhaps most conspicuous in theocracies, history is replete with examples of linkages between religion and politics. In contemporary conflicts, religion and politics are integrated enough to make it difficult to discern where one ends and the other begins. A case in point is the conflict in Northern Ireland, which, although it is often described as a religious conflict between Catholics and Protestants, is as much about historical grievances, social injustices, and issues of class and ethnicity as about religion (Cairns and Darby 1998).

As conflicts heat up, religious issues often come to the fore, setting the stage for the rise of more radical forms of religion. Radicalized forms of Christianity or Islam may call for believers to fight in order to purge the infidel, protect their religion, and achieve battlefield glory as a means of honoring their maker or achieving redemption for sin. Indeed, extremist religious leaders can pull people away from traditional forms of Christianity or Islam, rallying them into a radicalized form of religion that teaches that war is necessary, other religions are evil and must be resisted forcefully, and religious warriors, whether on a Crusade or a Jihad, will harvest divine rewards. Recognizing the power of religion to mobilize the masses for war, leaders often use religion in pursuit of their political aims. An important question, however, is why extremist forms of religion capture the public imagination. After all, radical leaders do not act in a vacuum; they achieve influence only if people back them. The answer is to be found in the intersection of social identity theory, political and social injustices, enemy imaging, and political ideology.

Many contemporary conflicts have been called identity conflicts because they arise not only out of competition over scarce resources (Klare 2001) but also out of threats to collective identity (Fisher 1997). Religion is a central element in people's social identities. It helps to answer the fundamental psychological issue, Who am I?, and provides a sense of place and meaning in the world (Tajfel and Turner 1986; Taylor and Louis 2004). In many situations people define themselves partly in religious terms, saying, "I am a Buddhist," or, "I am a

Muslim," although they may also define themselves by other markers such as their profession, nationality, or family of origin.

Although religious aspects of social identity do not in themselves cause conflict, they become potent sources of conflict when members of one's identity group are threatened. A vicious cycle can become established when a community feels its identity is threatened and responds by increasingly defining itself it terms that emphasize its difference from others, thus increasing the risks of isolation, discrimination, and deprivation. This has been seen in recent years in the United Kingdom, where an analysis of the race riots of 2001 suggested that communities of different religious and ethnic origin—while living in close geographic proximity—had developed as isolated social "silos" (Community Cohesion Unit 2003). The lack of integration led communities to feel that their culture and beliefs were threatened and to increasingly define their identity in terms that distinguished rather than linked them with their neighbors. As a result, tensions associated with mounting economic and social deprivation lead to blame of "others" and eventually erupted in prolonged street violence.

When injustices such as discrimination, deprivation, attack, detainment, or torture are directed toward a member of an identity group, the other members of the group also experience a sense of collective threat and victimization. Identity threats also arise from perceived or actual erosion of the group's core values, through, for example, the influx of infidels bringing values antithetical to local religious practices. Identity threats at once spark fear and the desire to protect oneself and one's group and heighten the sense of victimization, warranting action.

If one's identity group has been victimized by people from other religions, religion becomes a salient factor in the conflict. As religion becomes prominent, multiple factors come into play that amplify and prolong the conflict. First, people increasingly define themselves, for example, as "I am a Muslim," or "I am a Jew," thereby downplaying other aspects of social identity (such as "I am a parent," or "I am a teacher") in which common ground might have been found. Second, each religious community clings tightly to its sense of victimization, spreading memories of "chosen traumas" such as massacres or attacks by the other (Volkan 1997). These communal memories serve as conduits through which senior generations pass on their fear and hatred to younger generations, who are expected to carry the struggle forward. Third, social polarization increases, making it less likely that members of rival religious groups will have direct, positive contact (Rubin, Pruitt, and Kim 1994). As relationships beyond the group weaken, relationships within the group intensify, increasing internal dependence and reducing the opportunity for external reference. This provides a potent breeding ground for radicalization.

Fourth, and perhaps most important, radical religious leaders and groups sprout up, calling for the faithful to use violence to deal with the adversary and even portraying fighting as a divine duty. People experiencing identity threats and injustice are frequently drawn to extremist ideologies in an effort to make meaning out of an otherwise confusing situation and to rally with others against external threats. Extremist ideologies, visible in politically reconstructed forms of the religion having little to do with the religion per se, typically define the world in apocalyptic terms of good and evil, stirring people to fight against perceived or real enemies.

Supporting these processes is "enemy imaging," the tendency to go beyond objective enmity and portray the adversary as demonic, savage, and inhumane (Rieber 1991; Silverstein 1989; White 1984). Psychologically, dehumanized images of the "other" ignite fear, provide a subjective warrant for fighting lest that "evil other" prevail, and rationalize killings and atrocities. After all, if adversaries are sub-human, why should one experience moral qualms about killing them? In extreme conflicts, members of the "out group" are psychologically excluded from the moral universe (Opotow 1990; Waller 2002), making it possible to do horrible things to them. The commission of atrocities on both sides only cements the view of the "other" as implacably evil, stirring additional fears, identity threats, and cycles of violence.

Over time, these toxic psychological processes and the continuation of violence provide conditions ripe for further radicalization of religion. As has occurred in the Middle East and in other conflicts, extremist religious groups garner considerable political power and support political agendas such as war or increased autonomy, if not independence. In this manner religions become thoroughly politicized, lending the veneer of normality to extreme forms that had previously been unthinkable because they are so thoroughly at odds with the religious canon. As discussed below, many youth become willing agents of war through their engagement with radicalized forms of religion.

Children, families, and communities

For children, religion is a key point of intersection with important social ecologies such as the family and community. If religion is part of an intergenerational meaning system providing a sense of continuity across generations, it is also an important gateway to traditions, a means of bringing children fully into the social world and integrating them into their family, community, and society. Early in life many families give or expose children to religious instruction intended to impart the values, spiritual enlightenment, and perceived source of salvation that the family has enjoyed over the generations. For children, being a member of a particular family means acquiring its values, beliefs, and traditions, which occurs in no small part through exposure to religion. That one becomes a full member of the family by acquiring its religious traditions is evident in the importance many families attach to rite-of-passage rituals such as the bar mitzvah in Judaism or confirmation in Catholicism, not to mention marriage rituals conducted according to the dictates of particular faiths.

The mosque, church, or temple often provides children's first point of contact with the community beyond their immediate neighbors and with wider social institutions. There, children learn not only religion but also important lessons about morals, social behavior, and their own value as human beings. They also learn subtle messages about whether the world is a safe place, how to be a good person, and what their responsibilities are as members of a religious group. Their developing religious identity becomes part of the wider, collective identity that binds children and adults together into a people having a sense of collective meaning and place in the world.

Religious faith, stress, and basic psychological needs

We have seen how religion can interact with social identity and power at the macro level leading to radicalization and politicization, making children more vulnerable to violence and conflict. We have also highlighted the central role religion plays in societal processes of children's acculturization and socialization. Psychologists would argue that the tensions between vulnerability and resilience are also reflected in the micro world of the experiences of the individual. For example, Staub suggests that "cultural and societal conditions that frustrate basic psychological needs make violence more likely, whereas conditions that help fulfill these needs in constructive ways contribute to the development of peaceful relations" (Staub 2003, 1). He suggests that people have fundamental needs for security, a positive identity, a sense of effectiveness, positive connection to other people, autonomy, a comprehension of reality, and transcendence—to go beyond the self. It is the fulfillment of these needs that provides a basis from which the individual and the community are able to contribute to a culture of caring and peace. However, where these needs are frustrated, there is an increased vulnerability both to the negative psychological impact of violence and to extremist religious and political ideologies that invite participation in violence.

At the micro level, religious faith and practice is a double-edged sword; it can either increase children's vulnerability to violence or serve as a powerful resource to children, their parents, and the communities in which they live. Karl Marx suggested that religion "is the opium of the people," arguing that religious faith gives people an illusion of experience that protects or prevents them from experiencing the painful realities of their material lives (Marx 1844). Since then, Western psychologists have sought to explore the nature of the relationship among religion, health, and other measures of well-being using scientific methods. Meta-analyses of survey studies consistently report that religious faith and practice are linked with a range of positive measures of physical health, mental health, and even happiness (Beit-Hallahmi and Argyle 1997; Barnes et al. 2000; Koenig, McCullough, and Larson 2001). In the West, where most of these studies have been conducted, people of religious faith and practice generally experience higher levels of health and happiness than their nonreligious counterparts.

What factors create this link? Is it simply a question of denial of reality, as the opium analogy might imply? Religion certainly offers alternative ways of constructing meaning, of interpreting our experiences of the reality around us. Sometimes these calm and console, but images of vengeful, angry gods may also stir discomfort and action.

Models of coping borrowed from therapeutic practice offer a way of exploring the link between religion and well-being. Coping with stress can be understood in terms of three factors: the nature of the stressors experienced, attitudes and cognitive appraisal, and coping resources and behaviors (Koenig, McCullough, and Larson 2001). Our discussion above has suggested some of the complex social interactions through which religion influences children's exposure to stress. The following discussion explores how religion influences children's understandings—the ways in which they appraise the circumstances—and the extent to which these represent risk or protection. We then discuss the resources made available to children through their religious affiliations.

Religion is not only associated with certain beliefs, but also with particular practices and patterns of behavior, such as prayer or meditation, which themselves provide a protective effect. Most of the main religions encourage followers to look after their physical well-being, use their talents to help themselves and others, and maintain good relations with their neighbors. All these patterns of behavior promote good mental and physical health. Finally, psychologists have observed that religious affiliation influences the extent and nature of people's social connections, providing them with a sense of belonging, identity, and people to whom they can turn for support and advice.

Sources of Coping and Protection

As children become acculturated into their religion, they acquire valuable sources of coping with adversity and of protection in difficult circumstances. As outlined below, it is not the beliefs alone but also the practices and social networks that make religion a potentially powerful resource for children in war zones.

Beliefs

Like adults, children are active makers of meaning for whom religion offers a venue for developing spiritual dimensions (Coles 1991) and actively engaging with adversity. Research has shown consistently that children are not passive recipients whom war affects in a linear, billiard-ball model; rather, they are active in interpreting and engaging with their war experiences (Cairns 1996; Eyber and Ager 2004; Garbarino, Kostelny, and Dubrow 1991; Nordstrom 1999; Wessells, forthcoming a). Questions of veracity notwithstanding, religious beliefs offer enormous resources for coping with the vicissitudes of life in war zones. Religious beliefs may be a special means of coping because they are viewed as divinely sanctioned (Pargament, Magyar-Russell, and Murray-Swank 2005).

The unique advantages of religious beliefs as coping mechanisms are visible in the cognitive appraisals children and adults make regarding stressful situations. According to the cognitive-phenomenological model of coping (Lazarus and Folkman 1984), people cope with stressful experiences by making cognitive appraisals of what is personally stressful and then taking steps to manage or regulate their stress through actions such as seeking social support from adults or peers, avoiding thinking about negative events, praying, or reducing the sources of stress through problem-solving activity. Religious beliefs offer a means of making positive appraisals that contribute to the fulfillment of basic psychological needs. A sense of security is restored by appealing to the belief that a wise and benevolent Being is in control (Beit-Hallahmi and Argyle 1997). Appraisals such as "I know God has a reason why all this is happening to me" or "God is testing me through this situation" provide meaning for events and experiences that may otherwise seem unintelligible or random. People find meaning in suffering, which may even be seen as an opportunity for growth or redemption (Pargament, Magyar-Russell, and Murray-Swank 1997; Park 2005). They also may be able to protect their own positive identity by gaining freedom and absolution from the guilt either of committing atrocities or of failing to protect others from violence.

As Koenig, McCullough, and Larson suggest, the religious world view is likely to make the world seem like a friendly place (2001). It is difficult to overestimate the sense of emotional support derived from the belief that one is being watched over by a supreme Being who offers eternal love and salvation. Religion is typically a source of optimism through the promise of transcendence, because the faithful are promised a better life or eternal rewards beyond this life. Even in the face of death, believers take comfort in knowing they and those they love will enter an afterlife promising pleasures unattainable in their present lives. Arguably, the pain of other losses, whether material or emotional, is lessened when a person's sense of identity is rooted in the world of the spiritual rather than the temporal: "I am still a child of God even though I have lost my home, my family, and my community."

The benefits of religious faith are conspicuous among children in war zones. In Afghanistan, following the defeat of the Taliban in 2001, Wessells asked many children what had helped them endure the hardships experienced during the Mujaheddin period and the Taliban era. Children, like adults, reported that their faith had given them strength.

This anecdotal evidence fits with an expanding body of literature attesting to the protective effects of religion. Barber, for example, reported that negative Intifada experiences of the kind one would expect to produce adverse psychological effects on children had few negative effects on highly religious Palestinian children during the first Intifada. Barber concluded that "meaning is the most likely explanation for the absence of widespread negative experiences associated with a history of political violence," where the meaning is religiously derived (Barber 2001, 276). Complementing this observation is Punamaki's report that Israeli youth having strong ideological commitments showed no increase in anxiety and depression following exposure to political violence, whereas youth who lacked such ideological commitments did (Punamaki 1996). This is consistent with the literature that suggests that moral courage is strengthened by the belief that one's actions are approved of by God (Staub 2003). Although extensive evidence suggests that exposure to political violence can have adverse psychological effects on children and adolescents (e.g., Apfel and Simon 1996; Cairns 1996; Dawes and Donald 1994; Dyregov, Gjested, and Raundalen 2002; Garbarino and Kostelny 1996; Somasunandaram and Jamunanantha 2002; Yule et al. 2003), religious belief and other forms of ideology can protect children and support their resilience.

Even children who actively participate in political violence experience the protective effects of ideology. For example, Straker reported that South African youth who had participated in the anti-apartheid struggle and who had committed and experienced severe violence were remarkably normal in their psychological functioning and retained a sophisticated sense of morality (Straker 1992). This was particularly remarkable in the case of those children who displayed internalized belief systems that were not dependent on the approval of the group. This reflects a relationship between internalized belief systems and low levels of anxiety and depression reported in a number of studies (cited in Beit-Hallahmi and Argyle 1997). Research on child soldiers in many other countries also attests to the protective effects of ideology (Boyden 2003; Wessells, forthcoming a). This is not to deny the extensive psychological damage that can result from participation in armed conflict (see, e.g., Derluyn et al. 2004; Machel 2001) but to appreciate that in ideologically based conflicts youth may experience a sense of meaning through their participation in violence, a point developed further below. This sense of meaning has protective value. Overall, then, religious beliefs can be a valuable source of psychosocial support and a significant protective factor for children facing the hardships associated with war.

Practices and behavior

If religious beliefs offer a potent source of cognitive appraisals, they also point toward practices such as prayer and seeking the counsel of other believers. The power of religion as a coping device owes to this ability to simultaneously render stressful events intelligible and to point people to specific actions useful in restoring a sense of well-being.

Religion offers psychosocial support for people under stress by giving them specific activities for actively coping with their losses and stresses. For example, one of the primary means through which people cope with losses, even amid armed conflict, is by conducting religiously prescribed burial rituals (Batniji, van Ommeren, and Saraceno, forthcoming). Often, children see the completion of such rituals as essential for their psychosocial well-being. If funeral rites are important to people in industrial societies, they are particularly important in developing societies, in which spirituality is at the center of life and people understand their well-being as dependent on harmony with the ancestors, who, when honored through the practice of traditions, offer protection. During the recently ended Angolan wars, an eleven-year-old girl whose village had been attacked and whose parents had been killed reported her greatest stress was her inability to perform the appropriate burial ritual for her parents (Wessells and Monteiro 2004). According to the local beliefs, the failure to conduct the rituals made it impossible for her parents' spirits to move on to the realm of the ancestors, leaving the spirits in an upset state in which they might harm the living by causing crop failures or bad health. In situations of genocide and mass displacement, both children and adults often say their biggest stress was not the trauma but their inability to conduct the culturally scripted rites believed necessary for maintaining spiritual harmony and retaining the ancestors' protection. In countries such as Kosovo and Guatemala, mass exhumations are a key component of psychosocial support, both because they provide closure regarding the fate of people's loved ones and because recovery of the body enables the relatives to conduct the appropriate burial rite.

Many other kinds of religious and spiritual rituals and practices also contribute to children's well-being. In many parts of sub-Saharan Africa the transition into adulthood is marked by a rite of passage, typically conducted around fourteen years of age, having spiritual components. Successful completion of the rite of passage is necessary for entry into the socially prescribed roles for young women and men, respectively. To have completed the rite is to achieve a higher social status and to be in a position to marry, to own land, and to enjoy the positive social relations that help to define identity in a collectivist society (Triandis 2001). In contrast, not completing the rite of passage can mark young people as outcasts, make them unmarriageable, or consign them to a social limbo in which they enjoy neither the protection afforded to most children nor the prestige and options extended to most adults.

For former child combatants, effective reintegration and recovery in some contexts requires completion of appropriate rituals believed to purge angry spirits and impurities associated with death and killing (Honwana 1997; Honwana 1998; Wessells and Monteiro 2004; Wessells, forthcoming a). In the absence of these rituals former child soldiers are regarded not only as troublemakers but also as spiritually polluted people whose entry into the community could cause famine, misfortune, or additional fighting. The performance of a ritual of purification by appropriate local healers is believed to drive the angry spirits away, making the children acceptable for reentry into the community. This spiritual reconciliation is an important form of psychosocial support in the sub-Saharan context.

Aside from burial rites and cleansing rituals, local people in many societies conduct spiritual rituals believed to promote well-being. In Timor Leste rural people typically conduct rituals to honor the gods of the fields. They believe that failure to conduct such rituals can anger gods and cause crop failure, hunger, and poor health. The adverse effects of war on children include the disruption of these rituals, reminding us that the wounds of armed conflict are not only physical and psychological but also spiritual.

Religious practices also structure life and teach children modes of behavior regarded as locally appropriate. In many cases these are rooted in principles of individual and collective well-being. For example, the laws of Moses that underpin contemporary Jewish religious practice reflect the practical necessities of maintaining health and hygiene in a nomadic desert lifestyle, and the social necessities of ensuring harmony among the members of an ever-growing community. Most of the world's major religions promote positive social behavior that in itself will normally reduce children's exposure to violence. A child who is taught to turn the other cheek, for example, is less likely to seek a fight, though once in a fight this child could be more likely to suffer severe physical injury. Positive social behavior supports positive self-images and the building and maintaining of good social relationships, which in turn provide a resource and support.

In Afghanistan, where Islamic faith not only guides people's beliefs but the rhythms of prayer and fasting during *Eid* structure daily life for millions of people, socialization into Islam is a means through which families and communities transmit key values and practices, enabling children to learn proper behavior. Afghan children are expected to study the Qur'an, obey Islamic strictures, and demonstrate proper respect to mullahs and other Islamic leaders. Many Afghan parents regard training their children to be good Muslims one of their highest obligations (De Berry 2003).

It is important to note that forms of religious practice that support children relate also to actions to build social justice and peace. In many rural areas of developing countries the church is the arm of social justice and actively encourages youth to develop caring and outreach activities for people who are marginalized or less fortunate. In Latin America, liberation theology teaches youth that religion requires not only prayer and contemplation but also social action aimed at correcting social inequalities and injustices. These too are part of psychosocial support. At the individual level it has been demonstrated that altruistic behavior acts as an effective antidote to stress and depression (Koenig 2003). At the collective level religious faith can help to build peace, promote optimism, develop skills for addressing social problems, and provide active channels for overcoming adversity.

Social networks and resources

Much of the Western literature that associates religious faith and practice with well-being focuses on the associated benefits of enhanced social relationships. Social connection stemming from a shared religious faith, shared values, and a common world view provides a level of commitment beyond mutual attractiveness and shared history or geography. Studies comparing religious and nonreligious people in the United States indicate that people of faith express higher levels of commitment to their friends and higher levels of satisfaction with these relationships (Beit-Hallahmi and Argyle 1997). While these effects are less likely to be visible in non-Western societies, where religious commitment and community membership often share the same boundaries, nevertheless the quality of relationship within a community is likely to be enhanced by shared values and beliefs.

Religions typically provide a host of social networks and resources supportive of coping and protection. Through the church, mosque, or temple children develop social networks of people who can provide support in difficult circumstances. Key supports in these networks are religious leaders, whom children learn to respect and turn to for support and counsel. Traditional forms of spirituality also offer a host of networks and leaders such as healers, shamans, and herbalists to whom children can turn in times of crisis. These networks, of course, also offer support to parents, providing them with an additional resource for coping and potentially enhancing their parenting skills. It would be naive to suggest that all such intervention is experienced as positive; however, when parenting is strengthened, children certainly benefit.

In war zones children often turn to these networks of resources for support. For example, Afghan boys frequently report that when they encounter a problem or feel bad, they go to the mullah for advice (De Berry 2003). In Sierra Leone girls who survived abduction and rape and who said they had become spiritually impure said they needed to see a local healer and participate in an appropriate cleansing ritual (Wessells, forthcoming a). In Timor Leste children said they often went to the priest for advice and support (Kostelny and Wessells 2004). Among displaced children living in the welfare centers of central Sri Lanka, religious leaders were as likely be identified as sources of support as were teachers (Geisen, Strang, and Ruwanpura 2004). The power of religion to heal, to transform suffering into meaningful experiences, and to promote spiritual growth is due in no small part to the rich array of social resources it offers.

Sources of Harm and Damage

Despite these notable strengths, religion can also be a source of considerable harm and damage to children living in zones of armed conflict. In fact, each of the aforementioned sources of strength—beliefs, practices, and social networks—has its negative counterpart. It is worth reiterating that these negative facets result from how the religion is expressed and practiced in social contexts and cannot be viewed as paradigmatic features of religion.

Beliefs

Religious beliefs can themselves be sources of suffering and can encourage paralysis or ineffective action in dealing with adversity. To begin with, many religious beliefs depict adversities such as war, disasters, and famines as God's punishment for the sins of humankind. These beliefs often encourage pessimism and fatalism. After all, if the events are God's will, what can ordinary humans do to change them? Religious beliefs may also promote self-blame since practitioners may see themselves as having failed to live up to religious dictates and as being responsible for the suffering, thereby increasing their distress. Sometimes the expression of grief is problematic and seen as blame-worthy. For example, mothers of Palestinian children killed in active combat struggle with the advice that they should not cry because this will prevent their martyred child from being at peace in heaven (Habiballah 2004). Even the belief in the potency of religion can be problematic. For example, the belief that the main thing one needs to do to feel better or to mourn is to conduct an appropriate ritual can create enormous stress in situations where conducting the rituals is impossible. The promise of transcendence plays a part in encouraging an adolescent to wear the belt of explosives of the suicide bomber. Similarly, the belief that certain rituals confer impregnability to bullets sends many young people to their deaths (Wessells, forthcoming a).

Religious beliefs are problematic also because the mixture of faith and divine sanction increases the stakes of conflict and inclines people toward dogmatism. For example, transgressions committed by Muslims against Jews might be viewed not only as horrible violations of human rights but also as desecrations of one's faith and people, making it difficult to forgive and possibly demanding revenge as a means of redressing the wrongs. The idea that the transgressions may have resulted from wrongs committed by one's own group recedes in light of the perception of one's own group as good and the other group as evil or as the infidel. Further, beliefs in divinely sanctioned fighting can escalate the conflict and dampen any inclination toward conciliation, continuing the fighting that inevitably damages children.

Child recruitment

Worldwide, an estimated 300,000 children are members of armed groups (Machel 2001). Although many have been recruited forcibly, children themselves often decide to join armed groups in pursuit of security, food, and other necessities; to find a surrogate family; or for revenge, money, excitement, or power, among other motives (Brett and Specht 2004; Wessells, forthcoming a). In conflicts having strong religious dimensions, religion is often a deciding factor leading children to fight. In Pakistan and Afghanistan children traditionally received religious instruction not only in their homes but also in religious schools called madrassahs. Under the Taliban regime some Muslim extremists used madrassahs to teach children a highly politicized form of Islam calling for a Jihad against Western infidels. When US troops joined with Northern Alliance Forces in 2001, extremist religious leaders swelled the ranks of the Taliban by telling students in the madrassahs that it was their solemn obligation to fight in support of the Taliban (Brett and Specht 2004; Rashid 2000). To be sure, the children's willingness to fight was due to significant social influences by leaders and peers, but it also reflected their embrace of politicized religious ideology. The resulting risks to children's well-being indicate that the religious ideology is not always protective. In fact, the short-term protective effects of ideology discussed above may come at the price of longer-term harm.

Although the influence of religious ideology on youth has sometimes been attributed to brainwashing, this is only part of the story—and one that obscures youths' political consciousness and agency. As discussed earlier, extremist ideologies exist not in a vacuum but interact with identity threats, perceived or actual injustices, enemy images, and social mobilization by peers and leaders. Teenagers in war zones may seek to join armed groups when they believe their religious or social identity group is under severe threat or because they want to avenge wrongs done to their group. At a transitional time in their lives, when they are defining their own identity (Erikson 1968), youth may be attracted to groups having radical beliefs and identities since these may promise a better future and fit youths' idealistic conceptions. Talking among themselves, teenagers construct discourses about the conflict that influence how they position themselves in regard to it. If, following religious beliefs, they see the war as necessary or as a divine obligation, they may join the fight and derive a sense of meaning and identity from it. Nurturing enemy images in their own narratives, they may see themselves as fighting a holy war against the infidel. Seeing martyrdom as a form of spiritual fulfillment, or a "sacred duty" (Durkheim 1912) they may be willing to sacrifice themselves or take risks most people regard as unacceptable.

Cases in point include youth fighting in Iraq and Palestine. In Iraq during the early days of occupation, both Shiite and Sunni youth expressed seething anger over the occupation, viewing it as part of a wider US effort to dominate Muslim peoples. This identity threat, coupled with the injustices associated with the occupation, served to radicalize youth, leading some who claimed to have had no previous inclination toward violence to become jihadis vowed to purge the infidel (Wessells, forthcoming b). A more conspicuous, if sensationalized, case is that of Palestinian teenagers who have conducted terror bombings against Israelis. Contrary to popular images of suicide bombers as pathological or as living in depravity, recent evidence suggests that Palestinian suicide bombers are normal, well educated, and middle class or above (Pape 2005). Seeing themselves as warriors in a struggle not only about land but also religious identity, access to religious sites, social justice, and self-determination, they regard martyrdom as an appropriate means of fighting their religious enemy and achieving eternal salvation (Khosrokhavar 2005; Rosen 2005).

Both these cases attest to youths' political consciousness and agency and call attention to the fact that youth are not invariably passive victims or dupes manipulated by clever adults. Youth are actors who have identities shaped in no small part by religion, and they often respond to identity threats in the same manner as adults—with violence. Religious leaders' calls to war are not always needed to send children into the jaws of combat. Seeing violence in apocalyptic terms, children are often willing warriors who are at once willing to make the ultimate sacrifice and resistant to ideas about peaceful coexistence.

Damaging spiritual practices and behavior

Harm to children also occurs through some local spiritual practices. In Sierra Leone, for example, girl survivors of sexual violence were supported by the performance of rituals designed to rid them of spiritual impurities. However, there was also concern that in preparing the girls for the ritual, particular healers simultaneously identified whether the girls had been circumcised (Kostelny 2004). Like many other local practices, female circumcision (also called female genital mutilation) is a double-edged sword. In Sierra Leone circumcision is a symbol of womanhood and social acceptability; it is a prerequisite for social acceptance and entry into marriage and other adult roles. At the same time it is a significant violation of human rights, an extension of patriarchy, and one of the most damaging ways in which men have sought to control women's bodies. These and other harmful local practices caution against the tendency to romanticize local spiritual practices and warrant respect for human rights.

Social networks

We have discussed the protective effects of religion in facilitating the development of supportive personal relationships. However, in exploring the implications of social identity we have also pointed to some of the risks of isolation and radicalization associated with religious commitment. It seems that while religious commitment can stimulate the development of very positive relationships within a group, it can also serve to sharpen the boundaries between groups, thereby increasing the risk of conflict. The work of social-capital theorists illuminates this dual effect in terms of three levels of social relationship: "bonds" within groups, "bridges" between groups, and "links" with civil society (Colletta and Cullen 2000). Each level offers potential resources, such as the encouragement of close friends (bonds), trade with neighboring villages (bridges), or access to state health or education (links). Social capital is maximized where relationships are strengthened at all levels (Ager and Strang 2004; Ager, Strang, and Abebe 2005). However, there is always a danger that ideological commitment will strengthen "bonds" but neglect "bridges" and "links." This not only limits the resources to which the community has access, but, as we have seen, can increase social tension, radicalization, and the likelihood of conflict.

Conclusion

The contextual complexity of religion defies simplistic attempts either to malign religion as the problem or to portray religion as the solution. We hope, however, that this chapter has established the crucial importance of addressing religion as a key factor in understanding children's resilience and vulnerability in situations of armed conflict. The very complexity demands that humanitarians seek to explore the meanings that religion suggests and the resources that it offers. Since religion is a valuable resource and also a source of risk for children, it is crucial for practitioners to think carefully about how religious beliefs influence the ways that people in a community frame both the problems that they are experiencing and the solutions that they can envisage. Understanding religious beliefs is essential to the effective use of both religious and secular resources in programs of psychosocial assistance (PWG 2003; Strang and Ager 2003).

In light of the importance of religious and spiritual beliefs, practices, and networks, psychosocial assistance to children and families in conflict situations should map, support, and build upon the local resources already present. At the least outside humanitarians have a responsibility to learn about and support local resources, avoiding the imposition of outside approaches that tacitly marginalize local people and convert humanitarian action into a form of imperialism (Wessells 1999). In setting up camps for displaced people, for example, attention should be given to including spaces for supportive religious practices. Also, humanitarians should learn from local spiritual leaders what supports could be provided or strengthened as a means of enabling children's well-being. Outside humanitarians should also encourage spiritual leaders to conduct appropriate rituals such as burial rites and cleansing rituals, thereby making the humanitarian effort a partnership between outside humanitarians and local people. In longer-term peace building, humanitarian efforts should seek to engage religious resources, such as moderate leaders, in efforts such as peace dialogues and youth leadership projects in which youth from different sides of the conflict work together for peace.

In applying and supporting religious resources, practitioners also need to keep in mind the "do no harm" humanitarian imperative. Critical scrutiny is needed to avoid privileging particular religious groups; supporting religious practices that violate children's rights; or supporting groups, beliefs, practices, or leaders encouraging violence and war. The need for critical self-reflection has always been significant in humanitarian efforts. However, in an age of ideologically driven rhetoric, intolerance, and warfare, there is perhaps greater need of critical thinking about the uses and abuses of religion than ever before.

References

Ager, A., and A. Strang. 2004. Indicators of integration: Final report. Home Office Development and Practice Report 28.

Ager, A., A. Strang, and B. Abebe. 2005. Conceptualising community development in war-affected populations: Illustrations from Tigray. *Community Development Journal* 40 (2): 158–68.

Apfel, R., and B. Simon, eds. 1996. *Minefields in their hearts: The mental health of children in war and communal violence.* New Haven, CT: Yale Univ. Press.

Barber, B. 2001. Political violence, social integration, and youth functioning: Palestinian youth from the Intifada. *Journal of Community Psychology* 29 (3): 259–80.

Barnes, L. L., G. A. Plotnikoff, K. Fox, and S. Pendleton. 2000. Spirituality, religion, and pediatrics: Intersecting worlds of healing. *Pediatrics* 104 (6): 899–908.

Batniji, R., M. van Ommeren, and B. Saraceno. Forthcoming. Mental and social health in disasters: Relating qualitative social science research and the Sphere standard. *Social Science and Medicine.*

Beit-Hallahmi, B., and M. Argyle. 1997. *The psychology of religious behavior, belief, and experience.* London: Routledge.

Boothby, N., and C. Knudsen. 2000. Children of the gun. *Scientific American* 282: 60–66.

Boyden, J. 2003. The moral development of child soldiers. *Peace and Conflict: Journal of Peace Psychology* 9: 343–62.

Brett, R., and I. Specht. 2004. *Young soldiers: Why they choose to fight.* Boulder, CO: Lynne Rienner.

Cairns, E. 1996. *Children and political violence.* Oxford: Blackwell.

Cairns, E., and J. Darby. 1998. The conflict in Northern Ireland: Causes, consequences, and controls. *American Psychologist* 53 (7): 754–60.

Coles, R. 1991. *The spiritual life of children.* Boston: Houghton Mifflin.

Colletta, N. J., and M. Cullen. 2000. *Violent conflict and the transformation of social capital.* New York: World Bank.

Community Cohesion Unit. 2003. Community cohesion: A report of the independent review team chaired by Ted Cantle. Available online.

Dawes, A., and D. Donald. 1994. *Childhood and adversity: Psychological perspectives from South African research.* Cape Town: David Philip.

De Berry, J. 2003. *Children of Kabul.* Kabul: Save the Children US.

Derluyn, I., E. Broekaert, G. Schuyten, and E. De Temmerman. 2004. Posttraumatic stress in former Ugandan child soldiers. *The Lancet* 363: 861–63.

Durkheim, E. 1912. *The elementary forms of religious life,* trans. C. Cosman. Repr. Oxford: Oxford Univ. Press, 2001.

Dyregov, A., R. Gjestad, and M. Raundalen. 2002. Children exposed to warfare. *Journal of Traumatic Stress* 15: 59–68.

Erikson, E. 1968. *Identity, youth, and crisis*. New York: Norton.

Eyber, C., and A. Ager. 2004. Researching young people's experiences of war: Participatory methods and the trauma discourse in Angola. In *Children and youth on the front line: Ethnography, armed conflict and displacement*, ed. J. Boyden and J. de Berry, 189-208. New York: Berghahn.

Fisher, R. 1997. *Interactive conflict resolution*. Syracuse, NY: Syracuse Univ. Press, 1997.

Garbarino, J., and K. Kostelny. 1996. The effects of political violence on Palestinian children's behavioral problems. *Child Development* 67: 33–45.

Garbarino, J., K. Kostelny, and N. Dubrow. 1991. What can children tell us about living in danger. *American Psychologist* 46: 376–83.

Geisen, P., A. Strang, and E. Ruwanpura. 2004. Psychosocial support services in the welfare centres of Vavuniya. Evaluation report. MSF Holland.

Habiballah, N. 2004. Interviews with mothers of martyrs of the Aqsa intifada. *Arab Studies Quarterly* 27 (1): 15–30.

Hall, J. R. 2003. Religion and violence: Social processes in comparative perspective. In *Handbook for the Sociology of Religion*, ed. M. Dillion, 359–84. Cambridge Univ. Press.

Honwana, A. 1997. Healing for peace. *Peace and Conflict: Journal of Peace Psychology* 3 (3): 293–305.

———. 1998. *"Okusiakala O'Ndalu Yokalye": Let us light a new fire*. Luanda: Christian Children's Fund.

Huntington, S. 2003. *The clash of civilizations and the remaking of the world*. New York: Simon and Schuster.

Juergensmeyer, M. 2003. *Terror in the mind of God: The global rise of religious violence*. Berkeley and Los Angeles: Univ. of California Press.

Khosrokhavar, F. 2005. *Suicide bombers*. London: Pluto.

Klare, M. 2001. *Resource wars*. New York: Henry Holt.

Koenig, H. G. 2003. Religion, spirituality, and health. *The Medical Journal of Australia* 178: 415–16.

Koenig, H. G., M. E. McCullough, and D. B. Larson. 2001. *Handbook of religion and health*. New York: Oxford Univ. Press.

Kostelny, K. 2004. What about the girls? *Cornell International Law Journal* 37 (3): 505–12.

Kostelny, K., and M. G. Wessells. 2004. Community-based psychosocial assistance in a large-scale emergency: The challenges and lessons of East Timor. In *The mental health of refugees: Ecological approaches to refugee mental health*, ed. K. Miller and L. Rasco, 187–225. Upper Saddle River, NJ: Erlbaum.

Lazarus, R., and S. Folkman. 1984. *Stress, appraisal and coping*. New York: Springer.

Lewis, B. 2003. *The crisis of Islam: Holy war and unholy terror*. New York: Modern Library.

Machel, G. 2001. *The impact of war on children*. Cape Town: David Philip.

Marx, K. 1844. A contribution to the critique of Hegel's philosophy of right. In *Deutsch-Franzosische Jahrbucher*. February.

Nordstrom, C. 1999. Visible wars and invisible girls, shadow industries and the politics of not knowing. *International Feminist Journal of Politics* 1 (1): 14-33.

Opotow, S. 1990. Moral exclusion and injustice. *Journal of Social Issues* 46 (1): 1–20.

Pape, R. 2005. *Dying to win: The strategic logic of suicide terrorism*. New York: Random House.

Pargament, K. 1997. *The psychology of religion and coping*. New York: Guilford.

Pargament, K., G. Magyar-Russell, and N. Murray-Swank. 2005. The sacred and the search for significance: Religion as a unique process. *Journal of Social Issues* 61 (4): 665–87.

Park, C. 2005. Religion as a meaning-making framework in coping with life stress. *Journal of Social Issues* 61 (4): 707–29.

Punamaki, R. 1996. Can ideological commitment protect children's psychosocial well-being in situations of political violence? *Child Development* 67: 55–69.

PWG (Psychosocial Working Group). 2003. Psychosocial intervention in complex emergencies: A conceptual framework. Available online.

Rashid, A. 2000. *Taliban*. New Haven, CT: Yale Univ. Press.

Rieber, R., ed. 1991. *The psychology of war and peace*. New York: Plenum.

Rosen, D. 2005. *Armies of the young: Child soldiers in war and terrorism*. New Brunswick, NJ: Rutgers Univ. Press.

Rubin, J., D. Pruitt, and S. Kim. 1994. *Social conflict*. 2nd ed. New York: McGraw-Hill.

Silberman, I. 2005. Religious violence, terrorism, and peace: A meaning system analysis. In *Handbook of the psychology of religion and spirituality*, ed. R. Paloutzian and C. Park, 524–49. New York: Guilford.

Silverstein, B. 1989. Enemy images: The psychology of U.S. attitudes and cognitions regarding the Soviet Union. *American Psychologist* 44: 903–13.

Somasundaram, D., and C. Jamunanantha. 2002. Psychosocial consequences of war: Northern Sri Lankan experience. In *Trauma, war, and violence*, ed. J. De Jong, 205–58. New York: Kluwer.

Staub, E. 2003. Notes on cultures of violence, cultures of caring and peace, and the fulfillment of basic human needs. *Political Psychology* 24 (1): 1–21.

Stern, J. 2003. *Terror in the name of God: Why religious militants kill*. New York: HarperCollins.

Straker, G. 1992. *Faces in the revolution*. Cape Town: David Philip.

Strang, A., and A. Ager. 2003. Psychosocial interventions: Some key issues facing practitioners. *Intervention: International Journal of Mental Health, Psychosocial Work, and Counseling in Areas of Armed Conflict* 6 (3): 2–12.

Tajfel, H., and J. Turner. 1986. The social identity theory of intergroup behavior. In *The social psychology of intergroup relations*, ed. S. Worchel and G. Austin, 33–47. Monterey, CA: Brooks/Cole.

Taylor, D., and W. Louis. 2004. Terrorism and the quest for identity. In *Understanding terrorism*, ed. F. Moghaddam and A. Marsella, 169–85. Washington, DC: American Psychological Association.

Triandis, H. 2001. Individualism and collectivism. In *The handbook of culture and psychology*, ed. D. Matsumoto, 35–50. New York: Oxford Univ. Press.

Volkan, V. 1997. *Bloodlines*. New York: Farrar, Straus and Giroux.

Waller, J. 2002. *Becoming evil*. New York: Oxford Univ. Press.

Wessells, M. G. Forthcoming a. *Child soldiers: From violence to protection*. Cambridge, MA: Harvard Univ. Press.

———. Forthcoming b. The impact of U.S. anti-terrorism interventions on terrorist motivation: Preliminary narrative research on youth in Afghanistan and Iraq. In *Collateral damage: The psychological consequences of America's war on terrorism*, ed. P. Kimmel and C. Stout. Westport, CT: Praeger.

Wessells, M. G. 1999. Culture, power, and community: Intercultural approaches to psychosocial assistance and healing. In *Honoring differences: Cultural issues in the treatment of trauma and loss*, ed. K. Nader, N. Dubrow, and B. Stamm, 267–82. New York: Taylor and Francis.

Wessells, M. G., and C. Monteiro. 2004. Healing the wounds following protracted conflict in Angola. In *Handbook of culture, therapy, and healing*, ed. U. P. Gielen, J. Fish, and J. G. Draguns, 321–41. Mahwah, NJ: Erlbaum.

White, R. K. 1984. *Fearful warriors: A psychological profile of U.S.-Soviet relations*. New York: Free Press.

Yule, W., R. Stuvland, F. Baingana, and P. Smith. 2003. Children in armed conflict. In *Trauma interventions in war and peace*, ed. B. Green et al., 217–42. New York: Kluwer.

10

LAYERS OF SUPPORT

The social ecology of protecting children in war

Carl Triplehorn
and Catherine Chen

What is child protection?

Protection is a new and developing field of humanitarian research and practice, encompassing the prevention of abuse, restoration of dignity, and promotion of human rights. When first applied to the humanitarian context, protection was focused on preserving life and guarding against immediate harm and danger. Interventions included guarding refugee and internally displaced persons (IDP) camps and arranging military escorts for displaced people as they migrated to safer areas. This initial paradigm of protection also included the general acknowledgment of the international community's need to address grave physical abuse such as rape, attacks on civilians, and violence targeted at children.

From 1996 to 2000 the International Committee of the Red Cross (ICRC) conducted a series of consultations with leading humanitarian workers in Red Cross and Red Crescent chapters around the world to clarify the concept of protection. From these consultations *protection* was defined as "all activities aimed at obtaining full respect for the rights of the individual in accordance with the letter and spirit of the relevant bodies of law (i.e., human rights, humanitarian law and refugee law). Human rights and humanitarian actors shall conduct these activities impartially and not on the basis of race, national or ethnic origin, language or gender" (ICRC 2001).

While this definition provides a strong foundation for the principle of protection for all people, it does not address the specific vulnerabilities that children face in conflict. Instead, governments, humanitarians, and communities base their actions upon the rights set forth by the Convention on the Rights of the Child (CRC). As a specific means of protecting children from recruitment into armed groups in areas of conflict, the CRC's Optional Protocol establishes eighteen as the minimum age for compulsory recruitment and sixteen for voluntary recruitment. There are several additional international instruments that augment the protection delineated by the CRC, including the Rome Statutes, which declare rape, sexual violence, recruitment of children, and attacks on schools war crimes; the Geneva Conventions; the Genocide Convention; the 1997 Mine Ban Treaty; the 1951 Refugee Convention; the 1967 Protocol protecting refugee children; and Security Council Resolutions 1261, 1314, 1379, 1460, and 1539. Put together, these instruments constitute a strong and comprehensive legal structure to protect children in armed conflict (Save the Children Alliance 2005).

While these instruments establish a clear standard for how children are to be treated, they are too broad to be used to set priorities for programs on the ground. Most humanitarian organizations shy away from ranking the rights they intend to uphold, arguing that emphasis on one set of rights inherently de-emphasizes other equally important rights. At the field level, however, these decisions are made daily. The gap between field level action and a philosophical "all or nothing" approach leads to ambiguity about how protection is implemented.

Acknowledging the need to anchor these rights to programs on the ground, in 2004 the International Save the Children Alliance, a network of twenty-seven individually governed Save the Children members around the globe, developed *Child Protection in Emergencies*. In this framework the agency defines *child protection* as measures that "promote children's physical and emotional well-being, provide them equal access to services and safeguard their legal rights" (Save the Children Alliance 2005). Moreover, the framework prioritizes seven critical types of protection that children require in disaster and war-affected areas:

1. physical harm
2. exploitation and gender-based violence
3. psychosocial distress
4. recruitment into armed groups
5. family separation
6. abuses related to forced displacement
7. denial of access to quality education

Social ecology of protection

Conflict degrades the social structure or ecology that protects children. This degradation does not happen in isolation but is dynamically connected with other components of society and the natural environment. Social ecologies can be both protective and, more often than we would like to admit, harmful. Children harm one another. Parents and relatives harm children. Children are harmed in religious institutions or schools. Children are harmed by UN agencies, humanitarian agencies, and peace-keeping forces meant to protect them. To maximize their ability to protect children, humanitarian organizations should apply a social ecology model to identify programmatic entry points as well as areas to influence, strengthen, and protect.

Children: The foundation of protection

Children are at the center of their own protection. In conflict, children are not passive victims but active survivors. Children, even preschool age and younger, make day-to-day choices to protect themselves. In northern Uganda, according to Human Rights Watch, each night nearly forty thousand children "commute" from rural areas and IDP camps into urban areas to avoid being abducted into the Lord's Resistance Army. In Nepal youth migrate from Maoist-controlled villages across the border into India in search of security and livelihood (Hausner 2005).

From an external perspective children's choices often seem to increase their vulnerability. However, from experience we know that these decisions are often well considered. Children make choices to meet their immediate physical, emotional, and spiritual needs, often with a mind toward achieving their future goals. They might choose

FIG. 10–1. THE SOCIAL ECOLOGY OF PROTECTION

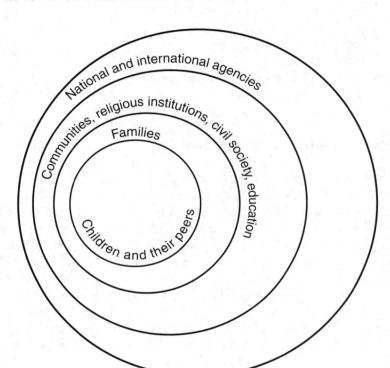

to engage in exploitative work or behavior as a means to an end they strongly desire, such as money, schooling, status, or safety.

Children protect themselves, and they also protect their peers. While dependence upon peers is a natural progression of childhood development, a child's changing family dynamics can accelerate and increase dependence on peers. For example, children who have been displaced or separated, such as the "Lost Boys" of South Sudan or street children in many post-conflict settings, often band together into protective "families." Understanding the developmental importance of peer networks, many humanitarian organizations initiate child-to-child programs.

Crisis often brings children, especially youth, to transcend their traditional roles in order to address the needs of their peers and community. During the Kosovo crisis, displaced youth, with support from the Albanian Youth Council, formed a network among forty-five refugee camps across the country. The Kosovo Youth Council took on a variety of tasks, ranging from activities for youth, such as concerts, sports, and classes in language and arts, to addressing humanitarian needs, such as identifying and assisting vulnerable community members, tracing families, and distributing humanitarian supplies (Lowicki 2001). Aside from ensuring children's protection, these activities built the youths' feelings of self-esteem and their capacity to organize and implement change.

While children often demonstrate that they are the first line of protection in their own lives, unfortunately children can also threaten and harm themselves and one another. Children often coerce their peers into substance abuse, unsafe sex, and other risky behavior. They subject others to significant abuse through bullying, discrimination, and harassment. Moreover, during times of extreme crisis, children may recruit children into exploitative situations such as soldiering or prostitution.

For these reasons children should be consulted with and integrated into the provisions of humanitarian assistance. Children often are able to identify threats within their environments as well as strategies to address them that have been overlooked by adults. In Afghanistan, Save the Children uses a child-centered assessment tool to determine priority areas for programming. When participants were asked to articulate what they were most afraid of, they acknowledged their fears of planes, bombs, landmines, and guns, but prioritized addressing the issues of traffic safety, wild dogs, and children being kidnapped and trafficked. Save the Children launched campaigns to address these issues, which led to the unraveling of other protection issues, such as traffic police abusing children on their way to school, school officials abusing children upon late arrival at school, and some instances of sexual abuse by other adults and peers when children were not allowed into school and, for fear of getting in trouble at home, sought other activities to fill their day.

Families: The second protective ecology

Families play an important role for children in conflict, especially for younger children. Parents are typically the primary caregivers and providers of food, shelter, and physical protection. Children also rely on their parents to provide psychosocial care and emotional support in times of uncertainty, violence, and displacement. Children who become separated from their families are more vulnerable to illness, exploitation, recruitment, abuse, and death. Moreover, without this support, children do not have the resources to rebuild their lives. In the absence of parental support, it is extended families, neighbors, and community members who often assume the role of caretakers.

While parents are widely known to be the best protection for children, instances of physical, sexual, and emotional abuse increase when instability and stress increase for caretakers. In addition, the placement of separated children with extended family members, older peers, and informal foster families may place children at risk for physical and sexual violence or exploitation. Foster children have been found to be sexually exploited and abused, trafficked or sold, or abused in a variety of other ways. Children whose parents participated in the conflict are particularly vulnerable when placed with foster families because the children may be viewed as indirect participants.

Communities: The third protective ecology

Communities offer the closest complement to the family's protective support. A community establishes the core norms for children's behavior. As children get older and begin to assert their independence from their parents, the community plays a greater role in raising them through example, as well as through educational and religious institutions. During times of crisis normal community structures are disrupted. Children and families, whether they remain in their home area or seek respite in refugee and IDP camps, form new social structures. These new social systems do not offer the same protective support, based as they are upon need rather than upon the deep social and familial structures that normally bind a community.

Though they are intended to provide humanitarian relief and protection, camps are some of the most dangerous places on earth for children. Lacking normal societal structures, children often are subjected to elevated levels of domestic abuse or attacks from rebel groups or hosting communities, and are susceptible to sexual abuse, trafficking, and exploitation. Lacking basic resources, refugee and IDP women and children resort to transactional or commercial sex to obtain desperately needed food and assistance when no other economic options exist. The full extent of sexual exploitation and abuse of children in camps is not known, but reports of abuse continue to surface. In 2004, for example, the UN Internal Oversight Services investigated the Department of Peacekeeping Operations in the Democratic Republic of Congo in Bunia and found that sexual relations between peace keepers and Congolese women and girls, some as young as thirteen, occurred regularly, usually in exchange for food or small sums of money (Lacey 2004).

Communities often prioritize the reestablishment of protective structures, choosing to rehabilitate or establish institutions for worship and education immediately. Aside from being institutions of faith, religious institutions provide strong psychosocial support and help reestablish societal norms. In any culture, worship provides an important way for those who have survived conflict to reconcile their experiences with their world view. It also provides closure for those who have lost loved ones to the conflict. Research on the role of religion in conflict reveals that those who have a strong link to some form of worship often exhibit strong resiliency and psychosocial coping abilities (Green and Honwana 1999).

Nonsectarian organizations are often uncomfortable partnering with religious leaders and groups, though these groups can play a strong protective role for children. In Africa the international community has become more aware of the power of using local healers to facilitate the reintegration of children into their communities. These protective dimensions can extend to children, parents, homes, and whole communities. In a variety of situations organizations have facilitated discussions with communities, scholars, and institutions to identify commonalities between religious doctrine and the CRC. As examples, many humanitarian organizations have supported Islamic scholars and institutions to find commonalities and gaps between local law and Qur'anic verses and use local religious leaders as advocates (IASC 2002).

War further deprives millions of children of the protection provided by being in school. Formal and non-formal education from preschool to secondary school, as well as extracurricular activities, can play a role in the protection of war-affected children. At their most basic, education programs protect children physically by providing a place to be under the supervision of an adult. As a process, education mitigates the psychosocial impact of the crisis, protects children's educational achievements, and prepares them to live in conflict and post-conflict environments.

Children's access to educational services may change for many different reasons. Schools may be closed by governmental mandate or lack of teachers' salaries, burned, or abandoned. Children, especially girls, may be unable to attend school due to a family's inability to pay school fees for all the children in the household (boys would be the priority) or due to security issues related to real or potential violence on the route between home and school—and potential vulnerability even within the school's walls.

Moreover, in areas of displacement, schools and other educational institutions are often limited. Adolescents are one of the most underserved groups. The Refugee Education Trust estimates that only 3 percent of the 1.5 million refugee children worldwide between the ages of twelve and seventeen have access to education, making them vulnerable to recruitment into armed groups or sexual exploitation—an ominous sign for the next generation of post-conflict leadership (UNOCHA 2004).

Education and religion can also play harmful roles in the lives of children. In some conflicts around the world simply walking to class may be endangering a student's life, especially when combatants target schools and educational facilities. Many conflicts are also fueled by disparate religious beliefs, and children bear the brunt of ensuing aggression.

Aside from educational and religious institutions, communities have preexisting or conflict-induced organizations that address the needs of children. These civil society organizations rise to the challenge of child protection and take a variety of forms. In Sierra Leone the local chapter of the Forum for African Women Educationalists (FAWE) organized a non-formal education program for displaced and marginalized children, most of whom were young mothers who had become pregnant due to rape or lack of birth control. For girls living outside the protective sphere of their families and communities, FAWE provided room and board, alternative formal education, and facilitated vocational training. Importantly, local organizations are often able to address the systemic legal issues that make children vulnerable. In Liberia, where there were no courts or correction facilities designed for children, the Association of Female Liberian Lawyers successfully advocated for the establishment of a juvenile court and for home-based care as an alternative to incarceration (Johnson 1997).

National and international policies:
The fourth protective ecology

In any emergency the state is the primary governmental body responsible for the well-being and protection of its citizens. This protection includes a functioning rule of law and corresponding judicial system, the military, and functioning education and social-service systems. In times of crisis these systems often cease to operate. Child-protection concerns escalate as state systems no longer enforce laws and established norms. However, this does not absolve the state of its responsibilities.

In many instances state structures have been maintained during conflict and have sought to ensure children's rights. For example, public education was highly valued in Sri Lanka throughout the conflict and, to this end, the state continued to hold national exams. Interestingly, a ceasefire was established during exam times. Similarly, ceasefires have been called in Sudan and other countries for vaccination campaigns during a crisis.

The international community assists when states are unable or unwilling to address the needs of citizens, particularly children. The international community has sought to protect children affected by armed conflict through the creation of a strong and comprehensive legal framework aimed at setting standards for the protection of children and urging states to abide by these standards.

The CRC provides a comprehensive framework of children's rights as well as mechanisms for accountability. The CRC recognizes children's right to be free from abuse and neglect, sexual exploitation, trafficking, abduction, torture, deprivation of liberty, and other forms of maltreatment at all times and provides for special protections during times of conflict. The Optional Protocol to the CRC on the involvement of children in armed conflict sets eighteen as the minimum age for compulsory recruitment and participation in hostilities and a minimum age of sixteen for voluntary recruitment.

The Rome Statute defines the "most serious crimes of international concern" to come under the International Criminal Court and classifies the following as war crimes: rape and other forms of sexual violence, recruitment or use of children under the age of fifteen in armed groups, and attacks against schools. In addition, the International

Labour Organization's Convention 182 declares child soldiering to be one of the worst forms of child labor and prohibits compulsory recruitment of children under the age of eighteen into armed conflict.

To support this legal framework, specific international organizations have been created. Under the direction of the UN, agencies such as the Office of Coordination of Humanitarian Assistance (OCHA), United Nations High Commissioner for Refugees (UNHCR), and the United Nations Children's Fund (UNICEF) all have protection of children as part of their mandate.

OCHA

Protecting children depends upon a coordinated humanitarian response. In 1991 the UN General Assembly adopted Resolution 46/182 to strengthen the UN's response to both large-scale natural disasters and complex humanitarian emergencies. The resulting Department of Humanitarian Affairs (DHA)—which later became OCHA—was mandated to coordinate humanitarian response, policy development, and humanitarian advocacy. OCHA's mandate includes responding to conflict situations and natural disasters. As a special focus, OCHA has developed the Inter-Agency Internal Displacement Division, which promotes systematic improvements in response to the needs of IDPs and also provides targeted support in specific country situations. In addition, OCHA has created the Inter-Agency Standing Committee Task Force on Sexual Exploitation and Abuse, which has issued a report and standards of conduct for personnel associated with the UN—both civilian staff and uniformed peace-keeping troops. The protection of vulnerable populations, especially women and children, is viewed as a priority in the organization.

UNHCR

Unlike the broad mandate of OCHA, the UNHCR has a specific mandate to protect refugees under the 1951 Refugee Convention. Under this convention UNHCR provides emergency food, water, shelter, and other non-food items as a first step to protection and survival for refugees. Additionally, UNHCR uses a wide body of international law to advocate for refugees' rights, including their rights to asylum, repatriation, and resettlement. UNHCR has global, regional, and field child protection officers to ensure the well-being of children and to support education and social services for children, women, and other vulnerable groups. In recent years UNHCR's mandate has been broadened to include programmatic support for the repatriation and reintegration of refugees. In specific situations UNHCR has been designated lead agency for IDPs based upon its rapid emergency response capacity.

UNICEF

UNICEF is the lead UN agency for children. Initially established in 1946 to meet the emergency needs of children in postwar Europe, its mandate was further broadened in 1953 to address the longer term needs of women and children in developing countries. Unlike its UN emergency response counterparts, UNICEF typically uses the emergency response to lay the foundation for long-term health, education, and protection programs. Like the UNHCR, UNICEF employs designated child protection officers. In many situations UNICEF takes the lead on specific child-protection issues such as reunification of separated children, demobilization of child soldiers, and community-based child care. UNICEF is often designated as the lead agency for IDPs based upon its mandate and existing infrastructure in these countries.

International NGO response to child protection in conflict

UN agencies work in close collaboration with governmental organizations and NGOs such as CARE, Christian Children's Fund, The International Committee of the Red Cross/Red Crescent, International Rescue Committee, Mercy Corps, Norwegian Refugee Council, Oxfam, Save the Children, The Women's Commission for Refugee Women and Children, and World Vision. These NGOs work in partnership with regional and local organizations to provide protection either by incorporating protective elements into existing, multi-sector, humanitarian relief programs or through stand-alone interventions.

Integrated humanitarian response

Humanitarian agencies have begun to adopt an integrated approach that includes the needs of children, women, and vulnerable groups in program development and implementation. In theory this means that humanitarian agencies include these concerns in all aspects of their assistance, including food distribution, water points, latrine locations, shelter construction, camp design and management, and educational activities.

For example, in some situations children gather water for their families. As they wait in line for hours, they often get into fights or are targeted in other ways. One creative solution was invented by Roundabout Outdoor, a public-private partnership with the Department of Water Affairs and Forestry in South Africa. To address the need for water collection coupled with the lack of opportunity for children to play, Roundabout Outdoor created a merry-go-round that pumps water. As children play on the merry-go-round (dubbed the Play Pump), the rotation activates a pump that drives water into an above-ground storage tank several meters away. The tank is also used to display safety and public health messages, such as HIV/AIDS prevention messages. Such an integrated approach can reduce the level of physical harm to children, support children in reestablishing peer relationships, address basic emotional well-being, and deliver lifesaving educational messages.

As part of an integrated response NGOs have joined the UN agencies in deploying child protection officers. These individuals are often tasked with assessing vulnerabilities, investigating reports of abuses, and establishing preventative measures. They also may address specific concerns such as demobilization of child combatants or family tracing and reunification. Ideally, child protection officers also ensure that protection is incorporated into all aspects of an organization's response.

Reunification and care for separated children

Recognizing that parents and extended families are the best sources of protection for children, humanitarian organizations often prioritize protecting children from family separation and identifying and reunifying children who have been separated from their families. Depending on the circumstances, tracing and reunification may be significant components of child protection during the acute phase of an emergency. Reunification is also important because general consensus within the humanitarian community is that residential care or orphanages are not conducive to the well-being of children (Tolfree 2004). Instead, efforts are made to establish fostering programs wherever possible.

Psychosocial well-being

There is consensus that children exposed to extreme violence require mental-health support. However, there is little agreement as to what this programming should be. In recent years agencies have begun to address mental health at the community level, emphasizing the psychological and social—or psychosocial—dimensions of recovery. These psychosocial interventions take a variety of forms from individual counseling or group therapy to reestablishing sports activities. In all cases psychosocial programs are designed to address the immediate impact and mitigate the long-term impact of the crisis.

In the Palestinian territories of West Bank and Gaza, Save the Children has established a school-based psychosocial program that uses a highly structured curriculum of fifteen sessions to address children's experiences through cooperative games, storytelling, sports, art, dance, and music. These activities help children regain a sense of normalcy and predictability to their days and support their natural resiliency. This community-based strategy enables children who would otherwise go without support to receive mental-health services. To date, over 100,000 children have received this intervention. The program is designed to build upon the primary and secondary protective ecologies by helping children to rebuild a sense of trust and camaraderie among their peers and families.

Education

In emergencies, educational programming often starts as protective "safe spaces" for children. The spaces provide psychosocial support but also maintain the children's educational momentum until formal schooling resumes. The form and implementation of the safe space varies depending upon the situation. Safe spaces range from daily activities surrounding a temporary shelter to camps conducted between the signing of peace agreements and the reopening of schools. These safe spaces typically make a transition into formal schooling, especially for primary-school-age children.

Humanitarian agencies support children's access to school but also improve the quality of education. Quality education protects children's future educational and employment opportunities and provides an incentive for school attendance and retention. To increase children's access to education, humanitarian support helps communities construct schools that vary from tents to mud-walled shacks to permanent cement structures. Other types of support for quality education include basic materials, teacher training, school management committee training and, where possible, support to the government.

Recognizing the threats that exist within educational programming, protection measures should be incorporated. These could include codes of conduct for teachers and school staff, escorts to and from school, improvement of school facilities (such as creating separate latrines for girls), and the implementation of building codes to encourage access for children with disabilities. Community involvement through school management committees is vital to ensuring that protection measures are implemented and that all children are able to access education relevant to their needs.

Restorative care

Conflict can affect children's roles and relationships within their families, communities, and society. Addressing the harm that has occurred to the children during the conflict and reintegrating them into their families and society is a delicate and long-term process. After the civil war in Sierra Leone, the International Rescue Committee (IRC) worked to disarm, demobilize, and reintegrate many of the ten thousand children who had been abducted and recruited into armed forces. The IRC facilitated the tracing and reunification of many of these children and provided them, as well as their home communities, with skills training, vegetable gardening, youth clubs, and cultural performance groups. The IRC also supported the identification and emotional support of girls who had become "wives" of former commanders and soldiers. Additionally, the IRC facilitated the identification of the girls' families and, where possible, assisted with their return through sensitization work with their families and community. The continued restoration of dignity for survivors of these abuses is a long-term process for both affected children and their communities.

Strategies to enhance the international response

Despite this extensive international network and protection programming, children in areas of conflict are largely unprotected. This is in large part due to a lack of understanding of the gravity and scope of their needs. Today, fifty-three million people have been uprooted by war; of these, some forty-two million are women and children. Every day, more than five thousand children are newly displaced by conflict. Political will and funding are essential to addressing the enormity of this challenge. This, however, is only part of the solution. To make an impact, humanitarian organizations must be diligent about including protection in their programs and deliberately choose to support children's protective social ecologies.

Incorporate children's voices and their needs into all aspects of policy and programs

International child protection is not provided to children equally. Although the CRC defines a child as anyone under the age of eighteen, humanitarian agencies have traditionally focused on children of primary-school age. This assumes children under age six are protected as long as they are in the care of their parents or guardians. This assumption overestimates the protective ability of the parents, who may be unable to give the proper care due to trauma or the need to rebuild their lives. It also underestimates the psychosocial impact of conflict on children and their need for support.

Similarly, this focus on primary-school-age children assumes that adolescents and youth do not need a comparable level of protective care. Relatively few programs address the specific protection needs of children aged thirteen to eighteen, even though this age group is often the most vulnerable to physical and sexual violence. Among school youth, especially female youth are dramatically under-served. This lack of support for youth and younger children is driven by the lack of age-disaggregated research on the impacts and interventions for these age groups.

Part of the solution to this dilemma is consulting children in the development, design, and implementation of all aspects of humanitarian programming and policy discussions. Practically, this means humanitarian organizations making a concerted effort to include children's voices in their work by using child-friendly assessment tools, establishing peer groups and child-to-child networks, and including children within community leadership. Through such actions humanitarian agencies, as well as children themselves, will be able to address the protection issues that threaten children's well-being. For example, Afghanistan's President Karzai has requested that children participate in the drafting of national plans of action on child trafficking, juvenile justice, and children at risk.

Increase support for education

While support is slowly growing, education is generally not seen as an instrumental component of humanitarian assistance or child protection. Of the estimated 104 million children out of school, half live in countries either in conflict or recovering from conflict (UNESCO 2005). Education should be supported alongside other humanitarian interventions during the acute, transitional, and developmental stages of an emergency. Donors often make the false assumption that education stops during conflict; thus they wait until the situation is stabilized to provide education. This assumption leads to large numbers of children in and outside areas of conflict being denied the protective benefit of education.

To this end donors and implementing agencies should embrace the Minimum Standards for Education in Emergencies, Chronic Crises and Early Reconstruction developed by the Inter-Agency Network for Emergency Education. These standards articulate how education should be provided at all stages of an emergency and for all education levels, including preschool, secondary school, and nonformal education.

Increase support for longer-term transitional programming

Protection is not a short-term intervention. During the acute phase of a crisis donors are more willing to support issues of child protection. However, donors have yet to prioritize protection throughout the course of an emergency. Typically, donors support protection programs for six months to one year, with a focus on addressing the most apparent and visible needs of children such as reunification of separated children, survivors of sexual assault, and child soldiers. This type of funding is not sustainable because it does not allow for the necessary time to build the capacity of governments and communities to address the longer-term, post-conflict protection concerns. Paradoxically, funding is typically at its highest in the acute phase of an emergency, during which time the absorptive capacity of local communities and governments is at its lowest.

For communities to address the immediate needs and long-term goals of protection, new strategies for long-term funding are needed. Funding periods should be extended and linkages to longer-term development funding must be established to correspond with the absorptive capacity of affected communities and governments. Additionally, in many emergencies countries and organizations have established trust funds to translate acute funding into long-term support.

Enhance support for governments and international communities to develop protective structures

As outlined in a recent report by the secretary-general of the UN, donors do not fund children's programs at the same level as other sectors in the UN Consolidated Appeals. On average, donors provide 73 percent of requested funding for other sectors in the appeals, but only 60 percent of requested funding for children's sectors over the same period of time. The report also notes that 60 percent of the UN and NGO staff surveyed in twenty-eight countries indicated that funding levels were insufficient to meet even the most basic protection needs of children in these situations (UN 2004).

Although the international community has established a set of laws and institutions to protect and assist refugees, there is no specific legal protection or specific agency mandated to protect IDPs—adults and children. In addition, the international legal structure created to protect children in conflict zones is only as meaningful as states have the political will to make it, and not all governments comply with relevant provisions of international humanitarian, human rights, and refugee law or provide their peace keepers with appropriate training in such law, including child and gender-related provisions.

On occasion warring countries also do not grant humanitarian agencies unimpeded access to civilian populations affected by armed conflict, making it impossible for them to ensure children's protection or survival. Additionally, there is no systematic global monitoring and reporting system in place to track the number of children affected by conflict, the specific threats they face, and the steps taken to address their needs. There also is no mechanism to ensure compliance at the field level or to ensure that governments comply with international law.

In order to address these shortcomings, governments, donors, and humanitarian agencies must make the protection of children a priority at every stage of a humanitarian response. This response must be based on an intimate knowledge of children's pre- and post-crisis social ecologies. Foremost, governments must ratify, enforce, monitor, and report on international treaties created to protect children. To enforce and monitor these treaties properly, governments need to support a systematic and comprehensive monitoring-and-reporting mechanism designed to provide timely, objective, accurate, and reliable information on violations against children. Peace-keeping mandates should include specific provisions to protect and assist children, and all military personnel should be required to sign codes of conduct that specify inappropriate behaviors, including abuse of power and resources and sexual relations with beneficiaries. In addition, governments need to provide adequate resources for child-protection activities. It is only with sufficient resources that the UN and humanitarian agencies can begin to meet children's most basic protection needs. Simultaneously, it is imperative for nation-states to recognize that children are central to a global peace-and-security agenda.

References

Green, E. C., and A. Honwana. 1999. Indigenous healing of war affected children in Africa. *Africa Policy E-Journal* 10. Available online.

Hausner, S. L. 2005. *The movement of women: Migration, trafficking, and prostitution in the context of Nepal's armed conflict*. Kathmandu, Nepal: Save the Children Federation.

IASC (Inter-Agency Standing Committee). 2002. *Growing the sheltering tree: Protecting rights through humanitarian action*. Geneva: UNICEF for IASC. Available online.

ICRC (International Committee of the Red Cross). 2001. *Strengthening protection in war: A search for professional standards*. Geneva: ICRC.

Johnson, A. 1997. Liberian law reforms will protect women. International Press Service. Available online.

Lacey, M. 2004. In Congo war, even peacekeepers add to horror. *The New York Times*, December 18, 2004.

Lowicki, J. 2001. *Making the choice for a better life: Promoting the protection and capacity of Kosovo's youth.* New York: Women's Commission on Refugee Women and Children.

Save the Children Alliance. 2005. *Protecting children in emergencies: Escalating threats to children must be addressed.* London: Save the Children Alliance.

Tolfree, D. 2004. *Whose children? Separated children's protection and participation in emergencies.* Stockholm: Save the Children Sweden.

UN (United Nations). 2004. *Comprehensive assessment of the United Nations system response to children affected by armed conflict.* Report of the secretary-general. A/59/331. September 3. Available online.

UNESCO. 2005. *Education for all by 2015.* Available on the unesco.org website.

UNOCHA (UN Office for the Coordination of Humanitarian Affairs). 2004. Burundi-Tanzania: Focus on secondary school education in refugee camps. November 24. Available online.

ABOUT THE AUTHORS

Alastair Ager is professor of clinical population and family health at the Mailman School of Public Health at Columbia University, working with the Forced Migration and Health program. He also holds honorary appointments with Queen Elizabeth House, University of Oxford; Tulane University; and Queen Margaret University College, Edinburgh, where he was formerly director of the Institute for International Health and Development. He holds degrees from the universities of Keele, Birmingham, and Wales. His international fieldwork experience as researcher and consultant spans Africa, South Asia, the Middle East, eastern Europe, and the Caribbean. Dr. Ager has worked with a wide range of international agencies, including UNHCR, UNICEF, WHO, and a number of nongovernmental agencies, both local and international. His publications include *Refugees: Perspectives on the Experience of Forced Migration* (1999) and papers on psychosocial intervention in complex emergencies for the medical journal *The Lancet.*

Cairo Arafat is director general of Aid Management and Coordination, Ministry of Planning, in the Occupied Palestinian Territory. She previously worked with UNICEF as an early childhood and children in difficult circumstances program officer and as director of the National Plan of Action for Palestinian Children. Her work has entailed developing national policies and programs to assist children in difficult circumstances to be able not only to cope but to relate effectively with their society and community. Dr. Arafat has conducted a number of different studies examining violence in the lives of Palestinian children and identification of childhood well-being indicators, and she has worked on reports on violations against children.

Neil Boothby, professor of clinical population and family health and director of the Program on Forced Migration and Health at the Mailman School of Public Health at Columbia University, is an internationally recognized expert on the care and protection of children in war zones. Prior to coming to Columbia University, Dr. Boothby held senior positions with UNHCR and Save the Children, during which time he developed programs and policy initiatives for war-affected children in Cambodia, Guatemala, Mozambique, Bosnia, Rwanda, the DRC, Sierra Leone, Liberia, Angola, Nepal, Indonesia,

243

and Afghanistan. Dr. Boothby is the author of numerous books and articles on the psychological impact of war and communal violence on children. He is also the recipient of a number of awards for his work with war and refugee children, including the Red Cross's Humanitarian of the Year Award, the Lyndhurst Prize, the Mickey Leland Award, and the Golden Achievement Award from the United Nations.

Catherine Chen is the anti-trafficking and exploitation specialist at Save the Children, focused on protecting children from exploitation, abuse, and trafficking in emergencies, conflicts, and post-conflict situations around the world. She has worked with survivors of commercial sexual exploitation, labor trafficking, rape, war, child labor, and physical and sexual abuse. Chen has a master's degree in public health in forced migration and health from Columbia University and a bachelor's in human biology from Stanford University.

Amy Hepburn is a policy professional who has researched, published, and programmed extensively on issues affecting children in complex humanitarian emergencies, including armed conflict and HIV/AIDS in the Balkans, eastern and southern Africa, and the Republic of Georgia. Her professional work includes projects with a variety of international NGOs, the UNHCR, the United States Department of State, the United States Agency for International Development, and the Duke University Terry Sanford Institute of Public Policy. Her primary research and programming interests include the education and holistic care of children orphaned by HIV/AIDS in eastern and southern Africa and the protection of refugee children in armed conflict. Hepburn currently co-directs and teaches at the Duke University–HEI Graduate Program on Global Governance and Policy in Geneva, Switzerland. She received both her undergraduate and graduate degrees with honors from Duke University.

Kathleen Kostelny is a senior research associate at Erikson Institute and a psychosocial consultant to national and international organizations, including Christian Children's Fund, Save the Children, and the World Bank. Her research focuses on the psychosocial effects of violence on children, and her work has taken her to war zones abroad, including Mozambique, Cambodia, Nicaragua, Israel and Palestine, Northern Ireland, Angola, Afghanistan, East Timor, Sierra Leone, Indonesia, and Sri Lanka, as well as urban war zones in communities in the United States. Dr. Kostelny has co-authored two books on children and violence: *No Place to Be a Child: Growing Up in a War Zone* (1991) and *Children in Danger: Coping with the Consequences of Community Violence* (1992). She is the recipient of a Kellogg National Fellowship award and a Fetzer Fellowship award for her leadership in the area of children affected by war and violence.

Siobhán McEvoy-Levy was born in Belfast, Northern Ireland. She received her master's and Ph.D. degrees from the University of Cambridge (UK) and a BA Honors degree from the Queen's University, Belfast. She is assistant professor of political science at Butler University in Indianapolis, Indiana. Since 2001 McEvoy-Levy has been researching, writing, and conducting workshops on war-affected children and youth, peace processes, and post-conflict peace building. She has written a number of articles and book chapters on youth and armed conflict, and she is the editor of and a contributor to *Troublemakers or Peacemakers? Youth and Post-Accord Peace Building* (2006). McEvoy-Levy's current research projects focus on children and issues of post-conflict public security, education, and reconciliation.

Susan McKay is a psychologist, nurse, and professor of women's studies and adjunct professor of international studies and nursing at the University of Wyoming in Laramie. For the past fifteen years she has taught and researched issues focused upon women and girls in armed conflict, women and peace building, and feminist issues in peace psychology. Her recent works include *Where Are the Girls? Girls in Fighting Forces in Northern Uganda, Sierra Leone, and Mozambique, Their Lives during and after War* (2004), *The Courage Our Stories Tell: The Daily Lives and Maternal Child Health Care of Japanese-American Women at Heart Mountain* (2002), *Raising Women's Voices for Peacebuilding: Vision, Impact, and Limitations of Media Technologies* (2001), and *Women and Peacebuilding* (1999). Dr. McKay is past president of the Division of Peace Psychology of the American Psychological Association. Recent awards include the Presidential Faculty Achievement Award for Research (2000), designation as a fellow of the American Psychological Association (2002), Extraordinary Merit in Research (2003), and selection as Seibold Professor in the College of Arts and Sciences at the University of Wyoming (2003–4).

Thahabieh I. Musleh is a UNESCO consultant with the Palestinian Ministry of Education and Higher Education. She is currently working on the preparation of a five-year plan (2007–11). Her research interests include child-protection policies and children's rights and welfare. She has a master's degree in international child welfare from the School of Social Work and Psychosocial Studies, East Anglia University, UK, and a BA in sociology from Birzeit University, Palestine.

Alison Strang is a research fellow at the Institute for International Health and Development, Queen Margaret University College, Edinburgh. She is a psychologist whose work has spanned the fields of education, training, and health, generally focusing on addressing the needs of marginalized groups. She is involved in applied research concerning the psychosocial consequences of conflict and disaster and the humanitarian response to health provision, education, and community development. Dr. Strang has worked with communities affected by conflict and disaster in the Balkans, Palestine, and Southeast Asia. She has also undertaken research on behalf of the UK government to explore the dynamics of community integration with asylum seekers and refugees. For the past five years she has coordinated the Psychosocial Working Group, a consortium of humanitarian agencies and academic institutions committed to promoting good practice in psychosocial interventions.

Carl Triplehorn is Save the Children's emergency education specialist. Prior to working for Save the Children, he was a consultant on humanitarian issues with a specific focus on child protection, education in emergencies, and youth programming. Triplehorn has more than thirteen years of field experience working for the International Rescue Committee in Kosovo, Somalia, Sudan, and Kenya, and initiating the Liberian Children's Initiative for UNHCR. Additionally, he has been a consultant on emergency education issues for Save the Children, International Rescue Committee, UNESCO, World Bank, and the Interagency Network on Emergency Education. He holds a master's degree in humanitarian assistance from Tufts University and is an adjunct professor at George Washington University and Tulane University's School of Public Health and Tropical Medicine.

Michael Wessells is senior child protection specialist for Christian Children's Fund, professor of clinical population and family health at Columbia University in the Program on Forced Migration and Health, and professor of psychology at Randolph-Macon College. He has served as president of the Division of Peace Psychology of the American Psychological Association and of Psychologists for Social Responsibility and as co-chair of the InterAction Protection Working Group. Currently, Dr. Wessells is co-chair of the UN Task Force on Mental Health and Psychosocial Support in Emergency Settings. His research on children and armed conflict examines child soldiers, psychosocial assistance in emergencies, and post-conflict reconstruction for peace. He regularly advises UN agencies, donors, and governments on the situation of children in armed conflict and issues regarding child protection and well-being. In countries such as Afghanistan, Angola, Sierra Leone, Uganda, Sri Lanka, East Timor, Kosovo, and South Africa, he helps to develop community-based, culturally grounded programs that assist children, families, and communities affected by armed conflict.

INDEX

DATE DUE

NOV 2 5 2007	

GAYLORD

PRINTED IN U.S.A.

 Kumarian Press, located in Bloomfield, Connecticut, is a forward-looking, scholarly press that promotes active international engagement and an awareness of global connectedness.